Corporate Victimization of Women

Advisor in Criminal Justice to Northeastern University Press

Gilbert Geis

CORPORATE VICTIMIZATION OF WOMEN

Edited by Elizabeth Szockyj and James G. Fox

Northeastern University Press   BOSTON

Northeastern University Press

Library of Congress Cataloging-in-Publication Data

Corporate victimization of women / edited by Elizabeth Szockyj and James G. Fox.
    p. cm.
    Includes bibliographical references and index.
    ISBN 1-55553-259-4 (cloth : alk. paper). — ISBN 1-55553-260-8 (pbk. : alk. paper)
    1. Women—Crimes against—United States. 2. Women consumers—Crimes against—United States. 3. Corporations—Corrupt practices—United States. 4. Products liability—United States. 5. Sex discrimination against women—United States. I. Szockyj, Elizabeth. II. Fox, James G. (James Gordon), 1939- .
    HV6250.4.W65C69   1996
    362.88'082—dc20   95-44839

Designed by Milenda Nan Ok Lee

Composed in Trump Mediaeval by Coghill Composition, Richmond, Virginia. Printed and bound by Thomson-Shore, Inc., in Dexter, Michigan. The paper is Glatfelter, an acid-free sheet.

MANUFACTURED IN THE UNITED STATES OF AMERICA

00 99 98 97 96   5 4 3 2 1

CONTENTS

ACKNOWLEDGMENTS

We are delighted to have assembled such a fine collection of authors whose work has focused on the corporate victimization of women. This book would not have been possible had they not all so kindly taken the time from their busy schedules to contribute a chapter to this collection. The outstanding quality of the contributors' work and their interest in the subject have made our job as editors easy and enjoyable. We are grateful for their participation.

Gilbert Geis has been instrumental in the development of this project; his thoughtful, expert advice at all stages of the project is greatly appreciated, as are his well-honed editorial skills. We are particularly indebted to him for his expertise in the field of white-collar crime and victimization; his numerous years of experience in these areas of study have guided the work of many scholars.

The insight and support we have received from our colleagues also has been of enormous benefit, and we would like to extend our sincere thanks to all of them. Specifically, we would like to acknowledge the contributions of Susan Plant, John A. Conley, Joan McDermott, and James Garofalo.

Financial assistance for the project was provided through the Faculty/Staff Development Endowment Fund awarded to us by the Buffalo State College Foundation. With this grant, we were able to employ a number of exceptional graduate research assistants. Our special thanks go to Christine Mathews for her diligent library research and her many contributions in getting this project off the ground. The enthusiastic efforts of David Kalish and Jennifer Upson also deserve recognition.

Finally, we would like to thank William Frohlich at Northeastern University Press for his patience on this project. His faith has provided us with the opportunity to expand on a topic that has so far received little attention from the academic community.

Corporate Victimization of Women

INTRODUCTION

Elizabeth Szockyj and Nancy Frank

On a global level, women are economically, legally, politically, and so-cially relegated to a lower status than men; and this makes them more susceptible to abuse. Corporate misconduct, notably the manufacturing and marketing of dangerous products related to reproductive needs and employment discrimination, is a major form of such abuse of women. Consequently, a book such as the present volume that deals with fe-male victimization fruitfully can explore the unique vulnerabilities and needs of women in a society in which corporations and males control power. Nonetheless, as Kathleen Daly and Meda Chesney-Lind remind us, "It is impossible to understand women's situations and gender rela-tions without examining masculinity, men's lives, and men's view-points."[1]

While corporations may harm consumers or employees indiscrimi-nately in some cases, in other instances women are disproportionately or differentially victimized. Or, as in the case of products related to reproductive needs, women are almost invariably the sole victims. These are the harms that occupy this book; harms, whether they be physical, psychological, or economic, that knowingly violate the rights of women and arise primarily in the domain of product liability or sex discrimination.

The organization of the book falls into three parts. This introduction and the first chapter propose a framework for thinking analytically about the corporate victimization of women, while the next four chap-ters illustrate that framework by focusing on specific corporate harms that women experience. The final two chapters examine the shaping of public policy and offer directions for change.

CONCEPTUALIZING VICTIMIZATION

The harms that women encounter from corporate acts or omissions need not be labeled criminal to be studied by white-collar criminolo-

4   gists. Victimization is not defined by legal parameters.[2] The broad view that "a victim is one acted upon adversely as a result of injustice" may extend from what most would view as annoyances, such as sexual innuendos in the workplace, to what most would view as serious criminal behaviors, such as the massacre of fourteen female engineering students at the Polytechnic of Montreal in 1989.[3] In between are corporate violations of civil or administrative laws, which, as Edwin Sutherland observed decades ago, produce serious harm.[4] It is primarily the violation of these laws that this book addresses.

The harms caused by corporations have not been typically recognized by the public as crimes, even though criminologists since the 1940s have claimed that they are.[5] Due to the close ties that corporations maintain with the state (political contributions, sources of former or future employment, lobbyists, stock ownership, economic and employment stability), their actions are rarely legislatively defined or handled as crimes.[6] The political and economic power that corporations possess led Sutherland to observe that in studying corporate crime the white-collar criminologist must examine civil and administrative harms, since investigating criminal violations would yield little information.[7]

While criminal prosecutions of corporations are rare, civil and administrative cases are more frequent.[8] However, even here corporate crimes are not severely sanctioned. When regulatory agencies, which monitor corporate behavior, find violations, the chances are that either no action is taken or that the case will be handled administratively with mild penalties such as warnings or fines.[9]

Adding to the problem is the fact that corporate crimes are difficult to detect.[10] Women are often unaware that they have been victimized or may not attribute their injuries to corporate behavior (for example, in cases such as respiratory problems or cancer as a result of workplace contaminants). In cases where female victims appreciate that there is a causal connection between corporate behavior and the harm they have experienced, and choose to initiate civil litigation on their own, they once again encounter a variety of obstacles: ignorance, skepticism, inadequate compensation and disability laws, difficulty in establishing causal links, statutes of limitation, delays, and so on.[11] If a case appears strong, corporations invariably prefer an out-of-court settlement, which the plaintiffs are encouraged by the system to accept. This way, any information regarding the harm experienced, amount paid, and evidence accumulated is kept under wraps, leaving the general public uninformed.[12] Limitations may be placed on attorneys and scientific experts as part of the settlement. Attorneys may be forbidden from handling such cases in the future, while experts may be prohibited from giving testimony in subsequent cases. The sealing of documents and gag orders are common tactics to stymie those harmed. By not having access to the material from prior cases, each victim must build the case anew.

As a result, the vast majority of corporate violations are hidden from the general public's view. When they do surface, it is typically in regard to some dramatic incident often termed a disaster. The ability of corporations to deflect responsibility and accountability for their actions is a direct consequence of the economic and political power they wield. As Sandra Walklate demonstrates, we need to reconceptualize our notion of victims of corporate offenses as ". . . not victims of accidents but victims of an economic and legal system which positions corporations in a different regulative and motivational environment than the young, black male who is subjected to differential policing priorities and behaviors of the police force."[13]

Those whose behavior is viewed as criminal are those who have been unable to mobilize political support for their interests—primarily minorities, the poor, and women.[14] Corporations, on the other hand, have been successful in having their views integrated into the political ideology as embodied by the statement, "What's good for General Motors is good for America." It is in the best interest of the state to protect and preserve the dominant means of production—the capitalist system.

But legislation—whether criminal, civil, or administrative—does not cover all serious harms; after all, it is passed by legislators, who are sometimes members of, and influenced by, the corporate elite. As a result, scholars have broadened the concept of corporate crime to cover acts that are not defined as illegal.[15] These more inclusive harms are identified by Herman and Julia Schwendinger as violations of human rights and include "imperialism, racism, sexism and poverty" as crimes.[16]

The failure of the state to protect society, when it is able, from social harms such as the ones depicted in this book can be viewed as state or political crime.[17] That is, women experience secondary victimization from a male-dominated political system that fails to support or protect them.[18]

Governments internationally have assisted, rather than deterred, corporations in their exploitation of women in economically disadvantaged regions.[19] In those areas where corporations (particularly those in

6 highly competitive industries) have set up shop, labor legislation and/ or enforcement is weak or nonexistent, the cost of labor is minimal, unionization is discouraged, and financial and tax incentives are offered. Women are targeted as a cheap and controllable work force for these typically low-wage, labor-intensive jobs. The preference for women workers is due not only to the expectation that they will work for lower wages than men but "to their socialized docility, lack of power, resources and organization."[20] For these reasons, it is estimated that women of childbearing age "comprise 80–90% of the workers in multinational-controlled light assembly work."[21]

The U.S. government has not been a leader in promoting the rights of women internationally. The Convention on the Elimination of All Forms of Discrimination Against Women, a U.N. document Jane Roberts Chapman considers to be "most central to the concerns of women," exemplifies this point.[22] The convention prohibits discrimination in various aspects of life—including employment, politics, health, and education. "One hundred and one countries have ratified this U.N. convention; the United States is not among them."[23] Likewise, Chapman's research shows that the United States has not ratified any International Labor Organization conventions that cover discrimination and equal opportunity and treatment.

From the Triangle Shirtwaist factory fire in New York City in 1911, in which over a hundred female employees lost their lives, to the 1991 fire at the Imperial Food Products chicken-processing plant in North Carolina, in which twenty-five employees—again primarily women— died as a result of unsafe working conditions, the U.S. government has been ineffective in protecting working women from corporate harm.[24] This failure is not surprising, since the government itself has a poor track record of protecting and serving women. Recent examples include the Tailhook episode, in which female naval officers were sexually accosted by their male colleagues, and the Senate Judiciary Committee's belated and reluctant investigation into the sexual harassment claims of Anita Hill during the hearings to confirm Clarence Thomas as a U.S. Supreme Court justice.[25] Likewise, the premier federal law enforcement agencies, the CIA and the FBI, both face sex discrimination charges.[26]

The women's movement has gained some ground in the public recognition of issues pertinent to women. However, despite affirmative action legislation, there has been little political action regarding the concerns of women.[27] Women have neither been heard in the political and criminal justice processes nor had their interests adequately protected.

This neglect can partially be explained by the vast underrepresentation of women in the legislative, judicial, and law enforcement areas of government.[28] Not being in positions of authority or control and lacking the capacity to exercise power, women have made only incremental steps toward achieving higher status.

While views and responses toward crimes against women in the form of rape, wife battery, and incest, for example, have undergone considerable reformation in the past two decades, Susan Caulfield and Nancy Wonders argue that the state perpetuates these harms by (1) not defining all forms of these behaviors as illegal, (2) not enforcing legislation aimed at reducing these harms, and (3) supporting the patriarchal social structure that results in practices harmful to women. For the most part, they claim, this political crime is conducted through acts of omission rather than acts of commission, that is, the state is consciously refraining from acting to eliminate or reduce harm to women.[29] Paralleling these individual acts of violence toward women is the harm corporations cause by advancing their power and profitability through targeting the employment, reproductive, and consumer vulnerability of women.

It is through the government's support of a capitalist patriarchy that the corporate victimization of women occurs. Because "far-reaching social harms, such as corporate transgressions and transgressions resulting from the symmetrical relationships between corporate America and the state remain largely unchallenged," corporations may victimize women with relative impunity.[30] Consequently, the government is intimately involved in, and ultimately shares some responsibility for, harms that corporations provoke—what Ronald Kramer and Raymond Michalowski have labeled state-corporate crime.[31] For these reasons this book defines white-collar crime as embracing transgressions that may not be defined politically as crimes. Yet, there is sufficient opposition to these acts that legislation has been adopted and applied, for the most part in the civil arena.[32]

CONSEQUENCES OF VICTIMIZATION

Concern for the victims of corporate malfeasance seems to have motivated much of the criminological interest in corporate crime. Definitions of corporate crime (specifically those that are not purely legalistic) are explicitly expressed in terms of harm to employees, consumers, or the general public.[33] But though the impact on victims has frequently been offered as a prime rationale for studying corporate crime,[34] most scholarly work on corporate crime has not examined the role or the experiences of victims in any systematic way.

Early in the development of the corporate crime literature, Gilbert Geis, a widely recognized expert, suggested that scholars ought to examine attitudes toward corporate victimization and corporate victims.[35] As early as 1980, others drew attention to such victims and the way in which they might influence societal reaction to corporate crime.[36] These scholars also highlighted the possibilities afforded through the growing field of victimology. Nonetheless, a sustained examination of corporate victimization never materialized. Given this lack of scholarly research into victims of corporate crime in general, the lack of attention to its female victims in particular is hardly surprising.

The harm that occurs as a result of corporate crime is often minimized in the public perception. Corporate crime is portrayed as taking place in an economic jungle where corporations, locked in a vicious competition for survival, commit such acts as corporate espionage, patent infringement, and misleading or false comparative advertising. Crimes of this nature harm other corporations or wealthy stockholders. When the consumer is harmed, as in cases of price fixing, the financial cost is diffused over the masses so that no one individual is greatly affected. However, as the many cases presented in this book illustrate, corporate victimization can be clear, substantial, and dramatic in its effect on the individual.[37]

Victims of corporate crime engage in a "long struggle to gain recognition of their victim status."[38] The causes of the victim's injuries are often hidden from view. Family, friends, and the official agencies of government may presume that the injury is just a random happenstance rather than a consequence of corporate misconduct. The individual who has been harmed must first overcome this presumption in order to be treated as a crime victim. The victim must then establish evidence that the corporation in question was responsible for the injury or health problems *and*, in many cases, that the corporation acted unreasonably and unlawfully. Only rarely will an act of corporate victimization be unambiguously determined to be the result of a crime.

Due to women's social status and society's cultural expectations, many female victims encounter a double standard. The tendency to attribute blame to female victims of corporate crimes often springs from stereotypical notions of the roles of men and women in society. The "madonna/whore" duality, the tendency to see women as either good girls or bad girls, increases the tendency for society to sort female victims into two groups: "bona fide, innocent victims," deserving of sympathy and justice; and "unworthy, undeserving victims." Victims who are viewed by criminal justice professionals and others as unworthy and undeserving are less likely to have their crimes seriously investigated or pursued in the courts.[39]

The process of victim blaming is a systematic, cognitive process. As Andrew Karmen describes it

First, and most basically, the victim blamer assumes that there is something "wrong" with victims. They are thought to differ significantly from people who have never been victimized. Either their attitudes or their behaviors, or both, distinguish them from the unafflicted majority. Second, the blamer assumes that these presumed differences are the source of the victim's plight. If they were like everyone else, the reasoning goes, they would not be singled out for attack. Third, and finally, the blamer argues that if victims want to avoid further suffering, they must change how they think and act.[40]

While victim blaming can occur in relation to any kind of crime, and often does, the application of victim blaming to crimes affecting women has been especially offensive and worrisome.

Female victims of sexual assault have been blamed for "miscommunicating" their sexual intentions. Female victims of domestic abuse have been blamed for provoking their husbands or boyfriends to violence. Even female child victims have been blamed; one judge in Wisconsin referred to a five-year-old victim as a "promiscuous young lady"! Such victim blaming appears to be an almost natural corollary to belief in a just world.[41] In order to "explain" why certain individuals become the targets of crime, those who espouse this notion of a just world suggest that victims deserve what they get.

Because common crimes in which women are disproportionately the victims—for example, sexual assault or wife battery—in many cases include some degree of victim involvement, society, rather than focusing on the behavior of the offender, often shifts responsibility to the injured party. When a woman's behavior or social position does not fit the stereotypical ideal of the "good woman," she is even more likely to be blamed for her own victimization. Similarly, corporate crime also often necessitates an examination of the circumstances around the offense to determine victim involvement.[42] Employment discrimination and sexual harassment cases, for example, revolve around the testimony and credibility of the female victim. Even consumer product litigation hinges on whether the victim used the product improperly or carelessly. The very notion of *caveat emptor* ("buyer beware") underscores the responsibility society places on victims of corporate crimes. Any evidence of blameworthy conduct by the victim tends to diminish the blame placed on the offender.[43]

In civil cases dealing with silicone breast implants, the Dalkon Shield, DES, and sexual harassment, the character, sexual practices, and lifestyle of female plaintiffs have been probed and judged. For example, a jury recently refused to rule in favor of a woman who claimed to have become ill from silicone breast implants. Interviews with the jurors after the trial suggested that the fact that the woman was a former topless dancer had influenced their decision.[44] In contrast, previous decisions had awarded other plaintiffs millions of dollars in punitive damages; and Dow Corning, the leading implant manufacturer, has been rebuked for its "corporate malice."[45]

Society's reaction to injury, both formally and informally, is likely to influence the victim's psychological adjustment as well. For the victim who never defines her victimization as criminal, it may be somewhat easier to adjust psychologically.[46] However, for the victim who comes to view the victimization as criminal, society's denial of her victim status, along with the absence of sympathy and support that such a status would otherwise engender, may further complicate psychological reactions to the experience. In this way the general lack of reaction to the crime is likely to influence the victim's *own* sense of self and responsibility. As with common crimes, female victims of corporate crimes may blame themselves for the victimization. They voluntarily underwent breast implantation surgery because they were dissatisfied with their appearance. Or they did not possess the willpower to be successful with diet programs. Or they voluntarily took DES during pregnancy to produce a healthier baby, and now their daughters have cancer. The guilt and shame attached to their participation in the harm and their complacent trust in corporations only increases the emotional trauma they experience.

There is a reluctance to see those harmed by corporate actions as victims of corporate crime. Few of the cases discussed in detail in this book have led to criminal indictments. Corporate crime is viewed not as illegal behavior but as savvy or shrewd business. There is rarely public outrage against corporations or clamor for criminal sanctions.[47] Rather, the harms are cast as accidents, debacles, disasters—thus diverting responsibility and blame away from the corporation. By refusing to prosecute cases, the criminal justice system implicitly promotes the view that these are not crimes. In addition, the negative treatment of victims by the criminal justice system and regulatory agencies aggravates the guilt that victims feel and increases their actual victimization. The common government attitude of indifference, ambivalence, or skepticism in regard to victims—or even the view that they "asked for it,"[48]—means that going public with victimization, either to a regulatory agency or in court, may have a greater negative impact on the victim than on the offender.

THE SOCIALIST-FEMINIST PERSPECTIVE

Research on the victimization of women is a growing component of criminology, and feminist theory has made a particularly strong contribution in this area.[49] Social structural explanations of victimization understand criminal victimization in terms of social structure and cultural expectations. The feminist theories discussed in Chapter 1 reflect this theoretical approach. One's position in the social structure influences one's vulnerability to crime. In relation to gender, sex role differences may explain why women are more vulnerable to certain kinds of crimes, such as employment discrimination and sexual harassment. In a society in which opportunities and expectations are differentiated by gender, it is only to be expected that the distribution and nature of victimization are gendered as well.

Some scholars have suggested that women's reproductive role in society may influence the types of corporate victimization women suffer.[50] For example, women's vulnerability to corporate crimes related to unsafe contraceptive products may be conditioned by societal norms that make contraception the woman's responsibility. The large number of women victimized as a result of using unsafe birth control devices may also reflect the targeting of female fertility for control by the pharmaceutical and medical industries. Women's vulnerability to certain kinds of industrial diseases is related to their occupational roles and is bound up with their opportunities relative to men. Women's vulnerability to victimization by breast implant manufacturers may have been caused by cultural values about beauty.[51]

The modified socialist-feminist point of view that Sally Simpson and Lori Elis advocate in Chapter 1 unites the relationship between capitalism and patriarchy. The two issues that this theoretical viewpoint highlight are women's reproductive and labor force potential as they are dominated, suppressed, or exploited by males and the capitalist system. The poor, of whom women comprise a majority, are more likely to be victimized by corporations. And both these corporations and the political system that permits these behaviors are controlled by men.

When examining the gender-based division of labor and sexuality as components of the social structure, however, the contributing effects of class and race cannot be excluded from the discussion.[52] Although experiences differ depending on a woman's social status and race, feminist theory has traditionally marginalized these issues by using a white, middle-class standard.[53] The perspective discussed by Simpson and Elis seeks to sensitize the reader to the necessity of integrating gender, class, and race dimensions.

Two elements, "women as reproducers" and "women as producers," form the thematic framework for the book. Individual chapters are devoted to the injuries sustained by women both as workers and as consumers of goods, whether pharmaceutical products aimed at responding to reproductive needs or products aimed at fulfilling perceived psychological needs.

Women as Reproducers

The burden of reproduction is uniquely female, but one over which women have little control.[54] Women have been encouraged to rely on products associated with pregnancy (thalidomide for morning sickness, DES to prevent miscarriages, the Dalkon Shield for contraception); menstruation (tampons with a risk of inducing toxic shock syndrome); beauty (silicone breast implants); psychological health (mood-altering drugs with adverse reactions[55]); and physical health (diet programs) without being informed of their possible dangers. It is the safety and effectiveness of such products that are of interest here.

Assessing the safety and effectiveness of products targeted exclusively at women has not been a natural priority. Due to paternalistic fears that medical experiments on women could have negative repercussions on their reproductive system or on fetal development, particularly in the early stages when the pregnancy may still be undetected, women were long excluded from many studies on the safety and effectiveness of various drugs. Prior to March 1993, the Food and Drug Administration (FDA) banned much of the early drug testing on women of childbearing age. Because women's physiological functioning—for example, circulatory and respiratory systems—was perceived as being identical to men's, results from studies on men were simply generalized to women. Consequently, women were excluded from up to half of all drug safety experiments. Although it was acknowledged that women were biologically different, and therefore in need of particular protective measures, when women were included in studies the results were not analyzed separately to see if they had a disparate response to the drugs or exhibited other side effects. Because many drugs react differently in the female body, the same dose of a drug that is effective for men may either be ineffective or constitute an overdose for women. Such inattention to female differences delayed the discovery that oral contraceptives can work to block the effect of some drugs and, conversely, that other drugs, for example, penicillin, inhibit the effectiveness of oral contraceptives.[56]

Pharmaceutical companies have capitalized on women's reliance on their products, sometimes with deleterious effects.[57] Reflecting on his work on corporate crime in the pharmaceutical industry, John Braithwaite states that "there has been little progress with criminal enforcement, which remains exceedingly rare in all nations of the world in spite of the fact that serious criminal conduct seems more common in the pharmaceutical industry than in perhaps any industrial sector in the world economy."[58] Repeated corporate crimes such as bribery, false advertising, fraud, inadequate testing, and neglect for safety make women's trust in pharmaceutical products worrisome.[59]

Problems with contraceptives, at this juncture primarily a female issue, best exemplify this point.[60] The Dalkon Shield tragedy of the 1970s and 1980s resulted in harm to hundreds of thousands of women—in some cases causing death and in many others serious health problems such as septic abortions, pelvic infections, pregnancy, and sterility—because the device was unsafe or ineffective. Its manufacturer, A. H. Robins, continued to sell the product in the United States even though it was aware of the potential risks, eventually declaring bankruptcy to avoid the financial burden of compensating the female victims.[61] After the Shield was banned in the United States, A. H. Robins exported its intrauterine device abroad, primarily to Third World countries.[62] Not only were women as a group vulnerable to this corporate transgression, but due to the stratification of power, forms of corporate conduct considered unacceptable for some (white, middle-class U.S. cit-

14 izens) were approved for others (poor, minority women in Third World countries).[63]

Pharmaceutical products, sold for their profitability, are marketed under the noble guise of offering women more control over their reproductive lives.[64] Control over one's body, though, requires knowledge of the risks involved in using a product. Poor labeling, inadequate warnings, and misleading advertisements are among the techniques manufacturers use to suppress information, misinform (particularly regarding effectiveness), or minimize risks associated with their products.[65] Also, because many products associated with reproductive needs require the services of a physician, product risks stated by the manufacturer may not be passed on by the doctor to the patient. Product liability legislation is a step toward correcting the power imbalance, providing some protection to female consumers knowingly deprived of information. However, the inadequacies of the regulatory and civil system of justice make this avenue for compensation and public dissemination of information problematic.[66]

Lucinda Finley describes the Dalkon Shield and DES tragedies caused by the pharmaceutical industry more fully in Chapter 2. She explains how women have been victimized by the pharmaceutical industry and the resultant regulatory response. In Chapter 3, at a broader level, Joan Claybrook analyzes the safety and effectiveness of general consumer products targeted at women buyers. Using a product liability framework, Claybrook illustrates the susceptibility of women to advertising tactics that exploit women's desire to be attractive and safe from crime.

The power of men to define sexuality shapes women as objects of the heterosexual male's desires. Women are sexualized as objects to be admired.[67] The patriarchal society represses women by overvaluing their physical appearance, and this overemphasis in turn has been internalized by women. Historically, women have chosen to subscribe to a number of culturally adored yet physically harmful practices, ranging from the Chinese practice of binding feet to the Western world's use of corsets.

As psychological studies have long shown, "what is beautiful is good."[68] And for women, physical appearance plays a more prominent role in their overall attractiveness than it does for men.[69] If women deemed attractive feel happier, are better adjusted, and have higher self-esteem than their counterparts who are deemed less attractive,[70] it is little wonder that women employ the latest technology to sculpt their bodies in an effort to match their appearance with the current, socially ascribed, male ideal of beauty. Collagen treatments make their lips fuller, liposuction makes their thighs slimmer, diet products reduce their weight, silicone implants augment their breasts, dyes improve their hair color, and cosmetics enhance their facial features.

A huge commerical outlet has been created that thrives on the standards of beauty as set for the benefit of men. The fashion, film, and magazine industries profit by creating a demand for their depiction of beauty, while manufacturers and plastic surgeons profit by supplying that demand. Women are targeted by corporations and manipulated into purchasing beauty products whose safety and/or effectiveness is questionable. As Laura Shapiro points out with regard to silicone breast implants, "to 'choose' a procedure that may harden the breasts, result in loss of sensation and introduce a range of serious health problems isn't a choice, it's a scripted response."[71]

Women as Producers

"Women make up over half the world's population and perform two-thirds of its work, but receive one-tenth of its income and own less than one one-hundredth of its property."[72] Taken by themselves, these figures are an indication of women's position in the international workplace and social structure. The work women perform, whether at home or in the marketplace, is undercompensated. In fact, women's work within the home is not compensated at all under the capitalist system. Instead, their services maintain and reproduce the work force at no additional cost to corporations, thus benefiting both men and the system. Women are the primary caretakers of the domestic responsibilities of housework and child care—whether or not they are employed outside the home.

As Susan Davis reveals in Chapter 4, women who work outside the home are not equally represented across job categories or wage scales. Even with equal employment opportunity measures in place, women are not fully integrated into the workplace. Although women have posted gains in some positions formerly dominated by men, they have suffered losses in others.[73] As Davis shows, women still cluster in service, administrative support (clerical), and education and health professions.

A variety of explanations has been proposed to account for the employment and wage differential. Barbara Reskin and Patricia Roos theorize that both employers and employees rank jobs according to prefer-

16 ence, resulting in a labor queue (for employers) and a job queue (for workers).[74] Corporations hire from the top of the labor queue and move down the queue, whereas workers move up the job queue by accepting the most attractive position available to them. While white men are the preferred group in the labor queue, when their labor becomes scarce or when the job becomes less attractive to them (for example, because of declining wages, hours, or working conditions), nonwhite men and white women become the next pool to be tapped. Minority women (primarily black women) move into those jobs that have now been vacated. When the job market shrinks, those in the lower-ranked groups, who were the last hired, are the first to go; and they move back into their former, less favorable jobs, displacing the current occupants. Reskin and Roos summarize the process:

> Despite the notion that African-American women particularly benefit from affirmative action, evidence increasingly documents what observers have long recognized: the joint effects of racial, ethnic, and sex segregation have made black women the last to profit from the opening of any doors into male lines of work.[75]

Preserving the gender queue bestows advantages on all men by reinforcing their dominant position in employment, and, by extension, in society.

Positions in the labor market are optimally filled by white males. Corporations have developed, and continue to maintain through evaluative criteria, abstract jobs that are not gender-neutral but are in fact tailored to men.[76] Attributes and standards (such as commitment to the job above all else and the higher value attached to money management skills than to human relations skills) are set according to a male norm designed to promote success for men. Women competing for these positions are compared to this "normal" standard.[77] Job evaluations reward skills and attributes that substantially match the existing structure and classifications. By maintaining this organizational structure, the replication of gender assumptions thus perpetuates the exclusion and subordination of women in the workplace.

The differences exhibited by women, whether real or stereotyped, are not valued or accommodated in the workplace but rather portrayed in a negative light.[78] "Women's bodies—female sexuality, their ability to procreate and their pregnancy, breast-feeding, and child care, menstruation, and mythic 'emotionality'—are suspect, stigmatized, and used as grounds for control and exclusion"; they are considered distracting and disruptive to the efficient functioning of the organization.[79]

As a result of these sexual and culturally maintained differences and the structural devaluation of women in the job market, women have distinctive work needs, problems, and conflicts. Patricia Gwartney-Gibbs and Denise Lach maintain that the gender differences in employment disputes and the manner in which they are resolved contribute to the inequity in employment.[80] These authors find that women are less likely to (1) seek formal resolution of their conflicts, (2) have access to unions or formal resolution mechanisms, and (3) have their complaints pursued by the dispute resolution gatekeepers. Since job attachment and performance are related to satisfactory resolution of workplace disputes, Gwartney-Gibbs and Lach suggest that women's higher turnover, lower earnings, and shorter work hours may be a reflection of unequal workplace dispute resolution. In traditionally female occupations, women experience more support, sympathy, and fewer disputes over discrimination and harassment than they do in traditionally male positions. If women are better treated in these jobs, Gwartney-Gibbs and Lach argue, it would explain why women tend to gravitate toward them.

Susan Davis also examines explanations for sex discrimination in employment in Chapter 4. She points to the economic advantages to men and to corporations as the primary beneficiaries of keeping women in low-paying, less desirable positions. Like Reskin and Roos, Davis argues for the need to maintain equal employment opportunity legislation and affirmative action programs to advance women's status.[81]

Combining Reproduction and Work

Occupational hazards inextricably link the issues of work and reproduction. The clerical, service, health, and education jobs females typically hold do not have high incidents of dramatic accidents or deaths like those found in traditionally male occupations such as mining, construction, logging, or steel refining.[82] Women's work is presumed to be "safe." However, scientific research, for the most part conducted by men, has rarely studied the occupational hazards and health of female workers in traditional occupations and has applied male standards to women.[83] The studies that have been conducted indicate that women's exposure to dangerous substances and physical activity is underestimated.[84]

The hazards women face are less observable, and more complex, than those confronting men. Conditions under which many women work include poor ventilation and lighting, noise, heat, rapid production pace, sexual harassment, sedentary positioning (standing or sitting for long periods of time), lack of autonomy, piecework, repetitive activity, continual lifting, stress, and inadequate training concerning handling substances, equipment, and proper safety procedures.

In a Canadian study, it was found that women sewing machine operators lifted more cumulative weight in one day than men working in a plastics factory.[85] Lifting for men was heavy but sporadic, with many opportunities for rest. For women, the lifting was moderate but continual, affecting isolated parts of their body (for example, the shoulder). The injuries that men sustained from lifting were acknowledged and compensated, whereas the accumulated pain that the women endured was not as easily identified as job-related. Compared with men, women are less likely to be unionized or to receive assistance from their unions when they are; and they receive less monetary compensation in damages from the court.[86]

Women are exposed to harmful substances even in traditionally female occupations. For example, dental assistants, nurses, and hygienists frequently work with radiation, anesthetics, and mercury; women textile workers breathe cotton dust resulting in byssinosis (brown lung); and women in electronics and the light assembly industry routinely handle toxic substances.[87] But only the effects of hazards on women's reproductive health have been consistently studied, and then only for women in nontraditional occupations.

Exclusionary policies restrict employment opportunities for women of childbearing years, it is argued, to protect their unborn children.[88] Corporations do not acknowledge that occupational reproductive hazards affect both men and women; reproductive health is viewed as strictly a female issue.[89] Dramatic cases that have been publicized illustrate that men are frequently harmed; they suffer from sterility and impotence and father babies with birth defects.[90] Men's exposure to reproductive hazards, however, is either ignored by employers or resolved through disclosure and informed consent. In the case of the pesticide dibromocloropropane (DBCP), "the response was to shut down the plant until the hazard was abated."[91] Only women are excluded from the typically higher-paying positions through restrictions or transfers.[92] "Excluding men is unthinkable."[93] Interestingly, there are no exclusionary policies related to the reproductive hazards that abound in the generally lower-paid, female-dominated occupations.

The harm women suffer from exposure to a vast array of toxic chemicals, solvents, and plastics in typically female occupations is evident from a study of the GTE assembly plant in New Mexico. A lawsuit filed against GTE listed over 250 employees, 95 percent of whom were female and 70 percent Hispanic.[94] A few of the ills they experienced included cancer, "frequent miscarriages, spontaneous abortions, excessive menstrual bleeding and hysterectomies, odd neurological problems and a strange array of other conditions."[95] Part of the lure to Albuquerque, New Mexico, for GTE was the low rate of workers' compensation and unionization. The women settled, signing the usual nondisclosure requirements as part of the agreement.

Donna Randall continues the discussion of corporate exclusionary policies in Chapter 5, analyzing the justifications corporations assert when implementing these policies and finding them lacking. The overarching humanistic concern (to protect the health of the fetus) has discriminatory repercussions. Nor does this concern ever seem to extend to men or women in predominantly female occupations, or to the institution of policies such as parental leave and paid maternal leave.

STRATEGIES FOR CHANGE

With all this information at hand, what then can be done to ameliorate the situation for women? At the federal level in the United States, sex discrimination legislation under Title VII of the Civil Rights Act of 1964 has led to affirmative action and sexual harassment policies. While both have received considerable public attention, an examination of affirmative action policies, which have been in place for some twenty years, provides the better gauge of success.

As pointed out in previous pages, the complete integration of women in the labor market has yet to be accomplished. Although this is a powerful argument for the continuation of affirmative action programs, it is apparent that these programs are not a panacea for women. Affirmative action has been most influential in helping women enter occupations in which (1) cost is a dominant factor, (2) men are not threatened and/or organized, (3) the job has become less attractive to men, and (4) the positions women occupy are low-level, dead-end positions.[96] Consequently, affirmative action has not resulted in employment equality for

20   women. Nonetheless, government affirmative action stipulations have increased the costs to corporations of hiring only white males, thereby serving a vital function in promoting the interests of women and minorities. As Reskin and Roos found, "In none of the occupations we studied did women impose sufficient costs to prompt employers to hire them for male jobs without the threat of government penalties."[97]

Legislative policies are necessary but not sufficient to alleviate corporate harms. These laws and regulations need to be enforced. More rigorous enforcement against corporate wrongdoing, however, runs counter to the economic and political relationship between government and business. Rather, state interventions should provide women with more economic and political power to enable them to respond to corporate crime effectively.

Corporations themselves may play a role in stifling corporate crime. Self-regulation, as proposed by John Braithwaite and Brent Fisse, places the primary responsibility for policy and enforcement on the shoulders of the corporation, an approach that is most in tune with the inner workings of its departments.[98] Using internal disciplinary mechanisms and structured accountability, Fisse and Braithwaite offer a model to improve compliance with the standards for the safety and effectiveness of products manufactured for women. Further suggestions for improvements to the working environment for women include more job-related and safety training, a slower production pace, more frequent breaks, sensitivity to harassment issues, greater attention to occupational health and safety, and access to successful dispute resolution mechanisms.[99]

Finally, women as consumers and employees should be encouraged to be more active.[100] A larger percentage of females need to form or join organizations to lobby for changes, such as better warnings or greater accessibility to information. Also, information that *is* available must be more widely circulated. One way to increase the dissemination of information is to limit by law the secrecy surrounding civil proceedings. Secrecy orders, especially when they affect health or safety, are being scrutinized by legislators, the Department of Justice, and the Judicial Conference of the United States. A legislative proposal, arguably the most promising approach, is before Congress.[101] It is incumbent upon women to fight for their right to a safe and equitable society and to pursue changes that further this goal.

Cultural ideology is difficult to overcome; it is almost always women, rarely men, who are faced with the conflicting needs of career and family.[102] Women are expected to meet the demands of the job, with little or no accommodation for the culturally ascribed work they perform in the home. While men's hours of work have decreased as women have moved into paid employment, women's hours of work have increased.[103] This ideology not only affects career aspirations and family responsibilities but strongly influences the way in which corporations treat women, as evidenced by examples given in this book.

Chapters 6 and 7 address the ways in which the government, courts, corporations, and female consumers and employees have reduced and can continue to reduce the corporate victimization of women. In Chapter 6 James Fox traces various legislative initiatives affecting women from the 1960s through to the 1990s. The political activism of the 1960s generated legislation favoring equal employment, while more recent public events have placed the issue of sexual harassment in the workplace in the legislative foreground.

Laureen Snider, in Chapter 7, rekindles the discussion of the relationship between government and business. The state, whether at the national, regional, or local level or in the form of regulatory agencies, is inextricably entwined with the needs and power of its corporate constituents. The influence that advocacy or consumer pressure groups exert is comparable to a fireworks display; there is momentary captivation, but only the most spectacular make a lasting imprint on the audience. For the most part, it is business as usual.

In 1992 Jurg Gerber and Susan Weeks published an article titled, "Women as Victims of Corporate Crime: A Call for Research on a Neglected Topic."[104] Although the idea for this book was conceived prior to that publication, this volume dovetails nicely with Gerber and Weeks's concerns. It explicates more fully the harms women encounter and what has been and could be done to address these harms. It is hoped that readers will be stimulated to further discussion. This is a topic requiring attention from both the academic community and the community at large.

A volume on the corporate victimization of women bridges several disparate bodies of literature: victimology, corporate crime, and feminism. The contributors as well come from diverse backgrounds, including law, economics, criminology, and business. This meld of perspectives enhances the unique flavor of this text and illustrates the need for more inter- and intradisciplinary discourse on this topic. Each individual chapter provides an insightful glimpse into one aspect of the theme; collectively the chapters reveal a portrait of unacceptable injustice.

22 NOTES

1. K. Daly and M. Chesney-Lind, "Feminism and Criminology," *Justice Quarterly* 5, no. 4 (1988): 497–535, 500.

2. M. A. Y. Rifai, "Victimology: A Theoretical Framework," in *The Victim in International Perspective*, ed. H. J. Schneider (New York: Aldine de Gruyter, 1982), 65–79.

3. Ibid., 67.

4. E. H. Sutherland, "White-Collar Criminality," *American Sociological Review* 5 (February 1940): 1–12.

5. Ibid.; G. Geis, "The Heavy Electrical Equipment Antitrust Cases of 1961," in *Criminal Behavior Systems*, ed. M. Clinard and R. Quinney (New York: Holt, Rinehart and Winston, 1967), 139–150; M. B. Clinard and P. C. Yeager, *Corporate Crime* (New York: Free Press, 1980); J. W. Coleman, *The Criminal Elite: The Sociology of White-Collar Crime*, 3rd ed. (New York: St. Martin's Press, 1994).

6. D. R. Simon and D. S. Eitzen, *Elite Deviance*, 4th ed. (Boston: Allyn and Bacon, 1993).

7. Sutherland, "White-Collar Criminality."

8. S. P. Shapiro, "The Road Not Taken: The Elusive Path to Criminal Prosecution for White-Collar Offenders," *Law and Society Review* 19, no. 2 (1985): 179–217.

9. Clinard and Yeager, *Corporate Crime*; Shapiro, "The Road Not Taken."

10. Coleman, *The Criminal Elite*.

11. R. B. Sobol, *Bending the Law: The Story of the Dalkon Shield Bankruptcy* (Chicago: University of Chicago Press, 1991); S. Fox, *Toxic Work: Women Workers at GTE Lenkurt* (Philadelphia: Temple University Press, 1991).

12. Fox, *Toxic Work*; P. Peppin, "Equality, Difference, Bodily Control and Harm Prevention: Gendered Aspects of Pharmaceutical Products Law" (paper presented at the Corporate Crime: Ethics, Law and the State conference, Queen's University, Kingston, Ontario, Canada, November 1992).

13. S. Walklate, *Victimology: The Victim and the Criminal Justice Process* (London: Unwin Hyman, 1989), 84

14. J. Reiman, *The Rich Get Richer and the Poor Get Prison: Ideology, Class, and Criminal Justice*, 3rd ed. (New York: Macmillan, 1990). Prostitution, child neglect, and certain cases of abortion would be examples of criminal legislation targeted at women.

15. R. M. Bohm, "Social Relationships That Arguably Should Be Criminal Although They Are Not: On the Political Economy of Crime," in *Political Crime in Contemporary America: A Critical Approach*, ed. K. D. Tunnell (New York: Garland, 1993), 3–29; R. Elias, *The Politics of*

Victimization: Victims, Victimology, and Human Rights (New York: Ox-   23
ford University Press, 1986); R. J. Michalowski and R. C. Kramer, "The
Space Between Laws: The Problem of Corporate Crime in a Transnational
Context," *Social Problems* 34, no. 1 (1987): 34–53.

16. H. Schwendinger and J. Schwendinger, "Defenders of Order or Guardians of Human Rights?" *Issues in Criminology* 5, no. 2 (1970): 123–57, 148.

17. W. J. Chambliss, "State-Organized Crime," *Criminology* 27, no. 2
(1989): 183–208; K. D. Tunnell, *Political Crime in Contemporary America:
A Critical Approach* (New York: Garland, 1993).

18. W. DeKeseredy and R. Hinch, *Woman Abuse: Sociological Perspectives* (Toronto: Thompson Educational Publishing, 1991).

19. J. R. Aulette and R. Michalowski, "Fire in Hamlet: A Case Study of a
State-Corporate Crime," in *Political Crime in Contemporary America: A
Critical Approach*, ed. K. D. Tunnell (New York: Garland, 1993), 171–206;
M. B. Kuumba, "Reproductive Imperialism: Population and Labor Control
of the Third World" (paper presented at the annual meeting of the American
Sociological Association, August 1994); Michalowski and Kramer, "The
Space Between Laws"; K. Ward, "Women and Transnational Corporation
Employment: A World-System and Feminist Analysis" (Women in Develop-
ment working paper no. 120, Office of Women in International Develop-
ment, Michigan State University, East Lansing, 1986).

20. Kuumba, "Reproductive Imperialism," 15–16.

21. Ibid., 12.

22. J. R. Chapman, "Violence Against Women as a Violation of Human
Rights," *Social Justice* 17, no. 2 (1990): 54–70, 58.

23. Ibid., 58.

24. Aulette and Michalowski, "Fire in Hamlet."

25. J. Mayer and J. Abramson, *Strange Justice: The Selling of Clarence
Thomas* (Boston: Houghton Mifflin, 1994).

26. "FBI Pays $647,000 Over Sex Harassment," *Chicago Tribune* (Febru-
ary 1, 1995): 4; M. Kilian, "Sex Bias Charges Latest Woe for CIA," *Chicago
Tribune* (September 8, 1994): 4; "CIA to Settle Sex Bias Claims," *Chicago
Tribune* (March 30, 1995): 4.

27. S. L. Caulfield and N. A. Wonders, "Personal AND Political: Violence
Against Women and the Role of the State," in *Political Crime in Contemporary America: A Critical Approach*, ed. K. D. Tunnell (New York: Garland,
1993), 79–100.

28. See Caulfield and Wonders, "Personal AND Political," for the United
States and DeKeseredy and Hinch, *Woman Abuse*, for Canada.

29. Ibid.

30. Tunnell, *Political Crime in Contemporary America*, xiii–xiv.

31. Aulette and Michalowski, "Fire in Hamlet"; R. C. Kramer, "The
Space Shuttle *Challenger* Explosion: A Case Study of State-Corporate

24 Crime," in *White-Collar Crime Reconsidered,* ed. K. Schlegel and D. Weisburd (Boston: Northeastern University Press, 1992) 214–43.

32. It should be noted that this book does not argue for the abolition of the capitalist system but rather acknowledges the necessity of corporate production and profitability for the improvement of the standard of living. What is objectionable is the abrogation of the rights of women in the process.

33. L. Schrager and J. F. Short, Jr., "Toward a Sociology of Organizational Crime," *Social Problems* 25 (April 1977): 407–19; N. K. Frank and M. J. Lynch, *Corporate Crime, Corporate Violence: A Primer* (New York: Harrow and Heston, 1992).

34. See M. D. Ermann and R. J. Lundman, *Corporate and Governmental Deviance: Problems of Organizational Behavior in Contemporary Society,* 4th ed. (New York: Oxford University Press, 1992); Simon and Eitzen, *Elite Deviance;* Coleman, *The Criminal Elite.*

35. G. Geis, "Victimization Patterns in White-Collar Crime," in *Victimology: A New Focus,* vol. 5, *Exploiters and Exploited,* ed. I. Drapkin and E. Viano (Lexington, MA: D. C. Heath, 1975).

36. M. E. Walsh and D. D. Schram, "The Victim of White-Collar Crime: Accuser or Accused?" in *White-Collar Crime: Theory and Research,* ed. G. Geis and E. Stotland (Beverly Hills, CA: Sage, 1980), 32–51.

37. D. Shichor, "Corporate Deviance and Corporate Victimization: A Review and Some Elaborations," *International Review of Victimology* 1 (1989): 67–88.

38. R. I. Mawbry and S. Walkgate, *Critical Victimology* (Thousand Oaks, CA: Sage, 1994), 190.

39. L. Holmstrom and A. W. Burgess, *The Victim of Rape: Institutional Reactions* (New York: Wiley, 1978).

40. A. Karmen, *Crime Victims: An Introduction to Victimology,* 2nd ed. (Pacific Grove, CA: Brooks/Cole, 1990), 121.

41. C. Smith, "Response to Victims: Are the Institutional Mandates of Police and Medicine Sufficient?" *Victimology* 10 (1985): 560–72.

42. Walsh and Schram, "The Victim of White-Collar Crime."

43. Ibid., 42–45.

44. J. Mears, "Jury Sides with Breast Implant-Maker in Lawsuit Brought by Topless Dancer," *Buffalo News* (June 12, 1993): A2.

45. See *Stern v. Dow Corning,* No. C83 2348 MHP (N.D. Cal. 1984); *Hopkins v. Dow Corning,* No. C88 4703 TEH (N.D. Cal 1991).

46. R. Janoff-Bulman, "Criminal v. Non-Criminal Victimization: Victims' Reactions," *Victimology* 10 (1985): 498–511.

47. J. P. Wright, F. T. Cullen, and M. B. Blankenship, "The Social Construction of Corporate Violence: Media Coverage of the Imperial Food Products Fire," *Crime and Delinquency* 41, no. 1 (1995): 20–36.

48. E. Moore and M. Mills, "The Neglected Victims and Unexamined Costs of White-Collar Crime," *Crime and Delinquency* 36, no. 3 (1990): 408–18; N. Shover, G. L. Fox, M. Mills, "Long-Term Consequences of Victimization by White-Collar Crime," *Justice Quarterly* 11, no. 1 (1994): 75–98.

49. Daly and Chesney-Lind, "Feminism and Criminology," 520.

50. J. Gerber and S. L. Weeks, "Women as Victims of Corporate Crime: A Call for Research on a Neglected Topic," *Deviant Behavior* 13 (1992): 325–47.

51. G. Troutwine, "Breast Implants: A Beauty Fraud," *Trial* 29 (August 1993): 48–51.

52. J. W. Messerschmidt, *Masculinities and Crime: Critique and Reconceptualization of Theory* (Lanham, MD: Rowman and Littlefield, 1993).

53. K. Crenshaw, "Demarginalizing the Intersection of Race and Sex: A Black Feminist Critique of Antidiscrimination Doctrine, Feminist Theory and Antiracist Politics," *University of Chicago Legal Forum* 1989 (1989): 139–67.

54. Again, the U.S. government has been intimately involved in decisions regarding women's bodies. Political agendas, particularly under the Reagan and Bush administrations, have taken decisions regarding abortion choice, for instance, out of the hands of women. One example is the ban (subsequently lifted by the Clinton government) on the French abortion pill RU-486, a potentially safe, less costly method of abortion (W. E. Leary, "Broader Uses Seen for Abortion Pill," *New York Times* [September 9, 1993]: A17).

55. These drugs are overprescribed to women. And, although women are physiologically smaller than men, the average prescribed dose is greater for women (DeKeseredy and Hinch, *Woman Abuse*).

56. P. Hilts, "FDA Ends Ban on Women in Drug Testing," *New York Times* (March 25, 1993): B8; "Drug Trials Are Criticized for Lack of Women," *New York Times* (October 30, 1992): A16; see Peppin, "Equality, Difference, Bodily Control," on the inadequacy of medical research on women in Canada.

57. D. Klein, "Violence Against Women: Some Considerations Regarding Its Causes and Its Elimination," *Crime and Delinquency* 27, no. 1 (1981): 64–80.

58. J. Braithwaite, "Transnational Regulation of the Pharmaceutical Industry," *Annals of the American Academy of Political and Social Sciences* 525 (January): 12–30, 13.

59. J. Braithwaite, *Corporate Crime in the Pharmaceutical Industry* (London: Routledge, 1984).

60. Not only does the current cultural ideology place the responsibility for birth control on women, but the types of birth control methods that

26   have been developed require medical involvement. The medical society is another male domain (S. Fisher, *In the Patient's Best Interest: Women and the Politics of Medical Decisions* [New Brunswick, NJ: Rutgers University Press, 1988]).

61. Sobol, *Bending the Law.*

62. M. Dowie and Mother Jones, "The Dumping of Hazardous Products on Foreign Markets," *Mother Jones* 4 (1979): 23–44.

63. Messerschmidt, *Masculinities and Crime.*

64. Braithwaite, *Corporate Crime;* DeKeseredy and Hinch, *Woman Abuse.*

65. Peppin, "Equality, Difference, Bodily Control."

66. Ibid.

67. Messerschmidt, *Masculinities and Crime;* Klein, "Violence Against Women."

68. K. K. Dion, E. Berscheid and E. Walster, "What Is Beautiful Is Good," *Journal of Personality and Social Psychology* 24, no. 3 (1972): 285–90.

69. G. Wilson and D. Nias, *Love's Mysteries: The Psychology of Sexual Attraction* (London: Open Books, 1976).

70. E. W. Mathes and A. Kahn, "Physical Attractiveness, Happiness, Neuroticism, and Self-Esteem," *Journal of Psychology* 90 (May 1975): 27–30.

71. L. Shapiro, "What Is It with Women and Breasts?" *Newsweek* (January 20, 1992): 57.

72. Chapman, "Violence Against Women," 57.

73. B. F. Reskin and P. A. Roos, *Job Queues, Gender Queues: Explaining Women's Inroads into Male Occupations* (Philadelphia: Temple University Press, 1990).

74. Ibid.

75. Ibid., 76.

76. J. Ackers, "Hierarchies, Jobs, Bodies: A Theory of Gendered Organizations," *Gender and Society* 4, no. 2 (1990): 139–58.

77. Also see L. M. Finley, "Transcending Equality Theory: A Way Out of the Maternity and the Workplace Debate," *Columbia Law Review* 86, no. 6 (1986): 1118–82; S. J. Kenney, *For Whose Protection? Reproductive Hazards and Exclusionary Policies in the United States and Britain* (Ann Arbor, MI: University of Michigan Press, 1992).

78. Kenney, *For Whose Protection?*

79. Ackers, "Hierarchies, Jobs, Bodies," 152.

80. P. A. Gwartney-Gibbs and D. H. Lach, "Gender and Workplace Dispute Resolution: A Conceptual and Theoretical Model," *Law and Society Review* 28, no. 2 (1994): 265–96.

81. Reskin and Roos, *Job Queues, Gender Queues.*

82. C. Brisson, M. Vezina, and A. Vinet, "Health Problems of Women

Employed in Jobs Involving Psychological and Ergonomic Stressors: The Case of Garment Workers in Quebec," *Women and Health* 18, no. 3 (1992): 49–66; DeKeseredy and Hinch, *Woman Abuse.*

83. L. Dumais, "Impact of the Participation of Women in Science: On Rethinking the Place of Women Especially in Occupational Health," *Women and Health* 18, no. 3 (1992): 11–25.

84. DeKeseredy and Hinch, *Woman Abuse.*

85. N. Vezina and J. Courville, "Integration of Women into Traditionally Masculine Jobs," *Women and Health* 18, no. 3 (1992): 97–118.

86. DeKeseredy and Hinch, *Woman Abuse*; Gwartney-Gibbs and Lach, "Gender and Workplace Dispute Resolution"; D. M. Randall and J. F. Short, Jr., "Women in Toxic Work Environments: A Case Study of Social Problem Development," *Social Problems* 30, no. 4 (1983): 410–23.

87. R. Guarasci, "Death by Cotton Dust," in *Corporate Violence: Injury and Death for Profit*, ed. S. L. Hills (Totowa, NJ: Rowman and Littlefield, 1987), 76–92; W. Chavkin, ed., *Double Exposure: Women's Health Hazards on the Job and at Home* (New York: Monthly Review Press, 1984).

88. Kenney, *For Whose Protection?*

89. Ibid.; Klein, "Violence Against Women."

90. Kenney, *For Whose Protection?*

91. E. Bingham, "Preface," in *Double Exposure: Women's Health Hazards on the Job and at Home*, ed. W. Chavkin (New York: Monthly Review Press, 1984), ix–xi, x.

92. E. Draper, "Gendered Constructions of Suitable Work," *Social Problems* 40, no. 1 (1993): 90–107.

93. Kenney, *For Whose Protection?* 2.

94. Fox, *Toxic Work*, 7.

95. Ibid., 8.

96. Reskin and Roos, *Job Queues, Gender Queues.*

97. Ibid., 311–12.

98. J. Braithwaite, "Enforced Self-Regulation: A New Strategy for Corporate Crime Control," *Michigan Law Review* 80, no. 7 (1982): 1466–1507; B. Fisse and J. Braithwaite, *Corporations, Crime and Accountability* (Cambridge, U.K.: Cambridge University Press, 1993).

99. Gwartney-Gibbs and Lach, "Gender and Workplace Dispute Resolution"; DeKeseredy and Hinch, *Woman Abuse.*

100. DeKeseredy and Hinch, *Woman Abuse.*

101. H. J. Reske, "Secrecy Orders at Issue," *ABA Journal* 80 (August 1994): 32–33.

102. S. J. M. Freeman, *Managing Lives: Corporate Women and Social Change* (Amherst, MA: University of Massachusetts Press, 1990).

103. C. Goldin, *Understanding the Gender Gap* (New York: Oxford University Press, 1990).

28   104. Gerber and Weeks, "Women as Victims of Corporate Crime,"
325–47.

REFERENCES

Acker, J. 1990. Hierarchies, jobs, bodies: A theory of gendered organizations.
Gender and Society 4(2): 139–58.

Aulette, J. R. and R. Michalowski. 1993. Fire in Hamlet: A case study of a
state-corporate crime. In *Political Crime in Contemporary America: A
Critical Approach,* ed. K. D. Tunnell, 171–206. New York: Garland.

Bingham, E. 1984. Preface. In *Double Exposure: Women's Health Hazards
on the Job and at Home,* ed. W. Chavkin, ix–xi. New York: Monthly
Review Press.

Bohm, R. M. 1993. Social relationships that arguably should be criminal
although they are not: On the political economy of crime. In *Political
Crime in Contemporary America: A Critical Approach,* ed. K. D. Tunnell, 3–29. New York: Garland.

Braithwaite, J. 1982. Enforced self-regulation: A new strategy for corporate
crime control. *Michigan Law Review* 80(7): 1466–1507.

———. 1984. *Corporate Crime in the Pharmaceutical Industry.* London:
Routledge.

———. 1993. Transnational regulation of the pharmaceutical industry. *Annals of the American Academy of Political and Social Science* 525(January): 12–30.

Brisson, C., M. Vezina and A. Vinet. 1992. Health problems of women employed in jobs involving psychological and ergonomic stressors: The
case of garment workers in Quebec. *Women and Health* 18(3): 49–66.

Caulfield, S. L. and N. A. Wonders. 1993. Personal AND political: Violence
against women and the role of the state. In *Political Crime in Contemporary America: A Critical Approach,* ed. K. D. Tunnell, 79–100. New
York: Garland.

Chambliss, W. J. 1989. State-organized crime. *Criminology* 27(2): 183–208.

Chapman, J. R. 1990. Violence against women as a violation of human
rights. *Social Justice* 17(2): 54–70.

Chavkin, W., ed. 1984. *Double Exposure: Women's Health Hazards on the
Job and at Home.* New York: Monthly Review Press.

CIA to settle sex bias claims. 1995. *Chicago Tribune,* March 30: 4.

Clinard, M. B. and P. C. Yeager. 1980. *Corporate Crime.* New York: Free
Press.

Coleman, J. W. 1994. *The Criminal Elite: The Sociology of White-Collar
Crime.* 3rd ed. New York: St. Martin's Press.

Crenshaw, K. 1989. Demarginalizing the intersection of race and sex: A black feminist critique of antidiscrimination doctrine, feminist theory and antiracist politics. *University of Chicago Legal Forum* 1989: 139–67.

Daly, K. and M. Chesney-Lind. 1988. Feminism and criminology. *Justice Quarterly* 5(4): 497–535.

DeKeseredy, W. and R. Hinch. 1991. *Woman Abuse: Sociological Perspectives*. Toronto: Thompson Educational Publishing.

Dion, K. K., E. Berscheid, and E. Walster. 1972. What is beautiful is good. *Journal of Personality and Social Psychology* 24(3): 285–90.

Dowie, M. and Mother Jones. 1979. The dumping of hazardous products on foreign markets. *Mother Jones* 4: 23–44.

Draper, E. 1993. Gendered constructions of suitable work. *Social Problems* 40(1): 90–107.

Drug trials are criticized for lack of women. 1992. *New York Times*, October 30: A16.

Dumais, L. 1992. Impact of the participation of women in science: On rethinking the place of women especially in occupational health. *Women and Health* 18(3): 11–25.

Elias, R. 1986. *The Politics of Victimization: Victims, Victimology, and Human Rights*. New York: Oxford University Press.

Ermann, M. D. and R. J. Lundman. 1992. *Corporate and Governmental Deviance: Problems of Organizational Behavior in Contemporary Society*. 4th ed. New York: Oxford University Press.

FBI pays $647,000 over sex harassment. 1995. *Chicago Tribune*, February 1: 4.

Finley, L. M. 1986. Transcending equality theory: A way out of the maternity and the workplace debate. *Columbia Law Review* 86(6): 1118–82.

Fisher, S. 1988. *In the Patient's Best Interest: Women and the Politics of Medical Decisions*. New Brunswick, NJ: Rutgers University Press.

Fisse, B. and J. Braithwaite. 1993. *Corporations, Crime and Accountability*. Cambridge, U.K.: Cambridge University Press.

Fox, S. 1991. *Toxic Work: Women Workers at GTE Lenkurt*. Philadelphia: Temple University Press.

Frank, N. K. and M. J. Lynch. 1992. *Corporate Crime, Corporate Violence: A Primer*. New York: Harrow and Heston.

Freeman, S. J. M. 1990. *Managing Lives: Corporate Women and Social Change*. Amherst, MA: University of Massachusetts Press.

Geis, G. 1967. The heavy electrical equipment antitrust cases of 1961. In *Criminal Behavior Systems*, ed. M. Clinard and R. Quinney, 139–50. New York: Holt, Rinehart and Winston.

———. 1975. Victimization patterns in white-collar crime. In *Victimology: A New Focus. Exploiters and Exploited*, vol. 5, ed. I. Drapkin and E. Viano. Lexington, MA: D. C. Heath.

30   Gerber, J. and S. L. Weeks. 1992. Women as victims of corporate crime: A call for research on a neglected topic. *Deviant Behavior* 13: 325–47.

Goldin, C. 1990. *Understanding the Gender Gap*. New York: Oxford University Press.

Guarasci, R. 1987. Death by cotton dust. In *Corporate Violence: Injury and Death for Profit*, ed. S. L. Hills, 76–92. Totowa, NJ: Rowman and Littlefield.

Gwartney-Gibbs, P. A. and D. H. Lach. 1994. Gender and workplace dispute resolution: A conceptual and theoretical model. *Law and Society Review* 28(2): 265–96.

Hilts, P. 1993. FDA ends ban on women in drug testing. *New York Times*, March 25: B8.

Holmstrom, L. and A. W. Burgess. 1978. *The Victim of Rape: Institutional Reactions*. New York: Wiley.

Janoff-Bulman, R. 1985. Criminal v. non-criminal victimization: Victims' reactions. *Victimology* 10: 498–511.

Karmen, A. 1990. *Crime Victims: An Introduction to Victimology*. 2nd ed. Pacific Grove, CA: Brooks/Cole.

Kenney, S. J. 1992. *For Whose Protection? Reproductive Hazards and Exclusionary Policies in the United States and Britain*. Ann Arbor, MI: University of Michigan Press.

Kilian, M. 1994. Sex bias charges latest woe for CIA. *Chicago Tribune*, September 8: 4.

Klein, D. 1981. Violence against women: Some considerations regarding its causes and its elimination. *Crime and Delinquency* 27(1): 64–80.

Kramer, R. C. 1992. The space shuttle *Challenger* explosion: A case study of state-corporate crime. In *White-Collar Crime Reconsidered*, ed. K. Schlegel and D. Weisburd, 214–43. Boston: Northeastern University Press.

Kuumba, M. B. 1994. Reproductive imperialism: Population and labor control of the Third World. Paper presented at the annual meeting of the American Sociological Association, August.

Leary, W. E. 1993. Broader uses seen for abortion pill. *New York Times*, September 9: A17.

Mathes, E. W. and A. Kahn. 1975. Physical attractiveness, happiness, neuroticism, and self-esteem. *Journal of Psychology* 90(May): 27–30.

Mawbry, R. I. and S. Walkgate. 1994. *Critical Victimology*. Thousand Oaks, CA: Sage.

Mayer, J. and J. Abramson. 1994. *Strange Justice: The Selling of Clarence Thomas*. Boston: Houghton Mifflin.

Mears, J. 1993. Jury sides with breast implant-maker in lawsuit brought by topless dancer. *Buffalo News*, June 12: A2.

Messerschmidt, J. W. 1993. *Masculinities and Crime: Critique and Reconceptualization of Theory.* Lanham, MD: Rowman and Littlefield.

Michalowski, R. J. and R. C. Kramer. 1987. The space between laws: The problem of corporate crime in a transnational context. *Social Problems* 34(1): 34–53.

Moore, E. and M. Mills. 1990. The neglected victims and unexamined costs of white-collar crime. *Crime and Delinquency* 36(3): 408–18.

Peppin, P. 1992. Equality, difference, bodily control and harm prevention: Gendered aspects of pharmaceutical products law. Paper presented at the Corporate Crime: Ethics, Law and the State conference, Queen's University, Kingston, Ontario, Canada, November.

Randall, D. M. and J. F. Short, Jr. 1983. Women in toxic work environments: A case study of social problem development. *Social Problems* 30(4): 410–23.

Reiman, J. 1990. *The Rich Get Richer and the Poor Get Prison: Ideology, Class, and Criminal Justice.* 3rd ed. New York: Macmillan.

Reske, H. J. 1994. Secrecy orders at issue. *ABA Journal* 80(August): 32–33.

Reskin, B. F. and P. A. Roos. 1990. *Job Queues, Gender Queues: Explaining Women's Inroads into Male Occupations.* Philadelphia: Temple University Press.

Rifai, M. A. Y. 1982. Victimology: A theoretical framework. In *The Victim in International Perspective,* ed. H. J. Schneider, 65–79. New York: Aldine de Gruyter.

Schrager, L. and J. F. Short, Jr. 1977. Toward a sociology of organizational crime. *Social Problems* 25(April): 407–19.

Schwendinger, H. and J. Schwendinger. 1970. Defenders of order or guardians of human rights? *Issues in Criminology* 5(2): 123–57.

Shapiro, L. 1992. What is it with women and breasts? *Newsweek,* January 20: 57.

Shapiro, S. P. 1985. The road not taken: The elusive path to criminal prosecution for white-collar offenders. *Law and Society Review* 19(2): 179–217.

Shichor, D. 1989. Corporate deviance and corporate victimization: A review and some elaborations. *International Review of Victimology* 1: 67–88.

Shover, N., G. L. Fox and M. Mills. 1994. Long-term consequences of victimization by white-collar crime. *Justice Quarterly* 11(1): 75–98.

Simon, D. R. and D. S. Eitzen. 1993. *Elite Deviance.* 4th ed. Boston: Allyn and Bacon.

Smith, C. 1985. Response to victims: Are the institutional mandates of police and medicine sufficient? *Victimology* 10: 560–72.

Sobol, R. B. 1991. *Bending the Law: The Story of the Dalkon Shield Bankruptcy.* Chicago: University of Chicago Press.

32   Sutherland, E. H. 1940. White-collar criminality. *American Sociological Review* 5(February): 1–12.

Tunnell, K. D. 1993. *Political Crime in Contemporary America: A Critical Approach.* New York: Garland.

Vezina, N. and J. Courville. 1992. Integration of women into traditionally masculine jobs. *Women and Health* 18(3): 97–118.

Walklate, S. 1989. *Victimology: The Victim and the Criminal Justice Process.* London: Unwin Hyman.

Walsh, M. E. and D. D. Schram. 1980. The victim of white-collar crime: Accuser or accused? In *White-Collar Crime: Theory and Research,* ed. G. Geis and E. Stotland, 32–51. Beverly Hills, CA: Sage.

Ward, K. 1986. "Women and transnational corporation employment: A world-system and feminist analysis." Women in Development working paper no. 120, Office of Women in International Development, Michigan State University, East Lansing.

Wilson, G. and D. Nias. 1976. *Love's Mysteries: The Psychology of Sexual Attraction.* London: Open Books.

Wright, J. P., F. T. Cullen and M. B. Blankenship. 1995. The social construction of corporate violence: Media coverage of the Imperial Food Products fire. *Crime and Delinquency* 41(1): 20–36.

THEORETICAL PERSPECTIVES ON THE CORPORATE VICTIMIZATION OF WOMEN

Sally S. Simpson and Lori Elis

Since Sutherland's call to study white-collar crime, there has been a great deal of discussion and research concentrating on definitions of corporate crime, its measurement, etiology, and control.[1] There has been less investigation, however, of corporate crime victims, and even less concern with the gendered nature of white-collar crime and victimization. For the most part, empirical research and theory tends to focus on offenders instead of victims. When the focus becomes more specialized, for example, corporate crime, it is the organization that is treated as the criminal actor, rather than the actually culpable decision makers (who tend overwhelmingly to be male). Consequently, with few exceptions[2] the ways in which gender structures offending patterns and victimization have been ignored.

This chapter develops a theoretical framework for the analysis of gendered corporate victimization. To lay out this perspective, we first review the ways in which corporate crime, victimization, and the potential for legal and other forms of redress are gendered. Second, corporate victimization is assessed from several different feminist perspectives. Finally, three case studies of corporate victimization highlight issues of women's health, occupational segregation, the "cult of domesticity and femininity," and gender inequality before the law—issues that are fundamental to understanding the problem of gendered corporate victimization.

GENDERED VICTIMIZATION AND CORPORATE CRIME

Corporate crime is ubiquitous.[3] Its victims are rich and poor, urban and rural, male and female, young and old, and members of all racial and ethnic groups. Yet there are discernible patterns of corporate vic-

34   timization by gender. One's chances of experiencing certain types of victimization are affected by the kind of work one does (which differs by gender), job-related restrictions (exclusions applying to women based on reproductive or other sex-based hazards or discrimination), the separation of home work from paid labor, and the cultural messages that are conveyed about masculinity and femininity in American society.

Gendered Victimization and Paid Labor

Male workers tend to be exposed to unsafe working conditions and toxic chemicals in basic manufacturing industries (steel, auto, chemicals, tire and rubber) as well as in farming, construction, and extractive industries like mining. Generally, these types of work have traditionally excluded females, thus increasing the male risk of victimization.[4]

Proportionally fewer women than men are employed full-time in the labor force, and female employment is concentrated in clerical, sales, and service work.[5] Within these occupations and among full-time workers—especially nonwhite and unmarried women—there are high levels of poverty.[6] Even though women's paid work is concentrated in relatively few industries, little is known about their occupational risks because women tend to be excluded from occupational health research. [7] Furthermore, for some occupations, such as private household work (an occupation that is disproportionately performed by black women), there is little information available from sources, such as workers' compensation claims, from which risk assessments can be calculated.[8] When standards are set in industries specifying worker tolerances and illness compensation, they tend to be based on male experiences and male tolerances.[9] As a consequence, the victimization risks of female employees, particularly those who belong to impoverished minorities, are difficult to assess accurately.[10]

Gendered Victimization and Home Work

Neither is the home a safe harbor for women. The dual role that women play in unpaid work (namely, as homemakers and mothers) increases their vulnerability to certain types of corporate victimization. The National Safety Council proclaims that one is more apt to be injured in the home than at work. For women, this translates into injuries from (1) household cleaning products that contain chemicals and can cause burns, systemic poisoning, and skin and eye irritations[11] and (2) tasks like cooking, moving furniture, cleaning windows, and so forth. Because these injuries occur at home, affecting unpaid ("unproductive") laborers or domestics, there is little protection for the victim. Because injuries are not covered by workplace laws or standards,[12] responsibility for maintaining a safe household is deferred from manufacturers (who provide very little information about product safety) to wives and mothers.[13] "Industry . . . prefers to imagine that home and work are two separate spheres. It can then ignore its responsibility for health and safety, and insist that this is the woman's responsibility."[14]

On the reproductive end, responsibility for birth control has shifted away from "moderately effective, coitus-related, male-dominated, nonmedical methods to highly effective, non-coital-related, female-dominated methods that need the involvement of medical authorities."[15] As a consequence of this shift, women have become increasingly vulnerable to corporate crime victimization from pharmaceutical companies, which have developed, in conjunction with physicians, drugs and devices that prevent reproduction through alteration of the hormonal composition of a woman's body, insertion of foreign devices into her uterus, and/or precipitation of spontaneous abortions.

One prominent scholar argues that women are disproportionately victimized by harmful drugs and medical devices.[16] Citing evidence from her review of case annotations described in the U.S. Code Annotated concerning multidistrict litigation, she discovered that while some cases were not gender specific (such as intraocular lenses and a swine flu vaccine) and a few others harmed mostly men (Agent Orange and asbestos), many cases documented harm to women from products supposedly designed "for their own good" (IUDs, tampons, silicone gel breast implants). There was not "a single mass tort in which men were injured by a product made for men to use or take, ostensibly to enhance their well-being."[17]

Gendered Victimization and Consumption

Examples of sexism in advertising are replete, and it is unnecessary to detail them here. An important consequence of the media's portrayal of the perfect woman as young, beautiful, and sexy is the negative effect this has on the female self-concept. If a woman somehow fails to measure up to this ideal (and few women can), a spate of cosmetics and beauty aids claim to assist her in the quest.

The health hazards of cosmetics are difficult to establish, partly be-

36   cause the FDA is restricted in how it can proceed in this area (only against contaminated and adulterated products) but also because the agency tends not to treat the cosmetic threat seriously. For instance, in the 1970s, although beauty aids ranked second among all classes of products causing injuries (the National Committee on Product Safety reported 60,000 persons injured yearly), only 17 of the 2,075 firms and products against which the FDA took action were cosmetics-related—a mere .08 percent of the total.[18]

Marketeers' conception and rendering of female beauty is also directly related to women's attempts physically to alter the way they look. Thanks to the medical profession, invasive surgeries are offered to women dissatisfied with their physical appearance: techniques that can trim fat from the body, remove lines from the face, and plump up breasts thought to be too small or sagging due to age, childbirth, or dieting. The current breast implant fad is but one of many unnecessary and dangerous surgeries historically advocated and/or supported by the medical profession. Others include hysterectomies, forced sterilization for minority women, and cesarean sections.[19]

Access to Redress

An important aspect of the gendered victimization of corporate crime has to do with reparation and punishment. A number of important questions about these processes are relevant for feminist theory: (1) Are female and male harms equally represented in the law? (2) How is access to legal systems and other means of redress distributed by gender? (3) Do females seek redress as often as males do? (4) How do case outcomes compare?

The process of redress for victims of corporate crime is clearly gendered. Workplace hazards are evaluated and assessed in the context of traditional basic manufacturing industries that historically excluded women and whose positions are still highly segregated by gender.[20]

Occupational segregation by gender (and race) affects the kinds of substances identified as harmful to workers as well as the workplace standards and classifications (for example, light versus heavy) related to factors such as exposure to heat[21] and toxins[22] and definitions of reproductive risk.[23] While female-dominated occupations are *assumed* to be safe and healthy[24] (even though the evidence suggests that they are not), empirical research on male-dominated occupations and workplace experiences sets the normative base for risk assessments, except where women work in male-dominated occupations. In these jobs a different kind of risk is assessed, namely, the threat to reproductive capacity—but primarily that of the female employee and not her male counterpart. These risks are then used to justify the exclusion of women from these jobs. Ironically, critics note that when reproductive threats to women emerge in female-dominated occupations, rarely are women excluded from employment in these jobs.[25] Equally troubling, however, is the failure to evaluate reproductive risks for males in male-dominated occupations.

One consequence of gendered laws, standards, and classifications is that females are denied or restricted access to legal redress when victimization occurs. We have already noted that female victims of corporate crime (as consumers and employees) may not be covered under workers' compensation or other product safety regulations. Similarly, because African Americans and other minorities tend to be employed in small businesses and shops, their on-the-job accidents and illnesses are not covered by federal regulations.[26] Additionally, women tend to be employed in occupations and businesses that lack formal dispute resolution mechanisms (such as access to unions); and women working in male-typed jobs (that is, tokens) have less access to informal and formal dispute resolution forums than do males working in female-typed jobs.[27]

Steinman argues that women victims in tort cases are the object of discrimination from the beginning of the legal process through to its conclusion.[28] Regulatory agencies, like the FDA, demonstrate an economic and attitudinal indifference toward women victims.[29] When cases are brought by individual plaintiffs, a double victimization occurs when the defense pursues a victim character assassination defense strategy. In the Dalkon Shield IUD cases, A. H. Robins's attorneys sought to blame the victims' sexual behavior (claiming promiscuity) for their physical injuries instead of acknowledging that the IUD had "wicking" problems that allowed bacteria to gain access to the uterus.

Female litigants also receive significantly smaller damage awards than do males.[30] In determining the appropriate compensation for damages, courts take into account the loss of productivity (future income) as well as the type of injury incurred (physical versus emotional). By focusing on labor market productivity as a basis for compensation, women are disadvantaged in two ways: (1) in general, women are paid substantially less than men and thus will be awarded smaller payments for their injuries and (2) a significant portion of women's labor is unpaid,

38 yet crucial. "Important services such as household management and child rearing are consistently undervalued or overlooked in a system which gauges damages to the market economy."[31]

Stereotypes about males and females have contributed to differential evaluations of the type of injury suffered by victims. Female injuries have often been dismissed as hysterical,[32] whereas males treated for similar injuries are assumed to be physically, not emotionally, damaged.[33] Recovery for physical damages is easier than for the more nebulous emotional distress category.[34]

Gender stereotypes even permeate the court (judicial) guidelines for the evaluation of impairment. Citing examples from Ellen Smith Pryor's (1990) book review of the American Medical Association's *Guides to the Evaluation of Permanent Impairment*, Steinman describes how whole-person sexual impairments are calculated by the AMA.[35] For males, penile impairment is considered 5–10 percent whole-person impairment when "sexual function is possible, but there are varying degrees of difficulty of erection, ejaculation, and/or sensation." Conversely, for females, impairment of the vulva-vagina rates a 0 percent whole-person impairment if "symptoms . . . do not require continuous treatment," "the vagina is adequate for childbirth," and "sexual intercourse is possible." Obviously, impairment of a man's enjoyment of sex can result in less than whole-person status, but as long as a woman can have sexual intercourse and bear children, her whole-person status remains intact.

In sum, corporate crime victimization, like many other forms of crime, is differentiated by gender. So too, the law and access to it reflect gender bias. Feminist theory offers some insight into this differentiation. In the next section, liberal, marxist, socialist, and radical feminist frameworks are applied to the corporate victimization of women.

FEMINIST THEORY AND THE CORPORATE VICTIMIZATION OF WOMEN

The development of feminist criminology parallels the development of feminist thinking in other disciplines. It began with criticism of female exclusion from the research and theoretical domain and/or the often blatant sexism in how females were portrayed when they were discussed. This early critique led to more investigations that put women and women's experiences at the center of the research endeavor.

More recently, however, feminist criminologists have shifted away from an exclusive focus on females. At the heart of this shift is the recognition that social organization is *gendered*, that male and female lives are interconnected materially, culturally, and structurally.

There is no single feminist theory or perspective. Rather, feminist criminology draws from several theoretical frameworks—including liberal feminism, marxist feminism, socialist feminism, radical feminism, and women-of-color feminism.[36] Each of these perspectives has something useful to say about the nature of gendered corporate crime victimization, but like Gerber and Weeks,[37] we believe that socialist feminism (with modifications from women of color) offers the keenest and broadest interpretations.

Briefly, each orientation differs as to (1) the historical development and source of gendered social organization, (2) who benefits from such social organization and how, and (3) tactics for change.[38] Liberals tend to view gender inequality as stemming from the separation of public and private spheres after industrialization. This separation, they claim, caused the development of distinct gender roles and attitudes that justified and reinforced differential treatment of males and females; men worked outside the home while women cared for the house and family. As society has modernized, however, this organization is outdated and exclusionary for both sexes—males who would like to develop a more nurturing side as well as females who want equal access to societal opportunities. Changes in attitudes and opportunities, liberals argue, can be achieved through legal interventions combined with basic changes in institutional socialization, such as the use of gender-neutral language in educational learning materials. Although liberal feminists (primarily those in the humanitarian camp) acknowledge that this type of gendered social organization has negative consequences for males, the focal concern of liberals is to gain equality for women, that is, they assume that women want what men have.

A liberal feminist approach to corporate victimization of women would analyze the problem in several ways. First, to the extent that males and females are treated differently as victims or plaintiffs, liberals advocate adopting gender-neutral legislation for equal protection under the law. For instance, they believe that reproductive harms should be studied and calculated for both males and females. If one or both sexes are affected by workplace exposure, instead of excluding women from employment in those positions, companies have an obligation to abate the hazard.[39] If abatement is not possible, job relocation at similar wages

40   should occur—a policy of rate retention.[40] Second, because few women are in positions of power and decision making within corporations, regulatory agencies, and court systems, female voices and concerns are not heard. Thus, liberals assert that better integration of women into these positions will offer more protection and support for female victims of corporate crime.[41]

Marxist, socialist, and radical feminist approaches offer more of a systemic critique of capitalist, patriarchal social organization that gives rise to gender oppression and subordination. Their perspectives differ as to whether the basis of gender conflict lies in relations of production, relations of reproduction and consumption, or a combination of the two. Marxist feminists cite the first, radical feminists emphasize the second, and socialist feminists combine both elements.[42] Recognizing the class basis of material relations in a capitalist society, marxist feminists would examine the ways in which women's victimization by corporations, general lack of protection, and limited access to redress serve the interests of capital. A shift from capitalism to socialist or communist social organization will eliminate class divisions (other types of stratification will necessarily follow), and the basis for corporate crime will be eradicated. Radical feminists, on the other hand, look to male subordination of women and control of women's sexuality to understand the ways in which women are victimized by corporations (for example, prescription drugs to prevent miscarriage that harm both the mother and fetus; birth control devices aimed at controlling female, not male, fecundity; protective legislation that excludes females, not males, from hazardous workplaces due to reproductive threats; and so forth).

A socialist-feminist perspective analyzes both social class and patriarchy as intersecting systems of dominance that allow males to appropriate the labor power of females (paid and unpaid labor) and to control their sexuality. Patriarchal gender relations structure criminality—both in terms of who does what kind of offending and the kind of victimization likely to occur. For instance, Messerschmidt hypothesizes that patriarchal capitalist societies produce two types of people: the powerless (women and the working classes) and the powerful (a group composed of men and the capitalist class). While both groups commit crimes, Messerschmidt argues that the greatest amount and most serious of these (corporate crime, sexual violence) are committed by the powerful against the powerless (working classes and women).[43]

From this viewpoint, corporate victimization of women represents the power of capitalist males to expropriate women's labor and reproductive power for the males' benefit. Thus, the fact that women's occupations have fewer health and safety standards and that some are not covered by workers' compensation demonstrates working women's relatively powerless status vis-à-vis working men. Women's occupations are seen primarily as an outgrowth of their roles in the home, namely, nurturing and providing service. Consequently, they tend not to be as well compensated, are assumed not to carry the same industrial risks as "real" jobs (read men's work), and therefore are not considered to be in need of special avenues for redress—in sum, all conditions that benefit capital. Men's work, in contrast, is more highly valued; is assumed (based on empirical studies of occupational hazards) to be riskier; and contains provisions that allow compensation, although limiting the amount injured workers may seek. Men benefit from this situation in that their contributions to production are acknowledged and given limited protection within the capitalist system. Capital benefits economically because workers' compensation places limitations on the amount of the award (thus, there is little substantial threat to capitalist profits). Capital benefits ideologically by demonstrating its concern for labor issues.

Because the domestic realm of housework, child care, and consumption (women's unpaid labor) does not directly contribute to production in capitalist societies, it is devalued. Moreover, because legally the home is viewed as a distinct and separate sphere, what happens in the home is often viewed as a private matter, beyond regulation and legal intervention. This view of the home benefits both capital and men. Capital benefits because reproduction, child care, homemaking, and consumption all reproduce the labor force with little cost to capital. Additionally, unemployed women make up a large portion of the reserve labor force that can be called into service as a means to increase competition among workers and depress wages. Finally, the isolation of women in the home (a private domain) reinforces the notion of *caveat emptor* (buyer beware). If a woman, as household consumer or domestic laborer, is injured by a household chemical (say, a cleaning product that is toxic, carcinogenic, or flammable), her home labor is not protected by a special body of law (such as labor law); nor does she have the kind of institutional supports, such as labor unions, offered to other types of workers. The home is not a regulated environment, and manufacturers are therefore less accountable to these kinds of victims.

Males, primarily husbands, benefit from these domestic arrangements. Studies demonstrate that the bulk of home labor is conducted

42   by women even if they are employed full-time outside the home.[44] Thus, males expropriate the productive labor power of women. While men do not directly benefit from the corporate victimization of women in the domestic realm, they do benefit from the lack of regulation and intervention into the private sector, where patriarchal power and privilege are normative.

So, too, do males benefit from modern birth control developments. While males benefit from the sexual freedom women gain as the threat of unwanted pregnancies is removed, women's actual freedom is curtailed and mediated through the medical community—typically, upper-class white males.[45] Medical controls over female reproduction reinforce the dominant gender stereotypes about sex and responsibility, namely, that women are responsible for male sexuality. The most direct benefit that males reap from the technological control of women's reproduction is that they themselves are spared similar experimentation and corporate victimization.

Socialist-feminist perspectives, while offering important insights into the problem of corporate victimization of women, are problematic for a number of reasons: First, they fail to incorporate race and racial oppression systematically as a distinct and intersecting system of dominance into the analytic framework.[46] All males and all females, with a salute to class differences, are viewed as essentially the same. Second, socialist-feminist perspectives are too macro in orientation and do not "account for the intentions of actors and for how action, including crime, is a meaningful construct in itself."[47] In other words, theory should provide insight into how individuals experience gender, race, and class relations and, in turn, how experiences shape social actions and social structures. Finally, socialist feminism does not reject marxist analytical categories but instead attempts to accommodate gender within them. Thus, production and reproduction are viewed as separate systems, one being the site of class relations and the other the site of patriarchy. Critics argue that these systems are reciprocal and complementary. "Reproductive labor is simultaneously productive labor and vice versa."[48]

A modified version of socialist-feminist criminology, one that is sensitive to micro processes and intragender diversity,[49] would better account for the ways in which all women, including minorities, are victimized by corporations and the extent to which access to redress is structured not just by gender but also by race. Further, differing conceptions of masculinity and femininity by race influence how females interpret their own victimization and how they are likely to respond to it. An example is helpful here.

The history of the birth control movement in the United States reflects two primary concerns: the individual freedom of women and population control.[50] These concerns were structured by race and social class in that it was primarily white, middle-class freedoms that were sought and the fertility of working-class and minority women that was controlled. "What was demanded as a 'right' for the privileged came to be interpreted as a 'duty' for the poor."[51] After decades of involuntary sterilizations, women of color came increasingly to view birth control as "genocide" and to reject its use. These different experiences, according to our modified theory, should influence both social action (that is, who is apt to use birth control) and aggregate patterns of victimization. We expect that the primary victims of unsafe birth control products are white middle-class women—those most apt to view birth control as a choice.

In the next section we apply our modified version of socialist-feminist theory to three case studies of women's corporate victimization. The corporations discussed are Imperial Food Products, Regal Tube Company, and Ortho Pharmaceutical Company.

CASE STUDIES OF CORPORATE VICTIMIZATION

Imperial Food Products

> There's a USDA inspector in every poultry plant to protect consumers from getting a stomachache, but there's nobody protecting people [employees] from getting killed.
>
> (Deborah Berkowitz, United Food and Commercial Workers
> International Union, *Time*, 1991:28)

In September 1991, a fire at an Imperial Food Products poultry-processing plant in Hamlet, North Carolina, killed twenty-five workers and injured fifty-six others. Although the cause of the fire was accidental, the resulting deaths and injuries were linked to violations of Occupational Safety and Health Administration (OSHA) workplace safety standards. Neither fire alarms nor sprinkler systems existed at the plant, and seven of the nine exit doors were either locked or obstructed.[52] Many of the workers who died were found next to locked exit doors or inside freezers where they ran to escape from the fire.[53]

44   The circumstances contributing to the deaths of twenty-five people were just one aspect of the hazardous working conditions at Imperial. The work force (consisting primarily of impoverished, black females) also had to cope with excessive heat from being forced to work in a room with no fans or windows, faulty equipment that management claimed was fine,[54] and periodic fires around the fryers.[55] Assembly-line workers were required to work so quickly cutting, bagging, and frying chicken that they were at risk of suffering severe cuts and diseases associated with repetitive hand movements (for example, carpal tunnel syndrome).[56]

In addition to facing hazardous physical conditions at the plant, workers were subjected to strict control by the management. For instance, the women were limited to two fifteen-minute breaks per day with an additional half hour for lunch. The consequence of taking an extra break, being absent, or arriving late was a warning. After five warnings an employee was terminated and given no chance to be rehired.[57]

Although the nature of work within the poultry industry has become increasingly dangerous recently, Imperial's plant had not been inspected by state or OSHA investigators in the eleven years it had been operating.[58] Had the plant been inspected, the accessibility of exit doors would have been checked.[59]

As a result of the hazardous working conditions initiated and left unchecked, twenty-five individuals died. An examination of the working conditions at Imperial illustrates the power differential between the owners and managers of Imperial Food Products and the paid labor force. It was this power differential that led to the victimization of the workers at Imperial.

The owner of Imperial Food, Emmit Roe, operated a business in an extremely competitive and dangerous industry. It was to his financial advantage to use a labor force that he could coerce into working under extremely hazardous and strictly controlled conditions. The position of impoverished, black females on the lowest rung of a labor force divided by gender, race, and social class left these women vulnerable to Emmit Roe and the management at Imperial.

Such women are more likely than other segments of the population to be kept in powerless positions in the labor market, and as a result of their economic dependence on their jobs, they are extremely vulnerable to exploitation.[60] At Imperial, the ability of the management to hire and fire, along with the knowledge that there were "always plenty of other poor people in town who would work on the poultry assembly lines if they got the chance,"[61] forced the workers to submit to the conditions set by Emmit Roe and the managers or face unemployment.

Additionally, two avenues of worker protection were inaccessible. The first, the labor union, possesses little power in the poultry industry. According to Thomas Geoghegan, a labor law attorney, the fire at Imperial "wouldn't have happened if there'd been a decent union there."[62] Second, the lack of external regulatory intervention at Imperial demonstrates the disregard regulatory agencies (OSHA) had for the health and welfare of Imperial's workers.

The only other avenue available for redress came into play after the fire, when surviving victims and families of those who died sued the insurance companies representing Imperial. The suit was settled for just over $16 million. Emmit Roe, the owner of Imperial, also pled guilty to twenty-five counts of involuntary manslaughter and was sentenced to twenty years in prison.[63]

Regal Tube Company

> Before this time, I was a happy and well-adjusted wife and mother. After working at Regal, I was afraid to leave my home and was unable to socialize. I was terrified that my former boss would find me and continue to assault me. I cut off all my hair to disguise myself.
>
> (Helen Brooms, quoted in Winston, 1990:407)

In 1983 Helen Brooms, a thirty-six-year-old black woman, was hired as an industrial nurse at Regal Tube Company, a subsidiary of Copperweld Corporation.[64] During her sixteen-month tenure at Regal, she was repeatedly subjected to sexual and racial harassment by Charles Gustafson, the human resources manager. After one incident, in which Gustafson directly propositioned her, Brooms experienced a physical illness linked to her emotional distress. After this incident, she informed her immediate supervisor of Gustafson's behavior. He directed her to tell Gustafson "that her husband had given her herpes and to tape-record her conversations with Gustafson."[65]

After dismissing that advice, Brooms met with a representative from the Illinois Department of Human Rights. She wrote a letter (after the meeting) detailing Gustafson's behavior and sent copies to several members of the management at Regal Tube and Copperweld Corporation. Upon receipt of the letter, Regal Tube Company attempted to handle the matter internally. An independent investigator was hired to examine the complaint, and Regal's general manager met with Helen Brooms and Charles Gustafson. Brooms asked for two things: an apology from the company and Gustafson and an end to the harassment. The general manager responded by warning Gustafson that he would be fired if he continued his behavior, postponed his merit salary increase, and required him to apologize. For a short period of time, Gustafson ceased the harassment.

However, soon thereafter the harassment began again. Gustafson showed Brooms a picture of a black woman engaged in sodomy and told her that "the photograph showed the talent of a black woman."[66] Brooms responded by filing a charge of discrimination with the Illinois Department of Human Rights and the Equal Employment Opportunity Commission (EEOC). Shortly after Gustafson received notice of the complaint, he showed Brooms a copy of a picture that contained a bestiality scene and told her that was how "she was going to end up."[67] Gustafson then grabbed her arm and threatened to kill her. As Brooms was running from the office, she fell down a flight of stairs.

After that incident, Brooms did not return to work. She received two months' disability compensation and then resigned. Shortly after Brooms's resignation, Gustafson tendered his resignation. On February 20, 1985, Brooms filed suit against Gustafson, Regal Tube, and Copperweld Corporation for sexual harassment and retaliation in violation of Title VII of the Civil Rights Act of 1964, and racial discrimination in violation of Section 1981 of the Civil Rights Act of 1866.

The harassment and retaliation claims were tried before a judge, while the racial discrimination claim was tried before a jury. The judge found for Brooms on the charge of harassment in violation of Title VII and awarded her back pay, but he also found that the response of Gustafson and Regal, after receiving notice of the complaint to the EEOC, did not constitute retaliation. The jury also denied Brooms's racial discrimination claims under Section 1981. Both Brooms and Regal Tube Company appealed the judgment. Brooms appealed on the grounds that her Section 1981 claims were denied, while Regal Tube Company appealed the finding of sexual harassment and the award of back pay. After consideration by the appellate court, these findings were affirmed.

The sexual and racial harassment of Helen Brooms in the workplace, her original attempts to deal with the matter internally, and her final attempt to resolve the matter in the court system illustrate the position of many black women in the workplace. Historical and economic factors render black women particularly vulnerable to racial and sexual harassment at work, and their tenuous economic standing (below that of white women) places additional pressure on them not to pursue charges because they may be more economically dependent on their jobs than white women.[68] In the case of Helen Brooms, this dilemma is evident. Helen Brooms tolerated the harassment by Charles Gustafson for an extended period of time before she informed her supervisor.

The male supervisors at Regal, however, did not support her attempts to deal with the matter internally. The response of her immediate supervisor (telling her to tell Gustafson she had herpes) indicated that he did not care enough about Gustafson's behavior to bring it to the attention of his supervisors. Rather, he imposed on Helen Brooms the responsibility to stop her own victimization. Additionally, the later decision of the general manager to warn Gustafson and postpone his merit salary increase was ineffective.

After several aborted internal attempts to change Gustafson's behavior, Brooms filed sexual and racial harassment charges. However, the inability of the legal system to recognize discrimination based on both gender and race, as opposed to either gender or race, left her in a unique position. Because the court did not recognize the dual sources of discrimination and treated the harassment as only gender-based, the only compensation for which Brooms was eligible was back pay.[69] Additionally, after leaving Regal, Brooms developed a severe case of depression, which led to her inability to work and required extensive psychiatric therapy. During her experience at Regal and thereafter, much of the harm she suffered was emotional, perhaps making it more difficult for the court to recognize it.[70]

Ortho Pharmaceutical Company

> You need not feel any urgency about removing the diaphragm. It is safe to let it remain in position for 24 hours. Should you forget to remove it for some hours, or should removal be inconvenient at any particular time, that is no cause for concern.
>
> (*Baroldy v. Ortho Pharmaceutical Company*, 1988:577)

The previous statements were included with the Ortho All-Flex diaphragm purchased by Roberta Baroldy in July 1982.[71] Believing that use of the diaphragm resulted in "no cause for concern," she wore it regularly for three days, removing and reinserting it repeatedly, but never

48 retaining it continuously for twenty-four hours. On the fourth day, she was taken to a hospital emergency room and diagnosed with toxic shock syndrome (TSS). She remained in the hospital for forty-one days, periodically comatose and near death.

In 1983 Roberta Baroldy and her husband filed a product liability suit against Ortho Pharmaceutical Company on the grounds that the diaphragm was defective. The basis of their claim relied on two key facts: (1) the booklet accompanying the diaphragm Roberta Baroldy purchased did not contain a warning about TSS and (2) the booklet contained false and misleading statements concerning the length of time the diaphragm could be left in place safely.

During the subsequent trial, medical experts for the plaintiffs testified that use of the diaphragm had caused Roberta's TSS. Additional testimony indicated that officials at Ortho Pharmaceutical Company were aware of evidence linking diaphragm use and TSS, yet did nothing to warn consumers.

Two physicians, Dr. William Dillon and Dr. Claire Wilson, testified that they had informed Ortho representatives about a link between diaphragm use and TSS well before Roberta Baroldy purchased her diaphragm. During a research study, Dr. Dillon had discovered a relationship between diaphragm use and an increase in the bacteria associated with TSS. In 1981 he reported his results to the Ortho salesperson who had provided the diaphragms.

In 1982 Dr. Wilson contacted Ortho and spoke with Dr. Arnold Yeardon, Ortho's director of medical services, about a possible connection between diaphragm use and TSS in one of her patients. In later correspondence, Yeardon indicated that the company was aware of other cases of TSS (reported in the *New England Journal of Medicine*) thought to be caused by diaphragm use. He also indicated that the company was considering changing the wording on the patient information booklet to indicate that there might be a connection between diaphragm use and TSS. This series of letters, too, was written several months before Roberta Baroldy purchased her diaphragm.

After the lawsuit was brought, Ortho Pharmaceutical responded to the charges by denying that its product caused Roberta Baroldy's TSS and arguing that support for the relationship between TSS and diaphragm use was based on a scientifically untenable theory. However, subsequent changes in the patient information booklet made by Ortho before the trial began indicate that the company was aware of a possible connection. With the first revision in July 1982, the wording on the booklet was changed from, "It is safe to let it remain in position for 24 hours" to, "The diaphragm should not be worn continuously for more than 24 hours."[72] It still did not mention a link between use of the product and TSS.

In May 1983 a second revision of the patient information booklet was produced. The booklet now recommended leaving the diaphragm in place for six hours after intercourse to protect against pregnancy and removing it as soon as possible after that time. It also stated that retention of the diaphragm for extended periods might cause the growth of bacteria, which had been linked to TSS under "certain as yet unestablished"[73] conditions. In addition, Ortho Pharmaceutical Company sent a letter to physicians in July 1983 about the possible association between diaphragm use and TSS.

Based on the information presented at the trial, the jury awarded the Baroldys $1.5 million in compensatory damages. Ortho Pharmaceutical appealed, but the appellate court affirmed the trial court's decision.

Baroldy illustrates the position in which women are placed when corporations and their [male] representatives are in control of women's reproductive health. Ortho Pharmaceutical Company had been in the business of manufacturing diaphragms for women for forty years,[74] and it controlled approximately 80 percent of the U.S. diaphragm market.[75] The firm's financial stake in the domestic diaphragm market was considerable, whereas its concern about its customers' health was not.

When information about a possible link between its product and TSS appeared, the corporation did not respond. In the words of the Baroldys' counsel, what happened was that "Dr. Yeardon sat on his duff, if you will, back at corporate headquarters, and let the information come in to him and didn't do anything with it."[76] The consequences of his (and the corporation's) inaction nearly resulted in the death of Roberta Baroldy.

When faced with a lawsuit over the use of the diaphragm, Ortho responded by denying that a link existed between its product and TSS, though the company had previously changed the wording on the information packet to indicate that a link "might" exist. The disregard shown by Ortho Pharmaceutical Company and its representatives for women's reproductive health, though they were in the business of manufacturing products designed to benefit women, resulted in the production of an unsafe product, which the company then had the power to leave on the market.

This case study also provides an example of victimization caused by a product developed exclusively for "a woman's own good." The victim

50   in this case purchased a contraceptive device developed and marketed specifically for women to provide protection against pregnancy. However, use of the product, according to the instructions in the published information packet, caused serious physical consequences. The corporation producing the device did not respond to evidence indicating that the product was unsafe; rather, they left it on the market in spite of the problems.

CONCLUSIONS

Drawing on empirical evidence, we have applied a modified socialist-feminist theory to account for gendered corporate victimization and gender bias inhibiting access to institutional redress (legal and otherwise). This theory explains victimizations that occur within both public[77] and private spheres.[78] It also explains the manner in which women's victimization and access to institutional means of redress vary by race and social class.[79]

Case studies reviewed in this chapter demonstrate how the occupational segregation of women into low-paying and nonunionized jobs increases their likelihood of exposure to hazardous work conditions in workplaces lacking adequate regulation. The gender stratification of the labor market concentrates women disproportionately at the bottom of the labor force and in less powerful positions, where they are vulnerable to the vicissitudes of the market and sexual harassment by male supervisors. Minority women, as shown in the Imperial Food Products and Regal Tube Company cases, are even more susceptible than whites to these conditions. By virtue of the jobs they do, women generally lack many of the legal protections accorded their better-positioned, better-studied, and better-protected male counterparts. But as Helen Brooms's experience at Regal Tube Company clearly illustrates, minority women who feel the sting of both race and gender discrimination at work are forced to seek redress within a legal system that fails to acknowledge and challenge dual discriminations. These societal arrangements generally benefit capital, since less regulation and greater worker competition yield higher profits; and white males, who get better jobs and workplace protections.

In the area of birth control, corporate America has consistently demonstrated the prioritization of profit over women's reproductive health by knowingly developing and/or marketing products that expose women to unacknowledged and unacceptable risks. Birth control for women (the pill, cervical caps, diaphragms, IUDs) is designed to free them from male-controlled contraceptive techniques (and ostensibly from male control over their sexuality). However, through their exposure to these products and in their treatment afterward, women who seek freedom from unwanted pregnancies often find themselves doubly victimized in a capitalist patriarchal system that is, at best, ambivalent about female sexuality. Roberta Baroldy's experience with Ortho Pharmaceutical Company—a firm that knew the risks of TSS associated with its diaphragm but chose not to do anything about it—is familiar to tens of thousands of women.

The problem of corporate crime in capitalist societies cannot be overstated. Millions of persons are harmed yearly by the illegal acts of corporations. In this chapter we have offered a modified version of socialist-feminist theory to explain the manner in which victims of corporate crime are stratified by gender, race, and social class. While this viewpoint and other feminist perspectives discussed herein are useful tools in rendering an account of corporate victimization, they are not comprehensive. Before a feminist theory of corporate crime victimization can be properly developed, it is imperative to conduct further feminist research on the gendered nature of corporate law, offenders, and victims.

NOTES

1. E. Sutherland, "White-Collar Criminality," *American Sociological Review* 10 (1940): 132–39; E. Sutherland, *White-Collar Crime* (New York: Dryden Press, 1949).

2. See, e.g., K. Daly, "Gender and Varieties of White-Collar Crime," *Criminology* 27 (1989): 769–94; J. Gerber and S. L. Weeks, "Women as Victims of Corporate Crime: A Call for Research on a Neglected Topic," *Deviant Behavior* 13 (1992): 325–47; L. Maher and E. J. Waring, "Beyond Simple Differences: White Collar Crime, Gender, and Workforce Position," *Phoebe* 2 (1990): 44–54; J. W. Messerschmidt, *Capitalism, Patriarchy, and Crime* (Totowa, NJ: Rowman and Littlefield, 1986); J. W. Messerschmidt, *Masculinities and Crime* (Lanham, MD: Rowman and Littlefield, 1993); S. S. Simpson, "Feminist Theory, Crime, and Justice," *Criminology* 27 (1989): 607–31; D. Steffensmeier, "Organization Properties and Sex-Segregation in the Underworld," *Social Forces* 61 (1983): 1011–32; D. Zeitz, *Women Who Embezzle or Defraud* (New York: Praeger, 1981).

52   3. S. E. Brown and C. Chiang, "Defining Corporate Crime: A Critique of Traditional Parameters," in *Understanding Corporate Criminality*, ed. M. Blankenship (New York: Garland, 1993), 29–56.

4. In one region of England, for instance, occupational exposures were responsible for 6 percent of male cancers but only 2 percent of female cancers (J. Higginson and C. S. Muir, "Environmental Carcinogenesis," *Journal of National Cancer Institute* 63 [1979]: 1291–98). In the United States, estimates suggest that occupational exposures account for between 5 percent and 10 percent of excess male mortality relative to females (I. Waldron, "Effects of Labor Force Participation on Sex Differences in Mortality and Morbidity," in *Women, Work, and Health*, ed. M. Frankenhaeuser, U. Lundberg, and M. Chesney [New York: Plenum, 1991]: 17–38). Studies also have indicated that employed men are five times more likely than women to have fatal accidents at work (J. P. Leigh, "Odds Ratios of Work-Related Deaths in United States Workers," *British Journal of Industrial Medicine* 45 [1988]: 158–66).

5. U.S. Bureau of the Census, *Statistical Abstract of the United States* (Washington, DC: Government Printing Office, 1993).

6. L. Mullings, "Minority Women, Work, and Health," in *Double Exposure*, ed. W. Chavkin (New York: Monthly Review Press, 1984), 121–38; J. M. Stellman, "The Working Environment of the Working Poor," *Women and Health* 14 (1988): 83–101.

7. V. R. Hunt, *The Health of Women at Work* (Evanston, IL: Program on Women, 1977); K. Messing, "Introduction: Research Directed to Improving Women's Occupational Health," *Women and Health* 18 (1992): 1–9.

8. Stellman, "The Working Environment."

9. C. Brabant, "Heat Exposure Standards and Women's Work," *Women and Health* 18 (1992): 119–30; Messing, "Introduction."

10. Potential health hazards for female workers include excessive noise, muscular and circulatory disorders, ventilation and temperature problems, exposure to toxic chemicals (e.g., photocopy toner, beauty products), VDTs, and carpal tunnel syndrome (Brabant, "Heat Exposure Standards"; Gerber and Weeks, "Women as Victims"; M. Love, "Health Hazards of Office Work," *Women and Health* 1 [1980]: 14–18; Mullings, "Minority Women, Work, and Health"; A. Palmer, "Respiratory Disease in Beauticians," *Women and Health* 1 [1978]: 14–18; Stellman, "The Working Environment"). Exposure to asbestos (less through installation and hands-on experience than via workplace exposure in schools, hospitals, and office buildings) and cotton dust—known hazardous substances—has produced asbestosis, silicosis, brown lung, lung cancer, and other respiratory diseases among women workers.

Minority women are particularly at risk. A study of the laundry and dry-cleaning industry conducted by the National Cancer Institute found that the death rate from various cancers (e.g., lungs, cervix, uterus, and skin) for African Americans is twice that of whites (Mullings, "Minority Women, Work, and Health," 129). A comparable situation exists in the textile industry, where the majority of workers (57 percent) are women and where sweatshops employ illegal aliens (typically women of color). "Minority workers tend to be concentrated in high dust areas, such as the opening, picking, and carding operations, and have disproportionate rates of respiratory disease" (ibid., 130; also see M. Davis, "The Impact of Workplace Health and Safety on Black Workers," *Labor Law Journal* 31 [1980]: 723–32).

11. H. G. Rosenberg, "The Home Is the Workplace," in *Double Exposure,* ed. W. Chavkin (New York: Monthly Review Press, 1984), 219–45.

12. Stellman, "The Working Environment."

13. Rosenberg, "The Home Is the Workplace."

14. Ibid., 24.

15. K. Hagenfeldt, "Reproductive Technologies, Women's Health, and Career Choices," in *Women, Work, and Health,* ed. M. Frankenhaeuser, U. Lundberg, and M. Chesney (New York: Plenum, 1991), 207–23, 210.

16. J. E. Steinman, "Women, Medical Care, and Mass Tort Litigation," *Chicago-Kent Law Review* 68 (1992): 409–29, 410–12.

17. Ibid., 412.

18. J. Weaver, "Government Response to Contraceptive and Cosmetic Health Risks," *Women and Health* 1 (1978): 5–11, 7.

19. B. Ehrenreich and D. English, *For Her Own Good* (Garden City, NY: Anchor Books, 1979), 294, suggest that two of these surgeries, hysterectomies and cesarian sections, increased as a consequence of the baby bust of the 1960s and 1970s. "Hospitals began to close their obstetrical wards; obstetricians compensated for the loss of income by performing more hysterectomies and (when a pregnant woman did come along) Caesarian sections."

20. Historically, women were often isolated in extremely hazardous, poorly paid, and nonunionized occupations. "When they became ill, women's symptoms would often be attributed to hysteria, to a combination of mental and physical weakness rather than to working conditions." (A. Bale, " 'Hope in Another Direction': Compensation for Work Related Illness Among Women, 1900–1960, Part 1," *Women and Health* 15 [1989]: 81–135, 83).

21. Brabant, "Heat Exposure Standards."

22. Stellman, "The Working Environment."

23. J. F. Katz, "Hazardous Working Conditions and Fetal Protection Policies," *Boston College Environmental Affairs Law Review* 17 (1989): 201–30; D. M. Randall and J. F. Short, Jr., "Women in Toxic Work Environments," *Social Problems* 30 (1983): 410–24; U.S. Department of Labor. Occupational Safety and Health Administration, *Lost in the Workplace: Is*

54   *There an Occupational Disease Epidemic?* Proceedings from a Seminar for the News Media, September 1979 (Washington, DC: Government Printing Office, 1980).

24. Messing, "Introduction."

25. U.S. Department of Labor, *Lost in the Workplace.*

26. Mullings, "Minority Women, Work and Health."

27. P. A. Gwartney-Gibbs and D. H. Lach, "Gender and Workplace Dispute Resolution," *Law and Society Review* 28 (1994): 265–96; union membership statistics from 1992 show the following disparities in union representation by gender and race breakdowns: Among whites, 20.6 percent of male employed wage and salary workers are represented by unions, but only 15 percent of their female counterparts have access to union representation. Among blacks, the numbers are 20.0 percent for males versus 13.8 percent for females. The disparities are somewhat less among Hispanic workers; 26.4 percent of the males and 22.1 percent of the females are covered (U.S. Bureau of the Census, *Statistical Abstract of the United States* [Washington, DC: Government Printing Office, 1993]).

28. Steinman, "Women, Medical Care."

29. She cites, for instance, the fact that public hearings on silicone breast implants were not held until 1991; the FDA chose to rely on the assurances of plastic surgeons and other interested parties (i.e., manufacturers) that the implants posed no danger (ibid., 422).

30. Illinois Task Force on Gender Bias in the Courts/ Illinois Committee for Implementation of the Gender Bias Report, *The 1990 Report of the Illinois Task Force on Gender Bias in the Courts*; Steinman, "Women, Medical Care."

31. L. M. Finley, "A Break in the Silence: Including Women's Issues in a Torts Course," *Yale Journal of Law and Feminism* 1 (1989): 41–73, 51.

32. Bale, " 'Hope in Another Direction'."

33. Finley, "A Break in the Silence."

34. Ibid., 65.

35. Steinman, "Women, Medical Care," 425–26.

36. K. Daly and M. Chesney-Lind, "Feminism and Criminology," *Justice Quarterly* 5 (1988): 497–538; Simpson, "Feminist Theory."

37. Gerber and Weeks, "Women as Victims."

38. See Simpson, "Feminist Theory," for a summary of this literature.

39. Katz, "Hazardous Working Conditions."

40. U.S. Department of Labor, *Lost in the Workplace.*

41. See, e.g., Steinman, "Women, Medical Care."

42. Daly and Chesney-Lind, "Feminism and Criminology"; Simpson, "Feminist Theory."

43. Messerschmidt, *Capitalism, Patriarchy, and Crime,* 156.

44. A. Hochschild, *The Second Shift* (New York: Viking, 1989).

45. L. Gordon, "The Politics of Birth Control, 1920–1940: The Impact of Professionals," in *Women and Health: The Politics of Sex in Medicine*, ed. E. Fee (Farmingdale, NY: Baywood, 1982), 151–75, 157–59.

46. S. S. Simpson, "Caste, Class, and Violent Crime," *Criminology* 29 (1991): 115–35.

47. Messerschmidt, *Masculinities and Crime*, 57.

48. Ibid., 59.

49. S. S. Simpson and L. Elis, "Sorting Out the Caste and Crime Conundrum," *Criminology* 33 (1995): 47–81.

50. Gordon, "The Politics of Birth Control," 151.

51. A. Y. Davis, *Women, Race and Class* (New York: Vintage, 1983), 210.

52. J. Jefferson, "Dying for Work," *ABA Journal* (January 1993): 46–51.

53. Facts on File, *Chicken Plant Owner Sentenced for Fire* (New York: Facts on File, 1991).

54. M. Tabor, "Poultry Plant Fire Churns Emotions Over Job Both Hated and Appreciated," *New York Times* (September 6, 1991): A17.

55. R. Smothers, "Twenty-five Die, Many Reported Trapped, as Blaze Engulfs Carolina Plant," *New York Times* (September 4, 1991): A1, B7.

56. Statistics from OSHA estimate that 20 percent of poultry-processing workers experience a severe injury to their hands, wrists or shoulders (R. Lacayo, "Death on the Shop Floor," *Time* 138 [1991]: 28–29).

57. Tabor, "Poultry Plant Fire."

58. Lacayo, "Death on the Shop Floor."

59. R. Smothers, "North Carolina Examines Inspection Lapses in Fire," *New York Times* (September 5, 1991): A15.

60. J. Winston, "An Antidiscrimination Legal Construct That Disadvantages Working Women of Color," *Clearinghouse Review* 25 (1991): 403–19.

61. Tabor, "Poultry Plant Fire," A17.

62. Jefferson, "Dying for Work," 50.

63. Ibid.

64. *Brooms v. Regal Tube Co.*, 881 F. 2d 412 (1989).

65. Ibid., 416, ft. 1.

66. Ibid., 417.

67. Ibid., 417.

68. Winston, "An Antidiscrimination Legal Construct."

69. Ibid.

70. Finley, "A Break in the Silence."

71. *Baroldy v. Ortho Pharmaceutical Corporation*, 760 F. 2d 574 (1988).

72. Ibid., 586.

73. Ibid., 586.

74. Ibid., 577.

75. G. Cox, "Diaphragm TSS Leads to Award," *The National Law Journal* (March 9, 1992): 3, 36.

56

76. *Baroldy*, 584.

77. Love, "Health Hazards of Office Work"; Palmer, "Respiratory Disease in Beauticians"; Mullings, "Minority Women, Work, and Health; Brabant, "Heat Exposure Standards"; Gerber and Weeks, "Women as Victims."

78. Hagenfeldt, "Reproductive Technologies"; Rosenberg, "The Home Is the Workplace"; Steinman, "Women, Medical Care"; Stellman, "The Working Environment."

79. Bale, " 'Hope in Another Direction' "; Mullings, "Minority Women, Work, and Health"; Stellman, "The Working Environment"; Winston, "An Antidiscrimination Legal Construct."

REFERENCES

Bale, A. 1989. 'Hope in another direction': Compensation for work related illness among women, 1900–1960. Part I. *Women and Health* 15: 81–135.

Brabant, C. 1992. Heat exposure standards and women's work. *Women and Health* 18: 119–30.

Brown, S. E. and C. Chiang. 1993. Defining corporate crime: A critique of traditional parameters. In *Understanding Corporate Criminality*, ed. M. Blankenship, 29–56. New York: Garland.

Cox, G. 1992. Diaphragm TSS leads to award. *The National Law Journal*, March 9: 3, 36.

Daly, K. 1989. Gender and varieties of white-collar crime. *Criminology* 27: 769–94.

Daly, K. and M. Chesney-Lind. 1988. Feminism and criminology. *Justice Quarterly* 5: 497–538.

Davis, A. Y. 1983. *Women, Race and Class.* New York: Vintage.

Davis, M. 1980. The impact of workplace health and safety on black workers. *Labor Law Journal* 31: 723–32.

Ehrenreich, B. and D. English. 1979. *For Her Own Good.* Garden City, NY: Anchor Books.

Facts on File. 1992. Chicken plant owner sentenced for fire. New York: Facts on File.

Finley, L. M. 1989. A break in the silence: Including women's issues in a torts course. *Yale Journal of Law and Feminism* 1: 41–73.

Gerber, J. and S. L. Weeks. 1992. Women as victims of corporate crime: A call for research on a neglected topic. *Deviant Behavior* 13: 325–47.

Gordon, L. 1982. The politics of birth control, 1920–1940: The impact of professionals. In *Women and Health: The Politics of Sex in Medicine*, ed. E. Fee, 151–75. Farmingdale, NY: Baywood.

Gwartney-Gibbs, P. A. and D. H. Lach. 1994. Gender and workplace dispute resolution. *Law and Society Review* 28: 265–96.

Hagenfeldt, K. 1991. Reproductive technologies, women's health, and career choices. In *Women, Work, and Health*, ed. M. Frankenhaeuser, U. Lundberg, and M. Chesney, 207–23. New York: Plenum.

Higginson, J. and C. S. Muir. 1979. Environmental carcinogenesis. *Journal of National Cancer Institute* 63: 1291–98.

Hochschild, A. 1989. *The Second Shift*. New York: Viking.

Hunt, V. R. 1977. *The Health of Women at Work*. Evanston, IL: Program on Women.

Illinois Task Force on Gender Bias in the Courts/Illinois Committee for Implementation of the Gender Bias Report. 1990. *The 1990 Report of the Illinois Task Force on Gender Bias in the Courts*.

Jefferson, J. 1993. Dying for work. *ABA Journal*, January: 46–51.

Katz, J. F. 1989. Hazardous working conditions and fetal protection policies. *Boston College Environmental Affairs Law Review* 17: 201–30.

Lacayo, R. 1991. Death on the shop floor. *Time* 138: 28–29.

Leigh, J. P. 1988. Odds ratios of work-related deaths in United States workers. *British Journal of Industrial Medicine* 45: 158–66.

Love, M. 1980. Health hazards of office work. *Women and Health* 1: 14–18.

Maher, L. and E. J. Waring. 1990. Beyond simple differences: White collar crime, gender, and workforce position. *Phoebe* 2: 44–54.

Messerschmidt, J. W. 1986. *Capitalism, Patriarchy, and Crime*. Totowa, NJ: Rowman and Littlefield.

———. 1993. *Masculinities and Crime*. Lanham, MD: Rowman and Littlefield.

Messing, K. 1992. Introduction: Research directed to improving women's occupational health. *Women and Health* 18: 1–9.

Mullings, L. 1984. Minority women, work, and health. In *Double Exposure*, ed. W. Chavkin, 121–38. New York: Monthly Review Press.

Palmer, A. 1978. Respiratory disease in beauticians. *Women and Health* 1: 14–18.

Randall, D. M. and J. F. Short, Jr. 1983. Women in toxic work environments. *Social Problems* 30: 410–24.

Rosenberg, H. G. 1984. The home is the workplace. In *Double Exposure*, ed. W. Chavkin, 219–45. New York: Monthly Review Press.

Simpson, S. S. 1989. Feminist theory, crime, and justice. *Criminology* 27: 607–31.

———. 1991. Caste, class, and violent crime. *Criminology* 29: 115–35.

Simpson, S. S. and L. Elis. 1995. Sorting out the caste and crime conundrum. *Criminology* 33: 47–81.

Smothers, R. 1991. North Carolina examines inspection lapses in fire. *New York Times*, September 5: A15.

58   ———. 1991. Twenty-five die, many reported trapped, as blaze engulfs Caro-
         lina plant. *New York Times,* September 4: A1, B7.
         Steffensmeier, D. 1983. Organization properties and sex-segregation in the
         underworld. *Social Forces* 61: 1011–32.
         Steinman, J. E. 1992. Women, medical care, and mass tort litigation.
         Chicago-Kent Law Review 68: 409–29.
         Stellman, J. M. 1988. The working environment of the working poor.
         Women and Health 14: 83–101.
         Sutherland, E. 1940. White-collar criminality. *American Sociological Re-
         view* 10: 132–39.
         ———. 1949. *White-Collar Crime.* New York: Dryden Press.
         Tabor, M. 1991. Poultry plant fire churns emotions over job both hated and
         appreciated. *New York Times,* September 6: A17.
         U.S. Bureau of the Census. 1993. *Statistical Abstract of the United States.*
         Washington, DC: Government Printing Office.
         U.S. Department of Labor. Occupational Safety and Health Administration.
         1980. *Lost in the workplace: Is there an occupational disease epi-
         demic?* Proceedings from a Seminar for the News Media, September
         13–14, 1979. Washington, DC: Government Printing Office.
         Waldron, I. 1991. Effects of labor force participation on sex differences in
         mortality and morbidity. In *Women, Work, and Health,* ed. M. Franken-
         haeuser, U. Lundberg, and M. Chesney, 17–38. New York: Plenum.
         Weaver, J. 1978. Government response to contraceptive and cosmetic health
         risks. *Women and Health* 1: 5–11.
         Winston, J. 1991. An antidiscrimination legal construct that disadvantages
         working women of color. *Clearinghouse Review* 25: 403–19.
         Zeitz, D. 1981. *Women Who Embezzle or Defraud.* New York: Praeger.

THE PHARMACEUTICAL INDUSTRY AND WOMEN'S REPRODUCTIVE HEALTH

The Perils of Ignoring Risk and Blaming Women

Lucinda M. Finley

Too many of the most tragic and preventable instances of unsafe drugs and medical devices have been products used in women's bodies, often in connection with sexuality and reproduction. The litany includes thalidomide; DES (diethylstilbestrol); the early unduly high-hormone birth control pills, which increased risks of strokes and cancer; intrauterine contraceptive devices (IUDs), with their huge toll of pelvic inflammatory disease and sterility; super-absorbent tampons, with their attendant risk of toxic shock syndrome; Parlodel, a drug to suppress lactation that has caused at least nineteen maternal deaths from stroke or heart attack;[1] and silicone breast implants, which leak or rupture and have been connected to debilitating autoimmune system diseases.

These drugs and devices were developed not in response to disease but for use in healthy women to enhance what nature had provided or to control the natural processes of reproduction. Medical science has long sought to control women's reproductive capacity and to surgically manipulate or technologically "improve on" women's bodies. Normal female attributes, such as small breasts or menopause, have been classified as disease conditions requiring treatment.[2] It is women exclusively who have faced the risks of iatrogenic injuries and disease from drugs and devices designed to alter the natural processes or shape of their healthy bodies. Drugs that have injured men are "gender-neutral"; developed to treat disease rather than healthy conditions, they can be used equally by men and women. As Professor Joan Steinman has noted, there has not yet been an instance of a "mass tort in which men were injured by a product made for men to use or take, ostensibly to enhance their well-being. It appears that women, far more than men, take it on the chin from products made ostensibly for our own good."[3]

60   Is the disproportionate number of drugs and medical devices that
have wreaked havoc on women's previously healthy bodies coinciden-
tal? I think not. The desire to control or "improve" women's bodies
reflects a devaluation of women and their health. One manifestation is
that pharmaceutical manufacturers have been lax about testing for or
heeding signs of danger to women.[4] Drug companies have often blamed
women themselves for any reported problems; and doctors and manufacturers have ignored complaints or attributed women's descriptions
of adverse effects to emotional reactions by stereotypically "hysterical"
women. Marketing and profit considerations have proved more important to the pharmaceutical industry than women's health and safety
concerns, and the corporate framework too readily allows for the evasion of individual legal or social accountability.

The mass product liability actions for injuries to women's reproductive health caused by such corporate behavior lead one to wonder
whether drug companies would have responded so callously to mounting evidence that a drug was harming men's reproductive or sexual
well-being. The federal judge who presided over many of the legal proceedings against A. H. Robins Company, the manufacturer of the Dalkon Shield, came to the same conclusion. In February 1984, Judge Miles
Lord called several A. H. Robins executives before him and castigated
them with remarks that aptly summarize the corporate victimization
of women:

> Today as you sit here attempting once more to extricate yourselves
> from the legal consequences of your acts, none of you has faced up to
> the fact that more than nine thousand women have made claims that
> they gave up part of their womanhood [or their lives] so that your
> company might prosper. . . . And there stand behind them legions
> more who have been injured but who have not sought relief in the
> courts of this land. I dread to think what would have been the conse-
> quences if your victims had been men rather than women, women
> who seem through some strange quirk of our society's mores to be
> expected to suffer pain, shame, and humiliation. If one poor young
> man were, by some act of his—without authority or consent—to in-
> flict such damage upon one woman, he would be jailed for a good
> portion of the rest of his life. And yet your company, without warning
> to women, invaded their bodies by the millions and caused them in-
> juries by the thousands. And when the time came for these women
> to make their claims against your company, you attacked their char-

acters [and] you inquired into their sexual practices. . . . Please, in the name of humanity, lift your eyes above the bottom line.[5]

This chapter will more fully explore these themes—the devaluation and trivialization of women's health, the blame laid on women and the use of the litigation process to harass them for speaking out, and the greater attention paid to marketing and short-term profit than to health and safety—in the context of case studies of DES and the Dalkon Shield IUD.

DES—"THE WONDER DRUG THAT YOU SHOULD WONDER ABOUT"[6]

Diethylstilbestrol—more popularly known as DES—is a synthetic estrogen first synthesized in Britain in 1938 by Sir Edward Dodds, the father of modern biochemical endocrinology. It was initially hailed as a wonder drug that would do everything from curing the problems of menopause, to treating prostate cancer, to making chickens and cattle plumper and more delectable for the dinner table, to serving as a "morning after" contraceptive pill, to preventing miscarriage and making babies (like chickens) plumper and healthier. But DES turned out to have tragic consequences for many of these babies, especially the female offspring, who were exposed in utero when their mothers took DES during pregnancy.

Natural estrogen is difficult to extract in large amounts, prohibitively expensive, and can be administered only by injection. Consequently, the synthetic compound, which could be made inexpensively into pills or capsules,[7] created great enthusiasm amongst doctors and pharmaceutical companies for its potential clinical and commercial promise to treat symptoms of menopause, suppress lactation after birth, and possibly inhibit miscarriage.[8] But in the midst of all the initial optimism about DES, there were notable voices of caution, including that of Dodds, the drug's developer. Estrogen was known to be a potent carcinogen in both animals and humans, and by 1939 there were over forty published articles in U.S. and European medical journals documenting carcinogenic effects in animals from natural and synthetic estrogens, including DES.[9] The growing evidence of carcinogenicity led the American Medical Association (AMA) Council on Pharmacy and Chemistry to issue a cautionary report on DES in December 1939, warning, "Be-

62 cause the product is so potent and because the possibility of harm must be recognized . . . its use by the general medical profession should not be undertaken until further studies have led to a better understanding of the proper functions of the drug."[10]

Early tests, including work by Dodds, also showed that DES could cross the placental barrier and adversely affect the fetuses of pregnant animals.[11] Dodds always remained an adamant opponent of using DES in conjunction with pregnancy, because he thought the hormone was too powerful and the female reproductive system too susceptible and complex to be manipulated by chemicals. In 1939 and 1940 a team of researchers from Northwestern University gave DES, supplied by the pharmaceutical manufacturer Squibb, to pregnant rats. The team reported that an alarming number of the female offspring had misshapen uteruses and structural changes in the ovaries and vagina, while some of the male babies had reproductive tract abnormalities such as tiny and malformed penises.[12] The drug companies did not regard these studies as necessitating caution about marketing DES for pregnant women.

In the same year that DES was synthesized, the FDA for the first time was given the authority to judge the safety of new drugs. The Federal Food, Drug, and Cosmetic Act of 1938 was passed in response to a 1937 scandal, caused when over a hundred deaths were traced to a liquid sulfa drug whose manufacturer had never tested its main solvent for safety. But the 1938 law did not require the FDA to consider efficacy as a criterion for drug approval. Effectiveness of new drugs was not made a regulatory factor until 1962, when thalidomide, a sedative that caused grossly deformed babies when given during pregnancy, much like the sulfa tragedy twenty-five years earlier, prompted Congress to strengthen the food and drug laws. At first the FDA was hesitant to approve DES because of the growing literature about carcinogenicity and the cautions raised by the AMA Council on Pharmacy and Chemistry. The FDA signaled to the drug companies that they should withdraw their applications and resubmit when they had more extensive evidence of safety. The FDA also urged the companies to coordinate their efforts and submit one joint application for the generic drug. A group known as the "Small Committee," headed by a doctor from Eli Lilly and with representatives from Squibb, Upjohn, and Winthrop Chemical Company, shepherded the preparation of a successful resubmission to the FDA.

The Small Committee submission was based principally on evidence gleaned from anecdotal clinical reports of individual cases rather than on controlled scientific studies. It also drew heavily on a questionnaire that the drug companies had distributed to carefully selected pro-DES doctors. The questionnaire focused on benefits to patients with menopausal problems and avoided the known weaknesses of DES, such as its carcinogenicity. The Small Committee's emphasis on clinical reports and its avoidance of animal studies enabled it to submit an application that focused almost exclusively on positive information, while ignoring or downplaying all the negative information about DES. Virtually none of the medical literature documenting carcinogenicity made its way into the FDA submission.[13]

Impressed and pressured by the extensive lobbying campaign from doctors and the pharmaceutical companies, and faced with the uniformly favorable Small Committee application, the FDA approved DES in September 1941 for four uses: to treat menopausal disorders, gonorrheal vaginitis, and senile vaginitis and to suppress lactation. Drug companies were prohibited from proclaiming other unapproved and thus experimental uses in their marketing literature, but their sales representatives who visited doctors were under no restrictions concerning the uses they could suggest.[14] They urged doctors to experiment with DES on women, including pregnant women, for unapproved uses; and the drug companies supported this experimental use by donating supplies of the drug.

Why did the pharmaceutical companies shun caution in their FDA submission and by encouraging widespread experimental use? In large part because of their excessive enthusiasm for the clinical and market potential of the new synthetic hormone and the burgeoning field of endocrinology. Hormone therapy was the newest development in medicine, subject to extensive "hype" because it promised the ability to better understand, regulate, and control the previously mysterious female reproductive system. The fact that the consumers of DES were to be women may also explain why contrary or cautionary evidence about safety was ignored. Women are simply not as highly valued by society as men (at least white men). The priorities and concerns of the medical profession and the pharmaceutical industry are shaped by and reflective of this social devaluation. Women have long suffered from insufficient attention to or understanding of their health needs, and inadequate concern for the impact of medical treatments and devices on their health.[15] The exclusive focus of the pharmaceutical industry on what DES might do *for* women, instead of also on what it might do *to* women, demon-

64   strates their greater concern for controlling the female reproductive system for profit than for the ultimate health and safety of women.

The exciting promise of estrogen therapy to regulate female reproduction prompted the pharmaceutical companies and clinicians vigorously to explore DES's potential to treat problems of pregnancy. A new medical theory posited that premature labor and miscarriage could be caused by a dearth of estrogen, and that DES might boost the body's natural production of this hormone.[16] As World War II came to an end, people were anxious to return to normal and start their longed-for families. DES rode this cultural pent-up desire of the baby boom period, with many medical researchers and pharmaceutical companies understandably eager to be credited with a miraculous cure for nature's tragedy of miscarriage.

In the early 1940s a Texas gynecologist, Dr. Karl Karnaky, experimented on women who arrived at his clinic with premature labor pains and bleeding, and he published a wildly enthusiastic article in 1942 opining that DES was an effective treatment for "premature labor, threatened and habitual abortion. . . . We can give too little stilbestrol but we cannot give too much."[17] A husband-and-wife team from Harvard Medical School, Dr. George Smith, a gynecologist, and Dr. Olive Smith, an endocrinologist, also tested DES on pregnant women broadly deemed at risk for pregnancy complications. In a 1946 article, the Smiths reported that a great number of these women delivered healthy, full-term babies than otherwise would have been expected given their medical histories.[18] Based on the case history of one patient, the Smiths recommended a massive dosage regimen involving far more estrogen than the body would ever produce naturally. Remarkably, neither many doctors nor the FDA questioned such huge dosages of a synthetic hormone known to be carcinogenic.

The Smiths also promoted DES as prophylactic treatment for any pregnancy, claiming that it "provid[ed] a more normal maternal environment at the very start."[19] The revealing, and inherently absurd, emphasis on a "more normal" maternal environment illustrates the medical desire to improve upon women's natural functions. The Smiths additionally posited that DES stimulated better placental function, thus producing bigger and healthier babies even when delivered prematurely.[20] These claims of a more enriched placenta, a "more normal" maternal environment, and bigger and healthier babies came to play a crucial role in the marketing of DES by pharmaceutical companies, forming the purportedly scientific basis for promoting the drug as the state-of-the-art enhancement for all pregnancies.

Some medical researchers and physicians greeted the work of Karnaky and the Smiths with skepticism and concern about health risks, but on the whole their theory was rapidly endorsed by large numbers of the medical profession. The largely uncritical acceptance of administering DES during pregnancy was partly attributable to the Harvard credentials and eminent reputations of the Smiths, but it was also fueled by the pronatalist enthusiasm of the baby boom era and the understandable excitement generated by claims that this "wonder drug" could salvage otherwise doomed pregnancies and help produce healthier babies. The prevailing medical and regulatory attitude toward drugs was also to emphasize benefits over risks. The pharmaceutical companies, faced with the potentially huge new market of pregnant women, emphasized only positive claims for efficacy and safety and excluded critical voices and adverse evidence. A Squibb medical director summed up this attitude with the observation that "anything that helps sell a drug is valid, even if it is supported by the crudest testimonial, while anything that decreases sales must be suppressed, distorted and rejected because it is not absolutely conclusive proof."[21]

The 1947 applications to the FDA seeking approval to produce and market larger doses of DES for treatment of "accidents of pregnancy" reflected this attitude. For evidence of safety, these new drug applications relied on the work of Karnaky and the Smiths, which hardly considered safety issues. As in 1941, the pharmaceutical companies did not mention the growing body of research reporting carcinogenic effects in animals or humans. Animal studies showing that DES could cross the placenta and produce reproductive abnormalities in the fetuses were also absent from the data the manufacturers supplied to the FDA. Nor did the applications cite the growing body of literature questioning whether DES was effective in preventing miscarriage. Within a couple of months of the submission, the FDA approved marketing DES for pregnancy-related uses, and dozens of drug companies jumped into the market for this generic, baby-saving drug.

Rather than being deterred by the quick FDA approval and the increasingly widespread use of DES, the skeptics were stimulated to do more research. At medical conferences and in journal articles several gynecologists and endocrinologists challenged the Smiths' methodology and conclusions: Their studies did not use properly selected control groups; they did not rule out the possibility that extra treatment, atten-

66   tion, bed rest, and psychological factors contributed to their results; and the results were not significantly better than those reported from using bed rest and enhanced nutrition without hormones. Following up on these criticisms, researchers then performed studies using control groups and placebos to ensure properly blind experiments, and offering no other treatment. Evidence against DES's effectiveness soon began to accumulate. A 1950 report in the *American Journal of Obstetrics and Gynecology* concluded that DES "is of no value in the treatment of threatened abortion."[22] In 1952, Columbia researchers also found that DES "is, in fact, a dismal failure in the general treatment of threatened abortion," and they lamented that "the public has been so frequently told of the virtue of this drug through articles appearing in lay journals that it now requires a courageous physician to refuse this medication."[23]

Two major controlled studies published in 1953 should have marked the end of DES use to prevent miscarriage. Both, larger in scope and methodologically more rigorous than any previous studies, showed conclusively that DES was not a wonder drug at all and could not prevent accidents of pregnancy. The first study, conducted by Dr. James Ferguson and colleagues at a New Orleans hospital, followed the Smiths' recommended regimen and administered the drug to 184 pregnant women while giving 198 pregnant women a placebo. They concluded that DES had no effect at all on the pregnancy outcomes, and their results also specifically refuted the Smiths' claims that DES produced weightier or healthier premature babies.[24] The second significant 1953 study was conducted by Dr. William Dieckmann and colleagues at the University of Chicago Lying In Hospital. This study used the largest group yet, and its results are therefore the most statistically significant. Dr. Dieckmann carefully adhered to the Smiths' dosage regimen and gave 840 pregnant women DES, while 806 women received a placebo. To rule out psychological factors or subtle treatment bias, the study was double-blind—neither the women nor those treating them knew who was getting DES and who was getting a placebo. To the extent the women were told anything, they were told they were getting vitamins.

Dieckmann's results were devastating to the claims that had been made for DES. The drug did not decrease the number of miscarriages; it had no effect on prematurity or toxemia; and it did not increase the weight, size, or health of premature babies. The conclusion was emphatic: DES "has no therapeutic value in pregnancy."[25] Twenty-five years later, the women in the Dieckmann study were tracked to find out what had happened to them, and two epidemiologists reanalyzed Dieckmann's data and found that the results were even more negative. Among the DES group, there was actually a statistically significant *increase* in the number of miscarriages, premature births, and neonatal deaths.[26]

The pharmaceutical companies acted unperturbed by the studies proving DES to be ineffective, and none sought further tests to refute or corroborate them. It obviously was not in their financial self-interest to follow up on these troubling results. They continued for the next fifteen years to list "threatened abortions" and "pregnancy accidents" as among the indicated uses of DES in the *Physician's Desk Reference,* the principal pharmaceutical reference manual relied on by virtually all physicians for information about drugs. In keeping with the practice of trumpeting any positive information and downplaying negative findings, the 1953 marketing literature from Eli Lilly, by far the dominant company in the DES market, described for several pages the positive indications that DES could help prevent miscarriage, all based on the now discredited studies from the early and mid-1940s. But the Lilly brochure slipped in only a single sentence mentioning the new, negative studies.[27]

As a result, U.S. physicians continued to issue an estimated 100,000 DES prescriptions to pregnant women every year for approximately eighteen years after 1953.[28] Thus, from 500,000 to two million offspring and up to two million mothers may have been exposed to DES and its carcinogenic dangers in the United States alone after it was proven to have no prophylactic value during pregnancy.[29] According to estimated sales data later compiled for litigation in the 1980s and 1990s, the peak years for DES use during pregnancy were 1954 through 1957, *after* the publication of the studies casting serious doubt on its effectiveness. Throughout the 1950s and 1960s DES was widely prescribed in routine pregnancies with no risk or history of miscarriage, because, as its marketing material claimed, it might "improve the maternal environment" and produce a plumper baby.

The demographics of DES use are worthy of note. Although quite inexpensive to produce, it was not sold nearly so cheaply. Considered the state of the art in high-level prenatal care, it was used by private physicians but rarely in clinics or public hospitals serving poor populations. Most of the those who were exposed to DES are middle- or upper-middle-class, white, well-educated women. The characteristics of the affected population, which came to be known as DES daughters, later

68   contributed to their grassroots activism, pursuit of medical information, and inclination to file a large number of lawsuits. The injured women had the education to do research and become involved in their own medical treatment; and they are from a racial and economic group that tends to regard legislatures and courts not with alienation and distrust but with the expectation that they will produce justice.

One reason DES remained the state-of-the-art pill for pregnancy long after the Dieckmann study is that no evidence of harm had yet surfaced. But the complacency about safety came to an explosive end in 1971. In the late 1960s two Boston gynecologists, Dr. Howard Ufelder and Dr. Arthur Herbst, treated a puzzling cluster of cases of a rare form of cervical and vaginal cancer in young teenage girls: clear cell adenocarcinoma. These young women had to undergo radical hysterectomies and removal of their vaginas, receiving skin grafts to reconstruct partially functioning vaginas. Some of them did not survive. Prior to this outbreak, this type of cancer had previously been seen only in postmenopausal women. Ufelder and Herbst enlisted the aid of an epidemiologist, Dr. David Poskanzer, to help them get to the bottom of what was causing these previously unheard-of cancers in such young women. After extensive analysis of medical and family histories, the only common factor in the cases was that each girl's mother had taken DES while pregnant. When Ufelder then heard of a few other cases of clear cell adenocarcinoma in young women reported elsewhere in the country, he learned from their physicians that these patients' mothers, too, had taken DES. After further study ruled out any factor other than DES as the causal agent, they published their results in the April 1971 issue of the *New England Journal of Medicine*.[30] It had an immediate impact, and popular media widely broadcast the findings, because this was the first confirmed instance of a human transplacental carcinogen. The Herbst article galvanized Dr. Peter Greenwald, director of the New York Cancer Registry of the state Department of Health, to check the state cancer registry. He located five recent cases of clear cell adenocarcinoma, all in women born between 1951 and 1953, three of whom were now dead from the cancer. Greenwald checked their medical histories and learned that all five mothers had taken DES. Four months after the Herbst article appeared, the *New England Journal of Medicine* published the results of Greenwald's confirming study.[31] The New York State health commissioner, Dr. Hollis Ingraham, responded swiftly to Greenwald and Herbst's findings, issuing a letter to all practicing physicians in New York State warning them about the danger of administering estrogens during pregnancy and urging them to send in information to aid in the surveillance and monitoring effort he had established. Ingraham also released Greenwald's findings to the FDA prior to their publication, urging the FDA to act swiftly to ban DES for use during pregnancy. The FDA did nothing for eight months, while an estimated 60,000 additional pregnant U.S. women received prescriptions for DES.[32] Then, prodded by alarmed members of Congress who scheduled hearings to investigate its slow response, in November 1971 the FDA declared DES contraindicated for use during pregnancy and notified all physicians to that effect.[33]

The startling revelation that DES could cause a rare and sometimes fatal form of cancer in female children exposed in utero prompted studies to track down and follow up on DES mothers and their children to learn what other health damage might have resulted from the more than twenty-five years of experimentation on women, which is what the DES experience can fairly be called. The pharmaceutical companies that had made and profited from DES did not contribute to these research efforts, in contrast to the free hand with which they had doled out pill supplies to support animal studies and clinical trials in the 1940s. The follow-up research burden fell largely on the federal government and on universities. In 1974 the National Cancer Institute established the national Collaborative DES Adenosis Project (DESAD), a longitudinal tracking study of a group of DES daughters and a control group of unexposed women. Prodded by DES Action, a grassroots advocacy organization of DES mothers and daughters, the federal Department of Health, Education, and Welfare set up a DES Task Force in 1978, which moved the surgeon general to issue an advisory on the health effects of DES and recommended physicians throughout the United States to provide follow-up care. In 1985, again under pressure from DES Action, the government established another DES Task Force to evaluate the ongoing medical findings and make research, education, and care recommendations. Still dissatisfied with the amount of public health attention and physician and victim education about DES, in 1992, when women's health suddenly became a hot legislative issue, DES Action successfully lobbied Congress for an appropriation for more education about DES. If not for the efforts of the victims' advocacy group, the devastations that DES continues to wreak on women's health might have been completely swept under the rug, and virtually all exposed people would remain ignorant of the risks they face.

Underlying many of these efforts by activist exposed women to get

70   public health authorities and physicians to learn more about the ravages
       of DES was the frustrating realization that many women did not know
       that they had been exposed to DES. In addition, many doctors did not
       know what to look for or what to do. When DES was in its heyday
       in the 1950s, giving full information to women patients was hardly a
       widespread medical practice. Many pregnant women were simply given
       a prescription slip by their doctors and told to "take this, it will help
       your pregnancy," or that it was special vitamins to help the pregnancy.[34]

       Women have learned about their exposure to DES in several circu-
       itous ways. Some mothers read newspaper or magazine articles about
       the problems associated with DES, which jogged vague memories of
       taking a pill while pregnant several years prior, and they took their
       daughters for checkups. Some young women read articles about others
       struggling with reproductive problems associated with DES, felt a pang
       of familiarity, and started making inquiries. Others were told by doc-
       tors, during a pelvic exam, that they had structural or cellular changes
       to their uterus, cervix, or vagina characteristic of DES exposure. And
       some young women learned after they started having strange bleeding
       and discharges and were suddenly confronted with the traumatic diag-
       nosis of clear cell adenocarcinoma.[35] One group of women found out
       when a letter from the University of Chicago informed them that they
       had been part of a study over twenty years ago and that unbeknownst
       to them, they had been given DES. When Dieckmann and his colleagues
       performed their definitive study, informed consent was not yet a univer-
       sally established legal or medical ethical requirement, although the fail-
       ure to seek informed consent was not without controversy. The eight
       hundred women who received DES in the Dieckmann study made
       many unwitting sacrifices for the sake of improved medical knowledge.
       First, doctors experimented upon them in an effort to learn more about
       the veracity of the claims for DES's effectiveness; later, they and their
       children were extensively studied as one of the few readily identifiable
       DES-exposed populations for whom precise information about dosage
       and duration of exposure was available. As many of the women from the
       Dieckmann study struggled with their own or their daughters' health
       problems caused by DES, they couldn't help noting the irony—that
       their experimental sacrifice should have spared millions of other
       women and children but did not; now they too were left to live with the
       adverse health and emotional consequences as they once again provided
       crucial medical knowledge about the effects of DES.

       The adverse health effects of DES on exposed women and their daughters are legion.[36] Women who took DES have a slightly higher risk than unexposed women of breast cancer, particularly at a relatively young age. Mothers also struggle with terrible feelings of conflict and guilt that they did something to hurt their child. It is estimated that one out of every thousand DES daughters may develop clear cell adenocarcinoma by her mid-thirties, although cases are now appearing in DES daughters approaching menopause. While some studies suggest that the cancer risk is greatest when DES exposure occurred early in pregnancy,[37] several DES-exposed women whom I interviewed stressed the apparent randomness of who gets cancer and who doesn't. This lack of a perceived pattern makes every pap smear—which they are recommended to have every six months—a time of distracting anxiety, when they can't help wondering whether "this will be the one that brings me terrible news." Particularly poignant was the case of one family in which three daughters were exposed to DES, two of them twins. One twin died from clear cell adenocarcinoma. The surviving twin, obviously exposed to the same amount of DES for the same duration, was apparently unaffected, with normal reproductive organs and several energetic children. The third sister had structural abnormalities of her reproductive system because of her DES exposure and was unable to bear children. Mixed in with the relief felt by the one unafflicted sister was a lingering sense of guilt. Why had she escaped the ravages of DES, while her beloved twin had died and her sister had to struggle with the lifelong pain of infertility?

For the women who have had clear cell adenocarcinoma, the treatment is traumatic and life altering, involving a radical hysterectomy and removal of all or most of the vagina, with a new vagina reconstructed from skin grafts. Some women have also had radiation treatments, resulting in infertility, altered sexual functioning, and radiation burns and scar tissue that affect the bladder and digestive system. For those women who had their cancer diagnosed and treated in their teens or early twenties, at an age when they were still gaining a sense of their incipient sexuality and feeling particularly insecure about their developing bodies, the experience has in many cases left them feeling sexually abnormal and dreading relationships. As one woman explained to me, the thought of when she would tell a man she liked that she didn't have a vagina was so intimidating and humiliating that she avoided the possibility of intimacy. And as Joyce Bichler wrote in her memoir *DES Daughter*, long after the pain and trauma of the cancer diagnosis and surgery has receded, the permanent alterations to her reproductive tract left a raw ache that she had to confront every night when she got into bed with her husband. And these are the lucky cancer victims, the ones who did not die from clear cell adenocarcinoma or its complications.

In addition to the cancer risk, DES daughters have several signature abnormalities of the reproductive system, as could have been predicted based on the previous animal studies. From 25 to 50 percent of DES daughters have malformations of the cervix or precancerous cellular changes in the cervix or vagina, or benign growths known as adenosis, compared with only 2 percent of women in the unexposed control groups.[38] The majority of DES daughters have an abnormally T-shaped narrower and smaller uterus space, or misshapen fallopian tubes. These structural abnormalities are so characteristic of DES exposure that DES specialists refer to them as the "fingerprint" of DES. Several DES-exposed women first learned of their exposure when a gynecologist reported to them after an internal exam, that they had the DES fingerprint.

These abnormalities have several implications. DES daughters have up to four times the rate of infertility, ectopic pregnancy, miscarriage, or severely premature delivery compared to unexposed women.[39] The DES-afflicted T-shaped uterus is too small to carry a normal pregnancy to term, and the hoods and ridges in the cervix make it medically "incompetent," unable to act as a plug holding the developing fetus in the uterus. The odd shapes of some DES daughters' fallopian tubes or the cellular changes in the uterine lining make ectopic pregnancies more likely or make it more difficult for a fertilized egg to implant successfully. This is perhaps the most tragic aspect of the DES story: The drug that was supposed to prevent pregnancy loss is now causing the next generation to suffer precisely those pregnancy accidents. Like the DES daughters afflicted with cancer, those rendered infertile because of these other abnormalities also have to deal with a damaged sense of sexual self, as well as the relationship stress and complications that infertility can engender. Many have encountered a medical system that tells them their difficulties are primarily emotional rather than physical in origin. DES daughters are today among the most frequent consumers of infertility drugs and reproductive technologies; and they are thus subjecting themselves and subsequent offspring to yet another round of pharmacological experimentation. Despite the high proportion of DES daughters seeking infertility treatment, there has been little research into the efficacy or safety of contemporary reproductive technologies for this particularly susceptible group of women.

For many DES daughters who do get pregnant, the experience of pregnancy is one not of anticipatory joy but rather of anxiety about a pregnancy deemed at high risk for miscarriage or premature delivery, of disruption and discomfort from being hooked up to a fetal monitor or confined to bed for months, of surgery to stitch the cervix closed. The number of severely premature deliveries to DES daughters has created what has come to be known as the "third generation" of DES victims. Severe lifelong mental and physical disabilities leave many of these third-generation children confined to wheelchairs, in institutions, or in need of round-the-clock special care and education. "What makes me so sad and angry about this whole DES experience," said one mother of a child with cerebral palsy and serious mental disabilities, "is that the third generation kids are the most damaged of all. I grew up normally, playing with friends, going to school, going to college, falling in love, having a career. But my daughter, because of what DES did to me, will never be able to experience any of what I have had."

Predictably, the DES saga has led to thousands of lawsuits filed on behalf of DES daughters against the major manufacturers of DES, such as Eli Lilly Company, Squibb, and Abbott Labs. These product liability lawsuits have been based on the theory that the pharmaceutical companies transgressed the legal duty to test DES adequately for safety and to warn physicians (and through them consumers) of the known risks to mothers and offspring of taking DES during pregnancy, based on scientific knowledge and methodology available in the 1940s. Many of the lawsuits have also asserted claims for breach of warranty because DES was not effective for treating pregnancy accidents, despite plaudits to the contrary, or claims that the drug companies misrepresented the safety data to the FDA and to physicians.

In the eyes of the judicial system, DES daughters are perhaps the quintessential innocent victims. Their mothers were either kept in the dark or were only doing what they were told would help save their baby; the injured daughters were fetuses when initially damaged, and so they obviously did nothing to contribute to their own misfortune. Sympathetic to these factors, several courts or legislatures have responded with flexibility and legal innovations to allow DES suits to survive numerous doctrinal barriers. If not for these legal innovations, the ability of DES manufacturers to evade financial responsibility for the injuries caused by the product would have been virtually complete.

The long time between fetal exposure and the resulting injury was the first barrier to DES lawsuits, because the statute of limitations tra-

74   ditionally required suit to be filed within two or three years of the date
of exposure to a toxic agent. Most courts or legislatures decided that
this "date of exposure" rule was fundamentally unfair because no DES
victims could realistically commence a lawsuit before they knew there
was anything wrong with them. Instead the courts adopted the date of
discovery of the injury as the relevant starting point for the lawsuit
clock.

Another significant hurdle facing DES daughters was that the drug's
generic nature, coupled with the passage of time, prevented many from
being able to identify which company made the pills their mothers took
years ago. Tort law traditionally requires that in order to prove causation, an injured person must identify the precise wrongdoer who supplied the injurious product. But when DES daughters and their mothers
tried to find information that could enable them to identify the particular manufacturer, they often ran into obstacles: lost or destroyed medical records, retired or dead doctors, and pharmacies that had long since
closed. Faced with the dilemma that genuinely injured parties might
never be able to obtain compensation, courts in several key states—
notably California, New York, Michigan, Wisconsin, and Washington[40]—fashioned further legal innovations allowing DES victims to
forego the manufacturer identification requirement. Instead, they could
recover prorated shares of their damages from several companies, all of
which acted in concert in creating the societal harm, or they could recover damages from several companies, in amounts proportional to
each company's share of the market for pregnancy-related DES use. The
New York Court of Appeals summed up the policy behind this market
share liability: "It would be inconsistent with the reasonable expectations of a modern society to say . . . that because of the insidious nature
of an injury that long remains dormant, and because so many manufacturers, each behind a curtain, contributed to the devastation, the cost of
injury should be borne by the innocent and not the wrongdoers."[41]

The pharmaceutical companies have bitterly protested that this new
principle of using market share is a radical departure from traditional
causation requirements and makes them responsible for injuries they
did not cause. But the alternative would be insulation from financial
responsibility for injuries they *did* cause, which is the result in several
states where courts have refused to adopt market share as a basis for
liability. The market share approach is based on commonsense recognition that DES was a generic drug from which many companies profited,
that the leading manufacturers cooperated through the Small Commit-

tee in obtaining FDA approval and in dictating what risks would be revealed, and that no company participating in the DES market paid sufficient attention to risks or ineffectiveness. Culpability is shared by all, even if a particular injured woman was exposed to some company's pills but not others. The market share allocation of damages also accomplishes a fair balance between the interests of victims in receiving some compensation and the interests of the largest DES manufacturers in not being the deep pockets that are always singled out to pay for the sins of the entire industry, since no woman who is unable to identify the precise manufacturer of her mother's pills is likely to receive 100 percent of her compensatory damages.[42]

Despite these important legal innovations, which have enabled many DES daughters who would otherwise have been foreclosed from court to pursue lawsuits, the litigation experience has hardly been entirely vindicatory for women injured by DES. Most courts have permitted a complete evasion of corporate responsibility for the lifelong injuries suffered by the third generation of DES children. Ruling that the chain of responsibility just has to stop somewhere, the courts have barred suits brought on behalf of the damaged severely premature children of DES daughters, ruling that the drug companies owed no legal duty to consider the risks to subsequent generations.[43] This reasoning is tantamount to saying that the greater the number of people harmed by risky corporate behavior, the less accountable the company should be, because paying for the full extent of the damage would just be too crushing a burden. It leaves the ultimate extent of the damage as the private responsibility of the injured families.

The overall financial liability of DES manufacturers has been relatively low, because women's reproductive injuries are not assessed at a high value by society or the legal system. While cancer victims have received several hundred thousand dollars, with a few multimillion dollar verdicts, most women who have had adverse pregnancy outcomes or have been unable to conceive have recovered in the range of $10,000 to $100,000. The tort system regards the most serious kind of loss to be out-of-pocket economic harm or lost earnings. Injuries to a woman's reproductive capacity, which do not have a ready market reference and are understood primarily in emotional rather than physical and economic terms, are minimized or trivialized as too subjective. While supposedly a priceless asset in cultural terms, economically speaking, a woman's reproductive capacity is virtually worthless. And the damage to a woman's sense of self-worth from not having "normal" reproduc-

76 tive organs is dismissed as purely her own emotional problem, not something for which drug companies should bear any financial responsibility.

Women also encountered an aggressive and frequently demeaning defense from the pharmaceutical companies. Led by Eli Lilly, by far the major participant in the DES market and the one involved in the most lawsuits, the companies used defense tactics that included interrogating women and their husbands or lovers about sexual habits and history, on the grounds, as Eli Lilly contended, that sexually transmitted diseases are the predominant cause of infertility. Some women were made to feel that they must have done something to make themselves infertile or to deform their own uterus. One woman who had lost her vagina to cancer when she was quite young and still a virgin was told by a drug company lawyer that her damages wouldn't be very much because she didn't know what she was missing. In depositions, DES mothers were closely interrogated about every possible factor in their lives that might have been responsible for injuring their child, thus exacerbating the profound guilt many mothers already endured. Another twist on the victim-blaming defense pursued by Eli Lilly was its claim that DES did prevent miscarriages, so that but for DES the plaintiff would not even have been born, and that she should therefore be grateful for her gift of life rather than complaining that her body was not perfect.

What lessons have been learned from the DES health disaster? The effects of DES have made many health professionals and women more cautious about taking drugs during pregnancy. But it has not cooled the enthusiasm for and human experimentation with drugs designed to alter women's hormonal balance or reproductive cycles. Potent drugs for treating infertility have not been thoroughly tested for their long-term effects on the mother or fetus, even though some are chemically related to synthetic estrogens. The desperation and emotional vulnerability of women who seek infertility treatment are easily exploited; many are inclined to discount information about known risks or how much is still unknown in the slim hope that they might get pregnant. As one DES daughter told me, "if tomorrow's theory is that jumping off a cliff would get me pregnant, I would jump off the cliff."

To this day, no pharmaceutical company has acknowledged any mistakes or lessons from the DES experience. Some spokespersons for Eli Lilly are adamant that DES did not cause harm. Others acknowledge the harm but say that the disaster was not preventable because they could not have foreseen the problems that came to light years later. But many juries have reached other conclusions, based on the fetal effects shown by animal studies, the drug's known carcinogenicity, and the evidence that DES was not effective in preventing miscarriage. It is too facile to claim that the effects of DES were all an unforeseeable tragedy when the pharmaceutical companies studiously avoided following up on clear evidence of possible danger. The lessons that should be learned from DES are that the female reproductive system should not lightly be tampered with and that pharmaceutical companies should routinely undertake greater research into the effects of drugs on women's reproductive health. Warning signs, adverse reports, and troubling animal studies should be diligently pursued, rather than regarded as a marketing problem to be finessed or buried.

THE DALKON SHIELD:
THE "PERFECT" CONTRACEPTIVE, MAIMED WOMEN,
AND CORPORATE DECEPTION

Just as the post–World War II baby boom fueled DES as a panacea for pregnancy, so the development of the Dalkon Shield IUD contraceptive was precipitated by the population control movement and the sexual revolution of the 1960s. It was beginning to be culturally acceptable for women, whether married or unmarried, to seek sexual intimacy and pleasure without the shackles of compulsory motherhood. While different cultural forces two decades apart propelled these two products, the factor they have in common is the constant medical search to control, manage, and "improve" women's natural sexual and reproductive functions and to leave as little as possible to women themselves. In the United States in the 1960s, the largely male doctors and population control advocates who brought about the birth control revolution were seeking the "perfect" contraceptive. This was defined as a device that was used by women rather than men; was nearly 100 percent effective in preventing pregnancy; was reversible; and was not subject to the agency, moods, or forgetfulness of women. Birth control literature of the 1960s is replete with discussions of the irresponsibility of women for their failures of diligence with barrier techniques, pill taking, or rhythm methods. Poor women, minority women, and of course women in Third World countries were particularly suspected of being intrinsically irresponsible in using birth control methods that required agency or regular action.[44]

78 Effectiveness in preventing pregnancy, rather than safety for women, has been the most salient criterion for judging the success of a contraceptive. While safety concerns have not been totally dismissed, a high rate of pregnancy prevention can lead birth control advocates to downplay or diminish adverse safety information. Bleeding, cramping, nausea, headaches, fatigue, and diminished libido are shrugged off as "normal" side effects, and women are given pain pills to manage the "temporary discomfort," because women are expected to make sacrifices for the good of humanity. For example, the opening speech at the 1962 First International Conference on Intrauterine Conception proclaimed:

> [IUDs] are horrible things, they produce infection . . . but suppose one does develop an intrauterine infection and suppose she does end up with a hysterectomy . . . ? How serious is that for the particular patient and for the population of the world in general? Not very. . . . Perhaps the individual patient is expendable in the general scheme of things, particularly if the infection she acquires is sterilizing but not lethal.[45]

Doctors and population control advocates working on developing IUDs seized on health concerns about the pill to increase public interest in their products, which they hailed as superior to the pill in terms of safety and efficacy, because they eliminated the "motivation" or "responsibility" problem of women who might forget or decide not to take a pill. Lost in the growing excitement over IUDs as the possible new answer to the problem of finding the perfect contraceptive was a fundamental fact that should have given pause: The very mechanism by which IUDs work to prevent pregnancy makes them inherently dangerous. As the 1968 FDA advisory committee on IUDs reported, IUDs provoke inflammation and infection in the endometrium, and it is this effect that apparently prevents implantation. In other words, inflammation and infection are not simply risks of IUDs but rather necessary conditions in order for the devices to be effective.[46]

Virtually no women who had IUDs inserted were ever informed that inflammation and stimulation of a low-grade infection were normal aspects of IUD efficacy, and the women's magazines that jumped on the IUD bandwagon also remained silent about how medical experts thought that it worked. Most women with whom I have spoken who once had IUDs inserted are horrified to learn that they worked by causing inflammation or infection. "If I had known that, I never would have let such a thing be put in my body!" is a typical reaction.

One doctor especially active in IUD development was Dr. Hugh Davis, an associate professor of obstetrics and gynecology and director of a family planning clinic at Johns Hopkins University in Baltimore. In the mid-1960s, he began experimenting with various IUDs, inserting them, usually without informed consent, on the poor, minority women from inner-city Baltimore who constituted most of the clinic's patients. None of his prototypes proved satisfactory, because they were too easily expelled by the body's natural drive to get rid of a foreign object. Ultimately, Davis and an engineering colleague, Irwin Lerner, perfected a design that was much harder for the body to expel. It was shaped like a shield, with downward prongs sticking out of each side. Because the prongs made it harder to pull the IUD out, Davis and Lerner also needed a tail string made out of stronger materials than those used in most other IUDs, which used a single strand of plastic, or a monofilament string. When Davis tried using a stronger and stiffer monofilament string with his pronged device, the male partners of women complained about its stiffness. The doctors then came up with a string composed of numerous nylon filaments enclosed in a nylon sheath. This multifilament string—adopted partly to appease men's needs during intercourse—proved to be the most deadly aspect of the Dalkon Shield design.

Davis and Lerner and their lawyer, Robert Cohn, formed the Dalkon Corporation in 1968 to manufacture, test, and market this newly patented IUD, which they named the Dalkon Shield. From the fall of 1968 through the next year, Dr. Davis tested the Dalkon Shield on 640 women, primarily Johns Hopkins Clinic patients. His highly laudatory article reporting the results of this twelve-month clinical trial was published in the February 1970 *American Journal of Obstetrics and Gynecology.*[47] Davis reported that only 1.1 percent of the women had become pregnant while using the Dalkon Shield—a rate comparable to the pill and significantly lower than that for other IUDs then on the market. As for adverse effects, he reported that out of the 640 women, only ten had expelled the device, nine had had it removed for medical reasons, and three had discontinued it for personal reasons. The article did not further elaborate. Davis did not reveal that he advised patients to use contraceptive foam for back-up for two or three months after the Shield was inserted, a fact that skewed any contraceptive claims for the Dalkon Shield. Davis also did not report that the average length of Shield

80 use among women in the study was only six months, hardly long enough to form any scientifically reliable conclusions about pregnancy or risk. The 1.1 percent pregnancy rate turned out to be false. While his article was still being reviewed, Davis did further follow-up and discovered that the pregnancy rate was now in excess of 5 percent—greater than for other IUDs. Yet Davis did not correct the manuscript and allowed publication with the inaccurate 1.1 percent figure.

Davis actively engaged in further publishing campaigns intended to stir up fear about the health risks of the pill and to promote the Dalkon Shield as a safer and more effective alternative. In 1971 he published as a supposedly objective medical textbook a tract called *Intrauterine Devices for Contraception: The IUD*, in which he again questioned the safety of oral contraceptives and compared the various IUDs on the market, concluding that the Shield was the superior device. Dr. Davis's expressed solicitousness for the health of women using the pill stands in sharp contrast to reports by some of his Dalkon Shield patients. One woman described her experience receiving a Shield from Dr. Davis in the early 1970s by recalling how he dismissed her complaints of severe cramping pain and heavy bleeding as normal, then told her that all her pain was in her head, and finally erupted at her in fury when she insisted on having the device removed.[48] Over the years, other doctors had similar reactions to women's complaints. Extreme cramping, shrieks of pain upon insertion, and profuse bleeding were dismissed as normal, and some women were even told that their reports of chronic pain were nothing more than probable yeast or bladder infections, or evidence that they were having severe emotional problems.[49] This tendency to trivialize women's complaints contributed to delayed awareness of the full extent of the Dalkon Shield's dangers.

The extravagant claims for the pregnancy prevention rate of the Dalkon Shield soon attracted corporate suitors for the small Dalkon Corporation. In 1970 the A. H. Robins Company acquired the rights, retaining Davis as a well-paid consultant. A. H. Robins was a major power in the pharmaceutical industry and maintained an extensive sales force, but the birth control market was completely new for the company, and no member of the corporate medical or research staff had any training or experience in gynecology or contraception. The A. H. Robins Company's handling of the Dalkon Shield is an appalling tale of indifference to safety, obsession with sales and cost concerns, misleading and fraudulent marketing, and unethical conduct in litigation. The Dalkon

Shield story has aptly been presented as a leading example of corporate crime and greed[50]—and a nightmare for women.[51]

Corporate misconduct and disregard for safety and effectiveness were evident from the outset. While negotiating to acquire the Shield, A. H. Robins officers learned that Davis's published pregnancy rate of 1.1 percent was false, but the company went ahead and extensively featured the fraudulent claim in its sales literature, distributing over one hundred thousand copies of the Davis article to its sales force and doctors, and prominently mentioning the 1.1 percent rate in its advertisements. Robins officials also learned that a smaller version of the device Davis and Lerner developed for nulliparous women (women who have never been pregnant) was completely untested. Nonetheless, the company aggressively promoted this version as safe and effective. Most IUDs were not recommended for nulliparous women; such women are thought to be at greater risk for perforations and infections, possibly because their unstretched uteruses are more vulnerable to foreign objects. Consequently, the claim that the Dalkon Shield came in a smaller version safe and effective for nulliparous women opened up a huge and lucrative market with relatively little competition.

A. H. Robins officials also covered up the fact that Davis and Lerner had made some design changes in the Shield that had never been tested. Most significantly, they had added copper to the molding mixture, both to make the Shield show up better on x rays and because of medical research suggesting that copper could enhance contraceptive effectiveness. Because the addition of copper was intended to have a medical effect, this should have brought the Dalkon Shield under the regulatory purview of the FDA. At that time, federal law gave the FDA premarketing approval authority only over drugs, not over medical devices. Consequently, manufacturers of medical devices did not have to demonstrate safety and efficacy to the FDA before selling a device to the public. But if a device contained active medicinal ingredients—known as a drug effect—then it would be subject to FDA premarket approval and proof of safety and effectiveness. The A. H. Robins Company was anxious to avoid FDA review, because the agency was closely scrutinizing birth control and the extensive testing required would have stood in the way of quick marketing.[52] In the course of reviewing another IUD, G. D. Searle Company's Copper-7,[53] the FDA had signaled that it would regulate as a drug any IUD that used copper to enhance contraceptive effect. Alarmed, Robins officials met with FDA staff to persuade them that the Dalkon Shield contained less copper than it actually did and that any

82   copper there was simply to augment strength and x-ray visibility. The FDA was convinced by this presentation, and A. H. Robins thus escaped the need to test the device and first prove its safety before marketing it.

A. H. Robins also rushed the Dalkon Shield to market despite other danger signs. Shortly after it purchased the device, Lerner, who had developed it with Davis, warned the company, in a memorandum that went to thirty-nine top executives, that there might be problems with the multifilament tail string. The string had a tendency to absorb fluid and bacteria and wick it up into the sterile environment of the uterus—a problem not caused by devices using single filament strings.[54] Soon after the company had begun marketing the Shield, Wayne Crowder, the quality control supervisor at the manufacturing plant, also warned about the wicking problem. Crowder conducted experiments that clearly showed that the tail string sucked up liquid and wicked it into the uterus, even when knots were put in the string. He suggested a simple and inexpensive corrective: a heat seal for the end of the string. Rather than reacting with concern to the reports of danger, Crowder's boss became angry, telling him that design and safety were not his responsibility and that his protestations of acting out of conscience were actually indications of insubordination.[55] Corporate officials rejected the suggestion for a heat seal on the tail string, because it would slow down production and create marketing problems for the existing supplies.[56] The corporation's attitude and priorities were starkly revealed in a memo sent by the head of the manufacturing division to the corporate director of pharmacy research, reassuring that they would not make any "unauthorized improvements" in the Shield. "My only interest in the Dalkon Shield," he wrote, "is to produce it at the lowest possible price, and, therefore, increase Robins' gross profit level."[57]

It turned out that Crowder's 1971 warning about wicking and bacteria was prescient—the unsealed multifilament tail string and its propensity to wick bacteria into the uterus was a principal reason the Dalkon Shield caused a significantly greater rate of sometimes fatal infections and pelvic inflammatory disease (PID) and sterility than other IUDs. In 1974 Dr. Howard Tatum of the Population Council, initially a Dalkon Shield enthusiast, conducted tests comparing the bacteria in Dalkon Shield tail strings with bacteria in monofilament IUD strings. These tests showed that a majority of Dalkon Shield strings contained infectious bacteria, while hardly any of the monofilament strings did. Tatum concluded that the Dalkon Shield was defective and unreasonably dangerous, but when he briefed A. H. Robins officials about his findings, the company took no corrective action.[58]

A. H. Robins's marketing strategy augmented the risks of the Dalkon Shield. Despite knowing that the tail string tended to deteriorate and become even more conducive to bacteria over time, in 1972 Robins changed its promotional material to encourage doctors to leave the Dalkon Shield in for five years or longer. The previous advice had been to remove and replace the Shield after two years, but Robins sales personnel reported that this recommendation made some doctors hesitant to use the Shield, when competing IUDs did not recommend replacement.[59] The company adhered to its insistence that it was safe to leave the Dalkon Shield in for lengthy periods even as medical evidence accumulated that the longer a Shield was in place, the greater the risk of PID.

A. H. Robins also actively promoted the Shield to general practitioners, refusing to limit its market to gynecologists. This marketing decision was directly contrary to the recommendation of the company's medical advisory board, which warned that complications were bound to arise if doctors not familiar with women's reproductive anatomy and unskilled in pelvic exams inserted Dalkon Shields. And despite warnings from physicians inserting the Shield in their patients that it could be fatal to leave it in place if a woman became pregnant because of a high rate of septic abortion,[60] in 1972 the company changed the promotional brochure distributed to patients to include a specific recommendation that the Shield should not be removed if a pregnancy resulted. Robins refused to change the patient brochure as reports from doctors about septic abortions accumulated, nor did the company order further tests or studies of the effect of Dalkon Shield use during pregnancy. Robins also remained silent about the mounting number of reports of perforated uteruses and virulent, sometimes fatal, PID, dismissing them as isolated incidents or attributable to poor medical practice and insanitary insertion techniques. Initially, the company did not recommend to doctors that an anesthetic and antibiotics be used during insertion, again ignoring its medical advisory board.

The company's promotional efforts paid off, as sales steadily increased from 1971 to 1973. Thanks to the patient brochures and publicity efforts targeted at popular women's magazines describing the Shield as the perfect, safe, modern contraceptive, many women specifically sought out the Dalkon Shield, rather than passively accepting their physicians' other recommendations. Between 1971 and 1974, according to

84   company estimates, approximately 2.2 million women in the United
       States and another 1 million women in other countries[61] received Dal-
       kon Shields.

       Although Robins officials attempted to suppress, dismiss, or down-
       play adverse reports coming into the company, they had no such control
       over independent doctors and medical researchers. Articles in medical
       journals reported not only high pregnancy rates of 5 percent or greater
       with the Dalkon Shield but also alarming rates of ectopic pregnancies,
       septic abortions, perforations, and infections—all attributable to the
       Dalkon Shield. One study, published in 1974, followed women with
       either the Dalkon Shield or Lippes Loop for a year after insertion and
       reported a pregnancy rate of 15 percent, with a 49 percent septic abor-
       tion rate among those who became pregnant.[62] In 1973 Dr. Donald
       Christian, the head of obstetrics and gynecology at the University of
       Arizona, wrote to A. H. Robins officials and contacted the FDA to report
       several cases of women who had died from septic infections after they
       became pregnant with Dalkon Shields in place. Neither the company
       nor the FDA followed up, and A. H. Robins continued to insist publicly
       that it had received no reports of any fatalities.

       When the company learned that Dr. Christian was going to publish a
       medical journal article about the fatalities, it was finally prompted into
       preemptive action. A. H. Robins acknowledged several deaths to the
       FDA, and in early May 1974 the company sent a letter to over 100,000
       U.S. and Canadian physicians advising them to remove Dalkon Shields
       from any women who became pregnant. The letter to doctors, however,
       did not inform them of the risk of pelvic infections in nonpregnant
       women, nor did it reach doctors in other countries where Shields were
       in use.

       In response to the advisory letter, the Planned Parenthood Federation,
       whose clinics were a major Dalkon Shield market, instructed its doctors
       to stop using the device because of its risks. And at the end of May, the
       Centers for Disease Control (CDC) reported that Dalkon Shield users
       had a 61 percent rate of pregnancy complications (compared with a 29
       percent rate for the next most dangerous IUD, the Lippes Loop), a 49.8
       percent rate of pelvic infections; and a 50.8 percent rate of other infec-
       tions.[63] Alarmed by all these negative reports, in June 1974 the FDA
       medical device bureau held hearings on the Dalkon Shield and recom-
       mended that it be withdrawn from the market. Pressured by A. H. Rob-
       ins officials, however, the FDA refused to order the company to recall
       all existing stocks; nor did the agency order removal of Shields already

in use. This agreement meant that existing supplies of Dalkon Shields already distributed to physicians could continue to be inserted in women, despite all the knowledge A. H. Robins officials had of its dangers. During the 1974 FDA hearings, company officials continued to suppress information about the multifilament tail string and the internal company studies that confirmed outside research demonstrating its dangerous propensity to wick bacteria. Had they revealed this information to the FDA, the agency might have been forced to take stronger steps to recall all Dalkon Shields, whether already inserted in women or on physicians' shelves.

In the wake of the domestic sales suspension, A. H. Robins publicly continued to defend the safety and efficacy of the Shield. It took another six years—with a mounting toll on women's lives, bodies, and reproductive health—before A. H. Robins wrote to U.S. physicians advising that they remove any Dalkon Shields still worn by their patients. Finally, in October 1984, a decade after it had stopped marketing the device, A. H. Robins undertook a massive media campaign recommending women wearing Dalkon Shields to have them removed and offering to pay some of the removal costs. In explaining this action, the company still steadfastly refused to acknowledge that the Shield was dangerous but instead attributed the recall to "new information" that long-term use might not be advisable.

Many of the injuries from the Dalkon Shield happened to women between 1974, when A. H. Robins stopped marketing it in North America, and 1984, when the company finally wrote to physicians and sponsored a media campaign aimed at reaching women to recommend its removal. If, at the time it first withdrew the Shield from the market, A. H. Robins officials had acknowledged the dangers and advised doctors and women of the need for its removal, the reproductive health of many women could have been preserved. Estimates of the number of U.S. women still wearing the Shield in 1983 range from 80,000 to 500,000.[64] By A. H. Robins's own undoubtedly conservative estimates, 4 percent of Dalkon Shield users suffered injury from it, and approximately 8 percent of the estimated number of Shield users eventually filed compensation claims from the victims' trust fund.[65] Approximately 5 percent of women wearing the Shield—110,000 women—became pregnant despite its insertion, and an estimated 60 percent of them suffered miscarriages. Over three hundred cases of septic abortion in the United States, some of them fatal, were attributed to the Shield. Studies published in the early 1980s estimated the rate of PID from Dalkon Shield use at from 8.3 to

86   15.6 percent for long-term Shield users,[66] precisely the group that could have been spared if A. H. Robins had recommended removal when it withdrew the device from the market in 1974. While there were several fatalities from severe cases of PID, those women who survived the infection continue to suffer from the lifelong psychological and physical effects of infertility.

Why, when the effect on sales obviously was no longer a consideration in the aftermath of the 1974 marketing suspension, did the company refuse at that time to recommend removal of all Dalkon Shields currently in use? Because now the corporate financial interest had shifted from marketing to defending litigation, and A. H. Robins was concerned that a removal campaign would be perceived as an admission that the product was defective and dangerous. The final capitulation in 1984 was prompted not by a suddenly acquired corporate conscience but by the realization that continued Shield use meant further successful litigation against the company. Several cases in the late 1970s and early 1980s resulted in punitive damages verdicts in excess of $1 million—a liability not absorbed by insurance. Jurors' reactions to the evidence of continued stonewalling by A. H. Robins officials and their failure to warn the public after 1974, as evidence of harm continued to mount, was a principal factor in these punitive judgments.[67]

In contrast to DES, where the litigation occurred long after the time when DES was used for pregnancy, Dalkon Shield litigation started soon after the Shield was initially marketed. Thus, it might have been able positively to effect corporate regard for safety—if A. H. Robins officials had chosen to react that way. There have been several instances in which corporations, presented with accumulating evidence of safety problems or threatened with an overwhelming number of lawsuits stemming from these problems, take corrective measures to improve product safety or recall and repair the defective product. Not surprisingly, given its history of denial and coverup of Dalkon Shield risks, A. H. Robins officials deliberately adopted quite the opposite course, pursuing a defense strategy of dragging out each case to make it expensive and difficult for the injured women and their attorneys, and of personally attacking the women plaintiffs by insinuating that their sexual and hygiene habits, rather than the Dalkon Shield, were responsible for their injuries. Company officials also instructed their lawyers to destroy incriminating documents and not to comply fully with their obligations to turn documents over to the plaintiff.

While the destruction of documents reveals the disregard of A. H.

Robins officials for the legal system in general, the company's deliberate defense strategy of vilifying and humiliating women plaintiffs speaks volumes about the corporation's attitude toward women in particular. As a crucial component of its victim-blaming strategy, in pretrial depositions and at trial, A. H. Robins's attorneys posed to women what plaintiffs' lawyers came to call the "dirty questions." This tactic was more prevalent in Dalkon Shield cases than in DES litigation. Ostensibly to explore whether their sexual histories and personal hygiene might have caused or exacerbated pelvic infections, the lawyers quizzed women in excruciating detail about the number of their sexual partners, the types of sexual activities they had engaged in, their toilet habits, and other sensitive and embarrassing questions. These attorneys forced married women, frequently in the presence of their spouse, to recount in detail their premarital sex lives and to divulge, under threat of perjury, whether they had engaged in sex with anyone other than their husband since marriage. One woman plaintiff described the experience of answering the dirty questions as akin to enduring an obscene phone call.[68] Many women reported the experience to be deeply humiliating or found that it provoked a feeling of self-blame and degraded self-worth.[69] The dirty questions did discourage some women from going ahead with their suits, prompting them to accept settlement offers they regarded as financially inadequate simply to avoid a repetition of the humiliation in the public forum of a courtroom. In addition to achieving precisely the effect that A. H. Robins hoped, this strategy also shifted the public focus away from the defects in the Dalkon Shield and onto the promiscuous transgressions of sexually active women.

Initially, A. H. Robins's legal strategy of trying to ride out and diminish the litigation by hiding information, attacking women, and offering cheap settlements appeared to work. Through mid-1979, the company had settled approximately three thousand lawsuits at an average cost of $11,000, which again reflects the low economic value attached to women's fertility.[70] Then, in 1979, a jury returned a huge verdict against A. H. Robins in the case of Carrie Palmer, who had almost died when she had a septic abortion after becoming pregnant with the Shield in place. The Palmer jury awarded $6.2 million in punitive damages, up to that time the largest single punitive damages judgment ever awarded against a pharmaceutical company.

This large verdict increased the subsequent average settlement value to $40,000 by 1982, but A. H. Robins also won defense verdicts in some cases where lawyers were able to raise doubts about whether the Dal-

88   kon Shield was actually the cause of a particular woman's infection. Then in 1983, angered by the company's humiliation strategy, Brenda Strempke, who suffered from infertility due to severe Shield-induced PID, rejected a $15,000 settlement offer and insisted on her right to a trial. The lawyers' dirty questions did not play well at trial, especially when the jury was presented with a newly released CDC study showing the rate of PID to be ten times higher in women with the Dalkon Shield than in those using other IUDs; they awarded Strempke $250,000 in compensatory damages and $1.5 million in punitive damages. The judge who presided over the Strempke trial, daunted by the large number of additional Dalkon Shield cases on his docket, then called in his colleague Judge Miles Lord to share some of the judicial burden. Judge Lord became much more actively involved in managing the litigation than previous judges, pushing hard on A. H. Robins to disclose fully documents it had long tried to keep out of plaintiffs' hands—including the internal tail string studies, which showed incontrovertibly that company officials were well aware of the wicking bacteria problem. Desperate to avoid having to comply with Judge Lord's order to turn over all documents, A. H. Robins offered to settle seven cases pending before Lord for $4.6 million—more than many jury awards and far exceeding the average value of all previous settlements.

The unprecedented settlement amount, coupled with the publicity given to Judge Lord's public condemnation of the company's behavior, stimulated more Shield victims to file lawsuits. By October 1984, Robins and its insurer Aetna had paid out $260 million for Dalkon Shield cases; yet they still faced over 3,500 claims—and dozens of new cases were being filed each week. The company's lawyers tried to have all Dalkon Shield cases consolidated and resolved en masse, with a single punitive damages determination for all time, preferably before a friendly federal judge, Robert Merhige, in the corporate hometown of Richmond, Virginia. This legal strategy was rebuffed by the courts, and in May 1985 a Kansas jury returned a $7.5 million punitive damages verdict—one of the largest ever awarded in a pharmaceutical products liability case—in the case of Loretta Tetuan, who had a hysterectomy in her twenties due to the ravages of the PID caused by her Dalkon Shield. The national publicity given to this huge punitive judgment stimulated another burst of new case filings by still more injured women. A few months later, with Dalkon Shield litigation expenses exceeding the amounts set in reserve to cover them and its stock price plummeting, A. H. Robins Company sought the legal protection of the U.S. bankruptcy court.

By filing a legal petition for bankruptcy reorganization, Robins was actually able to achieve its legal strategy of settling all Dalkon Shield cases once and for all in a single, Richmond-based proceeding before Judge Merhige. A bankruptcy filing automatically halts all litigation against a company, and the women injured by the Dalkon Shield were converted to creditors. Now they would have to stand in line for a portion of corporate assets along with bankers, suppliers, and stockholders. The bankruptcy filing also ensured that there would be significant delays before any more women injured by the Dalkon Shield received even a cent of compensation. It took almost four years of negotiations, legal wrangling, and appeals before payments of $725 started going out to Shield claimants. Injured women entitled to greater amounts had to wait several more years; women seeking the greatest damages—usually for the most serious injuries—are still waiting.

In reorganizing the company through bankruptcy, Judge Merhige's priorities appeared to be keeping financial assets in Richmond banks to be managed by Richmond people, assuring a healthy return for A. H. Robins stockholders, and continuing the company's safe and well-received product lines, such as Chapstick and Robitussin cough medicines. While establishing a fund to compensate women injured by the Dalkon Shield was essential to resolving the bankruptcy, critics of the bankruptcy process as a way to resolve injury claims point out that victims' needs wind up low on the list of priorities. For example, the U.S. Court of Appeals refused to approve an interim emergency fund to cover infertility treatment for women who would soon be too old to bear children, concluding that the potential diminution of estate assets for shareholders was a more compelling interest under the bankruptcy code than a woman's opportunity to bear children.[71] Individual women and the Dalkon Shield Information Network (DSIN), an advocacy group made up of victims, often found it difficult to get information about what was happening and how the proposed resolutions would affect them. The court refused to authorize the Claimants' Committee to send information about the status of the bankruptcy proceedings directly to the hundreds of thousands of Dalkon Shield claimants. Dalkon Shield victims themselves were sometimes treated as intermeddlers by the court. When Karen Hicks, a cofounder of DSIN who suffered severe PID and a total hysterectomy as a result of using the Dalkon Shield, sought to offer her views on how women's injuries had been valued in

90 estimating the funds to be allocated to Dalkon Shield victims, Judge Merhige refused to let her speak because of a legal technicality, even though as a claimant she had a right to participate directly without a lawyer as an intermediary. When she persisted in trying to present her views, the judge ordered a federal marshal to remove her from the court-room.[72]

Ultimately, the bankruptcy process was concluded when the American Home Products Company agreed to buy A. H. Robins and set up a fixed-value trust fund of $2.38 billion to pay Dalkon Shield claimants. Administrative and legal fees for administering the trust and resolving claims also come out of this fund. When this amount was selected for the trust fund, it was well below what the Claimants' Committee had estimated would be adequate to compensate victims. But with the price tag for Dalkon Shield liability now determinate, the price of A. H. Robins stock soared. When the sale of the company was consummated, and before any Dalkon Shield women had received any compensation, A. H. Robins shareholders received American Home Products stock equal to quadruple the value of their A. H. Robins stock before the bankruptcy filing. Robins family members and top corporate executives were among the largest shareholders, and they profited handsomely from the bankruptcy resolution.

The bankruptcy process, which focuses on the general financial interests of large, impersonal groups such as shareholders, claimants, and other creditors rather than on corporate or individual officials' knowledge of and disregard for risks, allows a far greater degree of evasion of corporate or personal accountability than the tort process. There were no uncomfortable depositions or incriminating document disclosures or hearings for personal sanctions and punitive damages to be endured in the bankruptcy process. Not a single individual responsible for covering up knowledge of the Shield's dangers, for refusing to change the deadly tail string, for suppressing information before the FDA and the courts, or for refusing to recall the dangerous product was ever held legally, personally, or financially accountable.

Most women victims of the Dalkon Shield, on the other hand, re-ceived trifling amounts as a result of the bankruptcy sale and trust fund. The compensation options established by the trust included an immedi-ate payment of $725, with no proof other than an affidavit of Shield use, intended for those with no or minimal injuries; a prompt but not immediate scheduled payment option ranging from $850 for heavy bleeding or induced abortion to $5,500 for hysterectomy, intended for those who had medical proof of Dalkon Shield–related injury but had other complicating causal factors; and a higher, individually tailored settlement offer of from $10,000 to $20,000, with the possibility of binding arbitration if the woman rejected the offer. This structure of payment options had the effect of giving priority to the least seriously injured women, while requiring those who had a strong need for other than de minimis compensation to wait for an indeterminate period of time. The trustees, constantly concerned about whether there would be sufficient trust assets to pay all claims, distributed literature designed to encourage women to take the quick and cheap payment options, regardless of what was medically and legally best for them. For example, trust literature highlighted and possibly exaggerated the delays and proof problems that might face women who held out for an individual settlement offer or arbitration, and it did not emphasize that the low payment fixed schedule was advisable only for women who would have significant problems proving a causal link. It is not surprising that nearly 100,000 claimants "chose" to receive only $725 as Dalkon Shield compensation.

Despite the overwhelming evidence of its dangers, the lessons of the Dalkon Shield have hardly been absorbed or heeded. Interest in IUDs is reemerging, and critics of the product liability system lament that it has reduced U.S. women's contraceptive options by driving all but a couple of IUDs off the domestic market. Never do they acknowledge that IUDs are inherently infectious. In the continuing search for the "perfect" female contraceptive, the desire to reduce women's agency and involvement as much as possible and to achieve a high pregnancy prevention rate are emphasized over adverse health effects. The latest panacea, Norplant, is distributed by American Home Products, the same company that wound up paying for the bulk of the Dalkon Shield carnage. Yet Norplant has not been adequately tested for its long-term effects on women or on children who may be conceived while exposed to any lingering chemical effects; and lawsuits are burgeoning in which women and doctors are claiming that they were not fully informed of the surgical difficulties, pain of removal, or side effects. Once again, common side effects such as severe nausea, migraine or other debilitating headaches, dizziness, and irregular menstruation are being dismissed as insignificant compared to the contraceptive promise.[73] The Dalkon Shield bankruptcy experience, rather than raising cautions about resolving issues of product safety and human injury through this process, has served as an inspiration to Dow Corning Corporation, the

92 leading manufacturer of silicone breast implants. Seeking a way out of the often punitive sanctions of juries in the form of a one-shot, fixed-value global resolution of the tens of thousands of tort claims it faces, Dow Corning recently filed for Chapter 11 reorganization. As it did in the Dalkon Shield cases, this maneuver will significantly delay any compensation that may go to injured women, while allowing the corporation to remain an ongoing and profitable concern.

THE FUTURE IS LIKELY TO REPEAT THE PAST

The cases of DES and the Dalkon Shield have much in common and paint sobering illustrations of the reasons and methods behind women's victimization by the pharmaceutical and medical device industries. Both cases demonstrate how cultural factors and attitudes toward women's bodies focus greater attention on possible benefits than on overwhelming dangers. A drug or device's ability to alter the normal functions of a woman's reproductive system is counted as a benefit. Evidence of harm is readily discounted as women's complaints are discredited or effects like heavy bleeding, pain, and nausea are considered insignificant or tribulations for women to bear. Damage to women's bodies is trivialized as merely emotional, or at any rate less worthy of significant compensation than injuries that keep people out of work.

This scenario is being repeated with silicone breast implants (to be discussed in greater detail in the next chapter). Capsular contracture—a sometimes painful and disfiguring puckering or hardening of the implant due to scar tissue that forms around it—is being virtually ignored as a harm in the current controversy over whether silicone implants are safe. The debate focuses solely on whether they are or are not epidemiologically associated with a higher incidence of immune system diseases. High rates of leakage and rupture, which may then necessitate expensive and risky removal surgery, are also not fully counted as a harm. Implant wearers' complaints of fatigue, dizziness, joint soreness, and depression are often ignored or attributed to emotional factors before they prompt medical examinations.

Both cases also illustrate the use of conscious strategies to blame and humiliate women who seek compensation for their injuries. Lawyers for DES manufacturers and for A. H. Robins vigorously pursued the possibility that a woman's own sexual history was responsible for her reproductive difficulties. The "dirty questions" were posed to DES daughters with cancer, T-shaped uteruses, and misshapen cervixes, even though there is not a shred of scientific evidence that sexually transmitted diseases or multiple sexual partners have anything to do with these afflictions.

The strategy of attacking women's lifestyle and character is also prevalent in the breast implant litigation. And as Norplant cases progress through the legal process, it is highly likely that once again the sexual activity that led women to seek out the product will be used to discredit them. A distinct "good girl/bad girl" dichotomy has developed in breast implant litigation. Of the cases that have gone to trial rather than being resolved through pretrial settlement, women who had implants because of reconstructive surgery after cancer treatment have prevailed in 80 percent of the cases. Women who used the implants for cosmetic breast augmentation, on the other hand, have been successful in only 50 percent of their cases.[74] While lawyers have been more reluctant to attack the lifestyle of sympathetic breast cancer survivors, it has been open season on women who had implants for cosmetic reasons, especially exotic dancers. Lawyers have sought to vilify women plaintiffs for having an active unmarried sex life and for having had abortions or out-of-wedlock births or placing children for adoption (all the available options if an unmarried woman should dare to get pregnant). Women who are strippers have been particularly vulnerable to attack, because their occupation so defies conventional norms of demure womanhood.

Postverdict interviews with jurors indicate that these defense tactics have successfully prejudiced some juries against injured plaintiffs.[75] For example, in two cases recently tried in Texas, one involving a breast cancer survivor and the other a woman who had implants for cosmetic reasons, the legal defense team thoroughly attacked the lifestyle of the latter plaintiff. The same medical and scientific evidence of injury and causation was presented in both trials, and many of the expert witnesses were the same. The jury in the cancer plaintiff's case returned a substantial plaintiff's verdict; the other jury found for the defense and made disparaging comments about the plaintiff in posttrial interviews.

Women are particularly vulnerable in ways men are not to the defense strategy of character assassination in cases involving products connected with sexuality and reproduction. The double standard for women and the double-edged sword of sexual freedom and the beauty culture are still quite potent; and with "traditional family values" resurgent, women who are sexually active outside marriage are even more likely to be castigated. "Loose" and independent women are not truly injured but have only themselves to blame when their breasts harden, their implants leak, their uterus is perforated, or an infection ravages their reproductive capacity. A strategy of attacking a man for having many sexual partners or for impregnating a woman outside marriage would be less likely to bias jurors against him, since these are considered normal and acceptable male behaviors. Drug and medical device manufacturers cynically manipulate these social attitudes and play on women's fears and vulnerabilities. Their marketing campaigns tantalize women with the promise of a perfect and more healthy baby, or the perfect contraceptive that will free them from mess, awkward situations, and responsibility. Women's lives, they claim, will be more fulfilled if they can have that baby, or engage in worry-free sex, or become more sexually attractive to men by augmenting their breasts. But when these wondrous devices cause cancer, deform their bodies, or erupt inside them, women are impugned for wanting to be sexually attractive and active in the first place.

Another common lesson is that the tort system can function as an important safety valve, prodding further regulatory action and mopping up after regulatory failure. The DES and Dalkon Shield cases were instrumental in stimulating more research into the health effects of these products, in getting more information out to women about the risks they faced, and in alerting doctors and the public. If not for litigation, documents that disclosed corporate disregard for safety and disseminated important safety information would never have been divulged.

This has also proved true in the breast implant situation. Much of our current knowledge about how Dow Corning officials covered up adverse animal studies and suppressed information about the tendency of implants to leak or rupture was derived through the discovery efforts of plaintiffs' lawyers. Like A. H. Robins, Dow Corning arduously resisted efforts to make it disclose information about risks.[76] The short-sighted corporate determination to protect a market at all costs, rather than cooperate in informing the public about risks, is not likely to dissipate. But the legal system offers powerful tools for forcing the disclosure of information. When adverse health and safety information is finally forced out, the corporate resistance to disclosure usually causes far more damage to the company's financial and sales position than a more forthcoming posture ever would. Just as A. H. Robins's coverup campaign outraged juries and motivated large punitive damages awards, jurors' and judges' reactions to Dow Corning's systematic efforts to keep damaging information private has played a large role in increasing puni- tive assessments.[77]

Although the tort system remains an important avenue for women injured by defective products to get more information and achieve some compensation, it can certainly be an abusive, disempowering, and inef- ficient way for women to have their health and financial needs ad- dressed. The tort system provides, at best, after-the-fact compensation, rather than prevention of the damage in the first place. Women also become subject to the agendas of lawyers for both sides, and their indi- vidual plights are often subsumed in the search for aggregate and finite resolutions. The creation of global settlement funds, either through ju- dicially orchestrated mass settlements, as with breast implants, or through bankruptcy court intervention, as with the Dalkon Shield and now breast implants, is likely to continue. Resource and political pres- sures are pushing the tort system away from individual, case-by-case resolution of mass injury problems. Global trust funds deliver some compensation to a far greater number of affected people than trying in- dividual cases could ever hope to do. But they tend to favor the least seriously injured or the uninjured over those with more compelling needs. While a lot of people get some compensation without regard to the severity of their injury, no seriously injured victims get close to what they need or what a jury is likely to think they deserve. Global settlements also leave unaddressed what is often women's most press- ing emotional need and initial reason for filing suit: the need to be rec- ognized as an injured individual, rather than an epidemiological sta- tistic.

Recent political and legislative trends to cut back on the reach of the tort system are likely to diminish whatever incentive it does offer to companies to be more attentive to safety. For over a decade, industry has been actively lobbying for tort "reform," which involves making liability harder for plaintiffs to prove, insulating companies from puni- tive damages, and capping the compensation injured people can receive. The likely and hoped-for result of this reform movement, which has borne fruit in many state legislatures and in the new Republican- controlled Congress, is that it will be more financially manageable for corporations to produce products that injure large numbers of people. And the consequences of suppressing adverse information that comes to light after initial regulatory approval will be less severe, because several reform bills—including one passed in 1995 by the U.S. House of Repre-

96   sentatives—give drug and medical device manufacturers immunity from punitive damages if the product received FDA premarket approval.

The tenor of tort reform is likely to have a particularly adverse impact on women's ability to recover full damages. The type of harm known as nonpecuniary or noneconomic loss has been under focused attack. Many states have passed laws capping the amount of nonpecuniary damages plaintiffs can receive. The U.S. House of Representatives recently passed a bill that would tie punitive damages to economic loss, leaving the extent of nonpecuniary harm out of the calculation. Nonpecuniary loss is a category of vital importance to women, however. Many of the injuries that happen disproportionately to women injure them primarily in ways legally considered to be of no economic value. Sexual harassment through a hostile environment, sexual assault, cosmetic disfigurement, depression, diminished sexuality, infertility, and pregnancy loss are all regarded as predominantly emotional injuries. Any resulting monetary loss is hardly the only, or the most significant, aspect of the injury. Rather, the harms also shred a woman's self-esteem and rob her of dignity and dreams and pleasure, but they do not as significantly cost her out-of-pocket expenses and deprive her of a paycheck. It is these gender-based injuries, precisely the principal types of injuries caused by drugs and medical devices that harm women's bodies, that are affected by the caps of the tort reform movement. All the efforts by lawyers and women's health advocates to get claims agents and juries to value women's reproductive capacity more highly will be pointless if an arbitrary cap is placed on the amount that any woman can recover. If the congruence of punitive damages protection and caps on noneconomic damages makes it even cheaper for pharmaceutical companies to cause injuries to women's reproductive health, they will have little financial incentive to pursue vigorously initial evidence of risks.

The pharmaceutical industry has been one of the most active lobbyists in the tort reform legislative debates, with insulation from punitive damages upon FDA approval their prized project. Recently, the pharmaceutical industry has cynically tried to use women's health as an argument for according the industry special protection from liability by immunizing companies from punitive damages. One suspects that once again, financial self-interest rather than a sincere concern for women's well-being is the prime motivation.

For the first ten years of congressional debates over tort reform, the possible impact on women of proposed legal changes was rarely considered. Then, starting in 1992, this author and a few other witnesses began to bring women into the debate. I argued before the U.S. Senate Judiciary Committee that given the track record of the pharmaceutical industry regarding drugs and devices used in women's bodies, the "FDA approval defense" would have an adverse impact on women's health. I also offered the critique of caps on damages for noneconomic loss outlined above. Some senators cited this information concerning the likely impact on women as grounds for opposing the legislation. Suddenly, women's health was the hot issue; consumer groups sensed that it was the new wedge that could forestall the worst aspects of tort reform, while industry groups perceived it as a threat that needed to be managed.

In response, the Products Liability Coordinating Council (PLCC), a group actively sponsored by the pharmaceutical industry, created a women's issues task force, which issued press releases containing egregious misstatements, such as "DES was never approved by the FDA" (so, according to them, the FDA defense would not have any effect on DES daughters). The basic thrust of the women's issues task force literature was that the product liability system was the real enemy of women's health. Cut back on tort suits and recoveries, they argued, and manufacturers will start investing more in contraceptive research. The reason, they asserted, that U.S. women have fewer contraceptive options than women in Third World countries (who might still be given DES while pregnant and have dangerous IUDs inserted) is U.S. tort law run amok. And it is tort law manipulated by greedy lawyers they claim, that has driven useful and safe products like the morning sickness drug Bendectin[78] and now breast implants off the market.

This industry effort to scare women into supporting legal reforms that would be seriously against their interests demonstrates that their overriding concern remains the protection of their financial and marketing interests and that their attitude toward women remains fundamentally the same: to manipulate their feelings about their bodies and sexuality; assume that pharmaceutical companies and doctors know better than women what's good for them; and, finally, to convince them that suing when they are injured undercuts other women's health needs. With this set of attitudes, the past examples of reproductive harms to women perpetrated by pharmaceutical companies are likely to crop up in different drugs in the future. For women, a healthy dose of caution about reproductive drugs and bodily devices will have to remain the best medicine.

NOTES

1. As the reports of adverse effects came in from doctors, the FDA withdrew its prior approval of lactation suppressants, but the agency has not required manufacturers to withdraw them from the market. See L. Neergaard, "FDA Sued Over Milk Inhibitor: 19 Deaths Connected," *Legal Intelligencer* (August 17, 1994): 9; "FDA Sued on Drug to Dry Mothers' Milk," *New York Times* (August 17, 1994): A15; "Lactation Drug Dropped for Postpartum Use," *Chicago Tribune* (August 19, 1994): 8.

2. See, for example, E. Martin, *The Woman in the Body* (Boston: Beacon Press, 1987), a fascinating study of the history and ideology of technological medical intervention in women's reproductive processes. An example of attributing pathology to women's natural bodily functions in order to promote the use of invasive devices is the denomination of small breasts as a disease, "micromastia," in the early 1980s by the doctor's group that stood to benefit most financially from breast implants, the American Society of Plastic and Reconstructive Surgeons (K. Cohen, "Truth and Beauty, Deception and Disfigurement: A Feminist Analysis of Breast Implant Litigation," *William and Mary Journal of Women and the Law* 1 [1994]: 149–82, 169).

3. J. Steinman, "Women, Medical Care, and Mass Tort Litigation," *Chicago-Kent Law Review* 68 (1992): 409–29, 412.

4. Women's health advocates have waged an ongoing political struggle to obtain more federal funding for research into women's health and to have women included in clinical drug trials so that more can be learned about the effects of drugs on women and whether dosages developed for male study populations are also safe for women. See, for example, V. Merton, "The Exclusion of Pregnant, Pregnable, and Once-Pregnable People (a.k.a. Women) from Biomedical Research," *American Journal of Law and Medicine* 19 (1993): 369–451; H. Gorenberg and A. White, "Off the Pedestal and into the Arena: Toward Including Women in Experimental Protocols," *NYU Review of Law and Social Change* 19 (1991–92): 205. While concerns about possible adverse effects if drugs are administered during pregnancy has been one of the most oft-repeated justifications for excluding women from clinical drug research, this concern has never stood in the way of pharmaceutical companies then marketing the same drugs, untested on women, for subsequent prescription to women.

5. Excerpts from courtroom statement of Judge Miles W. Lord, U.S. District Court for the District of Minnesota; remarks reprinted in full in "The Dalkon Shield Litigation: Revised Annotated Reprimand by Chief Judge Miles W. Lord," *Hamline Law Review* 9 (1978): 7–51. Rather than heeding Judge Lord's call to conscience, the A. H. Robins Company executives filed a complaint against him for violations of judicial ethical standards, contending that he had damaged their personal and professional reputations

without due process of law. Judge Lord had to endure the expense of hiring a lawyer for his defense and a public hearing before his judicial colleagues. Ultimately, the judges of the U.S. Court of Appeals for the Eighth Circuit, who had supervisory authority over Judge Lord, found that his statement was a governmental attack on the A. H. Robins officers' reputation without due process of law, and ordered it expunged from the official judicial records of the case (M. Mintz, *At Any Cost: Corporate Greed, Women, and the Dalkon Shield* [New York: Pantheon Books, 1985], 232–36).

Thus, it is important to use other forums, such as this one, to publicize Judge Lord's statement, so as not to have the Robins officials succeed in their ultimate goal of suppressing the painful truth in the judge's heartfelt appeal to the corporate and individual conscience.

6. "The Wonder Drug That You Should Wonder About" is a slogan used by the national DES victims' advocacy group DES Action in informational literature about DES.

7. According to government data, a gram of the natural estrogen estradiol costs $300, but a gram of DES costs $2 (R. Meyers, *DES: The Bitter Pill* [New York: Seaview/Putnam, 1983], 41, citing S. Bell, "The Synthetic Compound Diethylstilbestrol [DES] 1938–1941" [Ph.D. dissertation, Brandeis University, Waltham, MA, 1980]).

8. DES was never patented by Dodds or his research institute, because he believed that compounds with medical benefit should be in the public domain (ibid., 42). Consequently, it was a generic drug from its inception, and numerous pharmaceutical companies large and small—estimates are in the range of two hundred or more companies—participated in the DES market.

9. Studies performed by Dodds and his colleagues showed that DES caused breast and other tumors in rats and rabbits (D. B. Dutton, *Worse than the Disease: Pitfalls of Medical Progress* [Cambridge, U.K.: Cambridge University Press, 1988], 37). One study by Yale University researchers Edgar Allen and W. U. Gardner, published in the April 1941 issue of *Cancer*, showed that the administration of estrogen to test animals was "a very important factor" in causing cervical cancer—one of the cancers later to afflict the female offspring of the pregnant women who were given DES (Meyers, *DES: The Bitter Pill*, 55).

10. Dutton, *Worse than the Disease*, 37–38; Meyers, *DES: The Bitter Pill*, 77. This report was published as Council on Pharmacy and Chemistry, "Stilbestrol: Preliminary Report of the Council," *Journal of the American Medical Association* 113 (December 23, 1939): 2312.

11. In 1938 Dodds and some colleagues published a paper reporting that when they administered DES to pregnant rats and rabbits, it caused miscarriage, and they opined that in light of reproductive and hormonal system similarities, "the experimental conclusions arrived at should thus be appli-

cable to women" (Meyers, *DES: The Bitter Pill*, 42, quoting a study published in the September 10, 1938, *British Medical Journal*). Three years later, two U.S. researchers duplicated Dodds's results and published an article in the April 1941 journal *Endocrinology* explaining that DES caused the ova to disintegrate (H. O. Burdick and H. Vedder, "The Effect of Stilbestrol in Early Pregnancy," *Endocrinology* 28 [April 1941]: 629–32).

    12. Meyers, *DES: The Bitter Pill*, 54, 76.

    13. Dutton, *Worse than the Disease*, 43.

    14. The pharmaceutical sales force is known as "detail men," and many doctors are quite reliant on them for information about drugs. "Detail men" also ply doctors with free samples, gifts, and special deals on groups of a company's products to induce doctors to prescribe particular brands.

    15. See, for example, D. Scully, *Men Who Control Women's Health*, rev. ed. (New York: Teachers College Press, 1994); G. Corea, *The Hidden Malpractice*, updated ed. (New York: Harper and Row, 1985); S. Rosser, *Women's Health—Missing from U.S. Medicine* (Bloomington, IN: Indiana University Press, 1994); E. Nechas and D. Foley, *Unequal Treatment* (New York: Simon and Schuster, 1994).

    16. Subsequent medical knowledge has not borne out the Smith and Karnaky theories. Today, miscarriages are regarded as attributable more to fetal abnormalities or structural physical abnormalities in the mother (such as the reproductive tract malformations attributed to DES exposure) than to maternal hormone levels.

    17. Meyers, *DES: The Bitter Pill*, 51, quoting from K. J. Karnaky, "The Use of Stilbestrol for the Treatment of Threatened and Habitual Abortion and Premature Labor: A Preliminary Report," *Southern Medical Journal* 35 (1942): 838–47. Karnaky's experimental use of DES was prompted by representatives from the pharmaceutical company Squibb. After becoming aware of Karnaky's published theory, Squibb officials visited Karnaky in Houston, wined and dined him, promised him free samples of DES, and readily persuaded him to engage in research. Initially, Karnaky tested the DES on dogs, but he soon complained to Squibb that "the dang dogs were dying like flies" (Meyers, *DES: The Bitter Pill*, 53). Rather than reacting with alarm and caution to this troubling report, the Squibb doctors persuaded him to test the DES on women instead and sent him human experiment dosages of tablets ranging from .1 to 25 mgs. Unlike the dogs, the women did not immediately die from these lower dosages but instead showed an immediate temporary remission in uterine contractions. Karnaky concluded that dogs must be peculiarly sensitive to DES, and he was enthusiastic about its safety and efficacy for women.

    18. G. V. Smith, O. W. Smith and D. Hurwitz, "Increased Excretion of Pregnanediol in Pregnancy from Diethylstilbestrol with Special Reference

to the Prevention of Late Pregnancy Accidents," *American Journal of Obstetrics and Gynecology* 51 (1946): 411–15.

19. Meyers, *DES: The Bitter Pill*, 65, quoting from O. W. Smith, "Diethylstilbestrol in the Prevention and Treatment of Complications of Pregnancy," *American Journal of Obstetrics and Gynecology* 56 (1948): 821–34.

20. G. V. Smith and O. W. Smith, "The Influence of Diethylstilbestrol on the Progress and Outcome of Pregnancy as Based on a Comparison of Treated and Untreated Primigravidas," *American Journal of Obstetrics and Gynecology* 58 (1949): 994–1009.

21. Dutton, *Worse than the Disease*, 58, quoting remarks of Dr. Dale Console as reported in M. Mintz, "Squibb Doctor Faced Built-In Conflict," *Washington Post* (June 8, 1969): A9.

22. R. E. Crowder, E. S. Bills and J. S. Broadbent, "The Management of Threatened Abortion: A Study of 100 Cases," *American Journal of Obstetrics and Gynecology* 60 (1950): 896–99.

23. Meyers, *DES: The Bitter Pill*, 67–68, quoting from D. Robinson and L. B. Shettles, "The Use of Diethylstilbestrol in Threatened Abortion," *American Journal of Obstetrics and Gynecology* 63 (1952): 1330–33.

24. J. H. Ferguson, "Effects of Stilbestrol on Pregnancy Compared to the Effects of a Placebo," *American Journal of Obstetrics and Gynecology* 65 (1953): 592–601. When Dr. Ferguson reported his results at a 1952 professional conference, Dr. Greene, who had performed the Northwestern University animal studies of DES that showed reproductive abnormalities in rat fetuses, praised Ferguson's work, commenting that if the Smiths had used control groups and placebos, their conclusions might well have been far less glowing. "Dr. Ferguson has, I believe, driven a very large nail into the coffin that we will use some day to bury some of the extremely outsized claims for the beneficial effects of stilbestrol," Greene said in his commentary (Dutton, *Worse than the Disease*, 55; Meyers, *DES: The Bitter Pill*, 68).

25. Meyers, *DES: The Bitter Pill*, 69; Dutton, *Worse than the Disease*, 56, quoting from W. J. Dieckmann, M. E. Davies, L. M. Rynkiewicz and R. E. Pottinger, "Does the Administration of Diethylstilbestrol During Pregnancy Have Therapeutic Value?" *American Journal of Obstetrics and Gynecology* 66 (1953): 1062–81.

26. Dutton, *Worse than the Disease*, 56; Y. Brackbill and H. Berendes, "Dangers of Diethylstilbestrol: Review of a 1953 Paper," *Lancet* 2 (1978): 520.

27. Dutton, *Worse than the Disease*, 57–58.

28. See Meyers, *DES: The Bitter Pill*, 91–92, for insightful interviews with some doctors analyzing why they continued to prescribe DES. Some doctors reported that women, distraught at the prospect of losing a wanted pregnancy, would ask for the drug they had read about in a magazine, convinced that it could help. And the doctors, knowing that some studies said

102   it would help while others said it would not, were reluctant to withhold a drug that, even if it did no more than psychologically reassure and relax their patient, could possibly help protect the pregnancy.

29. These estimates are reported in Dutton, *Worse than the Disease,* 56–57, and are drawn from O. P. Heinonen, "Diethylstilbestrol in Pregnancy: Frequency of Exposure and Usage Patterns," *Cancer* 31 (1973): 576. It is difficult to derive exact reports on DES usage, because many medical records or prescription forms are no longer available due to passage of time or deliberate destruction, and many pregnant women were not told what pill they were prescribed, or cannot remember whether they took a drug during a long-ago pregnancy.

30. A. L. Herbst, H. Ufelder and D. C. Poskanzer, "Adenocarcinoma of the Vagina: Association of Maternal Stilbestrol Therapy with Tumor Appearance in Young Women," *New England Journal of Medicine* 284 (1971): 878–81.

31. P. Greenwald, J. Barlow and P. Nasca, "Vaginal Cancer After Maternal Treatment with Synthetic Estrogens," *New England Journal of Medicine* 285 (August 12, 1971): 390–92.

32. Dutton, *Worse than the Disease,* 71.

33. Despite these warnings, some U.S. doctors continued to prescribe DES to pregnant patients into the mid-1970s. Dutton (ibid., 74) reports that in 1974, U.S. physicians issued an estimated 11,000 DES prescriptions to pregnant patients. When I conducted interviews with several DES mothers and DES daughters, two of the mothers I interviewed had been given DES while pregnant in 1972 and 1973. One of these women had no prior history of miscarriage but reported that her doctor thought her first, normal, healthy child weighed too little at birth, so he gave her DES in the hope that her second baby would weigh more. The mother reported to me that her daughter weighed in two ounces less than her firstborn. "I guess my body just normally produces five and half pound babies, no matter what you try to do to it," she said. And, the only thing wrong with her second child is the reproductive tract abnormalities caused by DES.

DES also continued to be used throughout the 1970s, especially at college health services, as a "morning after" pill, with no warning to women about the risks if they turned out to be pregnant despite the contraceptive effort. While DES is no longer used for pregnancy in the United States, there are reports that even in the mid-1990s, some doctors in Eastern European countries are prescribing DES to pregnant women. And there is little or no monitoring by international health organizations of how it is being used in Third World countries.

34. One brand of DES, marketed under the name DESPlex, was mixed with vitamins B and C and aggressively marketed as "recommended for routine prophylaxis in ALL pregnancies" (emphasis in original). For a photo-

graphic reproduction of this ad as it appeared in obstetrics-gynecology journals, see R. Apfel and S. Fisher, *To Do No Harm: DES and the Dilemmas of
Modern Medicine* (New Haven, CT: Yale University Press, 1984), 26.

35. For a moving first-person account of what it is like for a young
woman who is just becoming sexually active, still sexually insecure, and
not yet used to pelvic exams, to go in for a checkup about a bleeding problem and emerge with a clear cell adenocarcinoma diagnosis, see J. Bichler,
DES Daughter (New York: Avon, 1981).

36. There is growing evidence of harm to DES sons, as well. There has
been much less research on the sons of DES mothers, perhaps because men
do not regularly go to the equivalent of a gynecologist to have their reproductive systems checked and because even fewer men than women know
they were exposed to DES. DES researchers and activists also report that
men are more defensive and more likely than women to deny that something may be wrong with their sexual organs, which in men's minds are
more bound up with sex and masculinity than with reproduction. The research that has been done suggests higher than average rates of testicular
cancer and malformations such as small penises, undescended testicles, or
enlarged testicular veins; and reduced sperm production, which can lead to
impaired fertility.

37. A. Herbst, S. Anderson, M. Hubby et al., "Risk Factors for the Development of Diethylstilbestrol-Associated Clear Cell Adenocarcinoma: A
Case Control Study," *American Journal of Obstetrics and Gynecology* 154
(1986): 814–22.

38. Dutton, *Worse than the Disease*, 86–87. The differing rates of these
conditions in the various studies may be attributable to the fact that the
women in each study group were exposed to different amounts of DES.

39. One 1980 study showed a successful pregnancy rate of only 66.7 percent among DES-exposed women and their partners who were trying to
have children, compared with a 90 percent rate among a similar unexposed
group (M. J. Berger and D. P. Goldstein, "Impaired Reproductive Performance in DES-Exposed Women," *Obstetrics and Gynecology* 55 [1980]: 25–
27). Another 1980 study by Dr. Herbst and colleagues, following the daughters of women in the Dieckmann study from the University of Chicago,
found that DES daughters had four times as many miscarriages, stillbirths,
and ectopic pregnancies as the unexposed women's daughters. Only 47 percent of the DES-exposed daughters had full-term, healthy live births, as
against 85 percent of the unexposed daughters (A. Herbst, M. Hubby, R.
Blough and F. Azizi, "A Comparison of Pregnancy Experience in DES-Exposed and DES-Unexposed Daughters," *Journal of Reproductive Medicine*
24 [1980]: 62–69). An additional Herbst study found a 21 percent miscarriage rate for those exposed to DES, compared with an 11 percent rate
among those without DES exposure (Meyers, *DES: The Bitter Pill*, 127).

40. *Sindell v. Abbott Labs*, 26 Cal.3d 588, 607 P.2d 924 (1981); *Hymowitz v. Eli Lilly & Co.*, 73 N.Y.2d 487, 539 N.E.2d 1069 (1989); *Abel v. Eli Lilly & Co.*, 418 Mich. 311, 434 N.W.2d 164 (1984); *Collins v. Eli Lilly & Co.*, 116 Wis.2d, 342 N.W.2d 37 (1984); *Martin v. Abbott Labs*, 102 Wash.2d 581, 689 P.2d 368 (1984).

41. *Hymowitz v. Eli Lilly & Co.*

42. *It is virtually impossible to sue enough companies to represent over 60 percent of the market, and market share estimation tables prepared in New York and California cannot account for almost 40 percent of the market in key years. If the companies a woman has sued together represent 50 percent of the total market for DES in the year she was born, then she will recover half of her damages. Most drug companies, thanks to the market share principle, have had to pay less than 8 percent of the verdicts or settlements. Eli Lilly has been assigned the largest market share, ranging from approximately 30 to 40 percent depending on the year and the pill dosage.*

43. *This principle is known as the no preconception duty rule. See, for example, Enright v. Eli Lilly & Co.*, 77 N.Y.2d 377, 570 N.E.2d 198 (1989).

44. As a 1968 FDA advisory committee report on intrauterine devices so tactfully put it, in enumerating the advantages of IUDs, "the underprivileged woman is more effectively served when the need for recurrent motivation, required in most other forms of contraception, is removed" (N. Grant, *The Selling of Contraception* [Columbus, OH: Ohio State University Press, 1992], 23, quoting from U.S. Food and Drug Administration, Advisory Committee on Obstetrics and Gynecology, *Report of Intrauterine Devices*. GPO Doc. No. 290-137-0-68-3 [1968], 1).

45. K. Hicks, *Surviving the Dalkon Shield IUD* (New York: Teachers College Press, 1994), 19, quoting from C. Tietze and S. Levitt, eds. *Proceedings of the First Conference on the IUCD*, April 30–May 1 (New York: Excerpta Medica, 1962), 3.

46. Grant, *The Selling of Contraception*, 25.

47. H. J. Davis, "The Shield Intrauterine Device: A Superior Modern Contraceptive," *American Journal of Obstetrics and Gynecology* 106 (1970): 455–62. Nowhere in the article did Davis reveal that he was one of the developers of the Shield or that he had a financial stake in its success. If he had divulged this information, it might have been apparent to readers that this supposedly objective medical research report was little more than elaborate sales promotional literature.

48. Hicks, *Surviving the Dalkon Shield IUD*, 27.

49. See Mintz, *At Any Cost* (New York: Pantheon Books, 1985), 13, 107; Hicks, *Surviving the Dalkon Shield IUD*, 27–33; Grant, *The Selling of Contraception*, 130–31.

50. J. Braithwaite, *Corporate Crime in the Pharmaceutical Industry* (Boston: Routledge, 1984); Mintz, *At Any Cost*.

51. S. Perry and J. Dawson, *Nightmare: Women and the Dalkon Shield*
(New York: Macmillan, 1985).

52. Mintz, *At Any Cost*, 55–56.

53. This IUD, too, turned out to very dangerous to women, producing a high rate of infection, perforation, and septic abortion. It generated extensive litigation, during which lawyers for plaintiffs proved that, like the A. H. Robins Company, Searle had suppressed evidence of dangers, submitted misleading information to the FDA, and made false advertising claims. See, for example, *Kociemba v. G. D. Searle Co.*, 707 F. Supp. 1517 (D. Minn. 1989).

54. R. Sobol, *Bending the Law* (Chicago: University of Chicago Press, 1991), 7; Mintz, *At Any Cost*, 138–39.

55. Mintz, *At Any Cost*, 141.

56. Ibid., 143.

57. Ibid., 143, quoting September 9, 1971, memo from Daniel French to Oscar Klioze.

58. Ibid., 143–44.

59. Sobol, *Bending the Law*, 8.

60. One particularly salient warning came in a June 1972 letter to Robins's sales manager from Dr. Thad Earl, a gynecologist who once had so enthused about the Shield that he invested in the Dalkon Corporation and became a paid consultant to A. H. Robins when it purchased the device. Dr. Earl reported septic abortions in five of his six patients who became pregnant with Dalkon Shields in place, and he urged the company to warn all physicians immediately to remove the device if a woman became pregnant. This dire report was circulated among several high-level company officials, but no corrective action resulted.

61. Mintz, *At Any Cost*, 4.

62. Grant, *The Selling of Contraception*, 56–57, citing R. Shine and J. Thompson, "The In Situ IUD and Pregnancy Outcome," *American Journal of Obstetrics and Gynecology* 119 (1974): 126–27.

63. Mintz, *At Any Cost*, 164–65.

64. Ibid., 6.

65. Ibid., 7; Grant, *The Selling of Contraception*, 68.

66. Grant, *The Selling of Contraception*, 66–67.

67. Those who doubt, in the current political climate of hostility to product liability lawsuits, that punitive damages can help improve safety should contemplate that within six months after the second punitive damages verdict against it, Robins notified physicians to remove Dalkon Shields, and after a few more punitive verdicts the company finally reached out to notify women of the danger implanted in their bodies.

68. Mintz, *At Any Cost*, 195.

69. Hicks, *Surviving the Dalkon Shield IUD*, 52–53.

70. Sobol, *Bending the Law,* 14.

71. Ibid., 129–135.

72. Hicks, *Surviving the Dalkon Shield IUD,* 69–70.

73. T. Lewin, "Dream Contraceptive's Nightmare," *New York Times* (July 8, 1994): A10; H. Little, "No Panacea: Norplant Suit Charges Failure to Educate Patients," *Chicago Tribune* (Oct. 31, 1993): Section 6, 1; G. Kolata, "Will the Lawyers Kill Off Norplant?" *New York Times* (May 28, 1995): Section 3, 1.

74. T. Koenig and M. Rustad, "His and Her Tort Reform: Gender Injustice in Disguise," *Washington Law Review* 70 (1995): 1–90, 44.

75. Cohen,"Truth and Beauty, Deception and Disfigurement," 172.

76. When Public Citizen, a consumer and health advocacy organization, sought release of animal study data that had been submitted to the FDA, Dow claimed that this research was confidential commercial information whose disclosure would cause substantial harm to its competitive position. A federal court rejected this defense and ordered public disclosure, criticizing Dow for erecting "unnecessary roadblocks" to an effort to help give the public crucial information about safety. The fact that the FDA allowed implants to stay on the market should not prevent women from getting all the information necessary for making their own informed decision, the judge observed (*Teich v. FDA,* 732 F. Supp. 17, 20 [D.D.C. 1990]). Dow also sought protective orders in many of the tort cases, which sealed the evidence from public availability. Dow Corning lawyers then invoked those protective orders to try to stop expert witnesses and former employees from complying with FDA requests for information.

77. As one court explained, in affirming a $6.5 million punitive damages award to Mariann Hopkins:

> Given the facts that Dow was aware of possible defects in its implants, that Dow knew long-term studies of the implants' safety were needed, that Dow concealed this information as well as the negative results of the few short-term laboratory tests performed, and that Dow continued for several years to market its implants as safe despite this knowledge, a substantial punitive award is justified (*Hopkins v. Dow Corning Corp.,* 33 F.3d 1116, 1127 [9th Cir. 1994]).

78. Whether Bendectin was a teratogen or not has been the subject of intense scientific and legal controversy. Most juries in Bendectin cases have found that Bendectin did not cause a baby's birth defects, or courts have ruled that without conclusive epidemiological evidence plaintiffs did not have sufficient proof based on animal studies and toxicology alone to warrant presenting the case to the jury. While Bendectin may not have caused birth defects, its effectiveness in alleviating morning sickness was also hotly debated. To the extent that it may have helped some women feel bet-

ter, its active ingredients were available in much less costly over-the-counter preparations such as vitamin B-6. Moreover, Merrell-Dow's decision to withdraw it from the market was attributable in large part to significantly declining sales fueled by adverse publicity, for which tort suits were only partially responsible (M. Green, *Bendectin and Birth Defects: Lessons for Mass Toxics Litigation* [Philadelphia: University of Pennsylvania Press, forthcoming]. Thus, the example of Bendectin does not provide a compelling case for concluding that tort suits can drive a totally safe product of unquestioned benefit off the market. Even if it were, it is the only such example that the pharmaceutical industry possibly has. See S. Garber, *Product Liability and the Economics of Pharmaceutical and Medical Devices* (Santa Monica, CA: RAND Institute for Civil Justice, 1993).

REFERENCES

American Medical Association Council on Pharmacy and Chemistry. 1939. Stilbestrol: Preliminary Report of the Council. *Journal of the American Medical Association* 113: 2312.

Apfel, R. and S. Fisher. 1984. *To Do No Harm: DES and the Dilemmas of Modern Medicine.* New Haven, CT: Yale University Press.

Bell, S. 1980. "The Synthetic Compound Diethylstilbestrol (DES) 1938–1941." Ph.D. dissertation, Brandeis University, Waltham, MA. Cited in R. Meyers, *DES: The Bitter Pill* (New York: Seaview/Putnam, 1983), 41.

Berger, M. J. and D. P. Goldstein. 1980. Impaired reproductive performance in DES-exposed women. *Obstetrics and Gynecology* 55: 25–27.

Bichler, J. 1981. *DES Daughter.* New York: Avon.

Brackbill, Y. and H. Berendes. 1978. Dangers of diethylstilbestrol: Review of a 1953 paper. *Lancet* 2: 520.

Braithwaite, J. 1984. *Corporate Crime in the Pharmaceutical Industry.* Boston: Routledge.

Burdick, H. O. and H. Vedder. 1941. The effects of stilbestrol in early pregnancy. *Endocrinology* 28: 629–32.

Cohen, K. 1994. Truth and beauty, deception and disfigurement: A feminist analysis of breast implant litigation. *William and Mary Journal of Women and the Law* 1: 149–82.

Corea, G. 1985. *The Hidden Malpractice: How American Medicine Mistreats Women.* Updated ed. New York: Harper and Row.

Crowder, R. E., E. S. Bills and J. S. Broadbent. 1950. The management of threatened abortion: A study of 100 cases. *American Journal of Obstetrics and Gynecology* 60: 896–99.

Davis, H. 1970. The Shield intrauterine device: A superior modern contraceptive. *American Journal of Obstetrics and Gynecology* 106: 455–62.

108   Dieckmann, W. J., M. E. Davies, L. M. Rynkiewicz and R. E. Pottinger. 1953. Does the administration of diethylstilbestrol during pregnancy have therapeutic value? *American Journal of Obstetrics and Gynecology* 66: 1062–81. Quoted in D. Dutton, *Worse than the Disease: Pitfalls of Medical Progress* (Cambridge, U.K.: Cambridge University Press, 1988), 56.

Dutton, D. B. 1988. *Worse than the Disease: Pitfalls of Medical Progress.* Cambridge, U.K.: Cambridge University Press.

"FDA Sued on Drug to Dry Mothers' Milk," *New York Times* (August 17, 1994): A15.

Ferguson, J. H. 1953. Effects of stilbestrol on pregnancy compared to the effects of a placebo. *American Journal of Obstetrics and Gynecology* 65: 592–601.

Garber, S. 1993. *Product Liability and the Economics of Pharmaceutical and Medical Devices.* Santa Monica, CA: RAND Institute for Civil Justice.

Gorenberg, H. and A. White. 1991–92. Off the pedestal and into the arena: Toward including women in experimental protocols. *NYU Review of Law and Social Change* 19: 205.

Grant, N. 1992. *The Selling of Contraception: The Dalkon Shield Case, Sexuality, and Women's Autonomy.* Columbus, OH: Ohio State University Press.

Green, M. 1995. *Bendectin and Birth Defects: Lessons for Mass Toxics Litigation.* Philadelphia: University of Pennsylvania Press.

Greenwald, P., J. Barlow and P. Nasca. 1971. Vaginal cancer after maternal treatment with synthetic estrogens. *New England Journal of Medicine* 285: 390–92.

Heinonen, O. P. 1973. Diethylstilbestrol in pregnancy: Frequency of exposure and usage patterns. *Cancer* 31: 576.

Herbst, A., S. Anderson, M. Hubby et al. 1986. Risk factors for the development of diethylstilbestrol-associated clear cell adenocarcinoma: A case control study. *American Journal of Obstetrics and Gynecology* 154: 814–22.

Herbst, A. and H. Bern, eds. 1981. *Developmental Effects of Diethylstilbestrol (DES) in Pregnancy.* New York: Thieme-Stratton.

Herbst, A., M. Hubby, R. Blough and F. Azizi. 1980. A comparison of pregnancy experience in DES-exposed and DES-unexposed daughters. *Journal of Reproductive Medicine* 24: 62–69.

Herbst, A. L., H. Ufelder and D. C. Poskanzer. 1971. Adenocarcinoma of the vagina: Association of maternal stilbestrol therapy with tumor appearance in young women. *New England Journal of Medicine* 284: 878–81.

Hicks, K. 1994. *Surviving the Dalkon Shield IUD: Women v. The Pharmaceutical Industry.* New York: Teachers College Press.

Karnaky, K. J. 1942. The use of stilbestrol for the treatment of threatened and habitual abortion and premature labor: A preliminary report. *Southern Medical Journal* 35: 838–47. Quoted in R. Meyers, *DES: The Bitter Pill* (New York: Seaview/Putnam, 1983), 51.

Koenig, T. and M. Rustad. 1995. His and her tort reform: Gender injustice in disguise. *Washington Law Review* 70: 1–90.

Kolata, G. 1995. Will the lawyers kill off Norplant? *New York Times,* May 28: Section 3, 1.

"Lactation drug dropped for postpartum use," *Chicago Tribune* (August 19, 1994): 8.

Lewin, T. 1994. Dream contraceptive's nightmare. *New York Times,* July 8: A10.

Little, H. 1993. No panacea: Norplant suit charges failure to educate patients. *Chicago Tribune,* Oct. 31: Section 6, 1.

Lord, M. W. 1978. The Dalkon Shield litigation: Revised annotated reprimand by Chief Judge Miles W. Lord. *Hamline Law Review* 9: 7–51.

Martin, E. 1987. *The Woman in the Body.* Boston: Beacon Press.

Merton, V. 1993. The exclusion of pregnant, pregnable, and once-pregnable people (a.k.a. women) from biomedical research. *American Journal of Law and Medicine* 19: 369–451.

Meyers, R. 1983. *DES: The Bitter Pill.* New York: Seaview/Putnam.

Mintz, M. 1985. *At Any Cost: Corporate Greed, Women, and the Dalkon Shield.* New York: Pantheon Books.

———. 1969. Squibb doctor faced built-in conflict. *Washington Post,* June 8: A9. Quoted in D. Dutton, *Worse than the Disease: Pitfalls of Medical Progress* (Cambridge, U.K.: Cambridge University Press, 1988), 58.

Nechas, E. and D. Foley. 1994. *Unequal Treatment: What You Don't Know About How Women Are Mistreated by the Medical Community.* New York: Simon and Schuster.

Neergaard, L. 1994. FDA sued over milk inhibitor: 19 deaths connected. *Legal Intelligencer,* Aug. 17: 9.

Perry, S. and J. Dawson. 1985. *Nightmare: Women and the Dalkon Shield.* New York: Macmillan.

Robinson, D. and L. B. Shettles. 1952. The use of diethylstilbestrol in threatened abortion. *American Journal of Obstetrics and Gynecology* 63: 1330–33. Quoted in R. Meyers, *DES: The Bitter Pill* (New York: Seaview/Putnam, 1983), 67–68.

Rosser, S. 1994. *Women's Health—Missing from U.S. Medicine.* Bloomington, IN: Indiana University Press.

Scully, D. 1994. *Men Who Control Women's Health: The Miseducation of Obstetrician-Gynecologists.* Rev. ed. New York: Teachers College Press.

Shine, R. and J. Thompson. 1974. The in situ IUD and pregnancy outcome.

110   *American Journal of Obstetrics and Gynecology* 119: 126–27. Cited in N. Grant, *The Selling of Contraception: The Dalkon Shield Case, Sexuality, and Women's Autonomy* (Columbus, OH: Ohio State University Press, 1992), 56–57.

Smith, G. V. and O. W. Smith. 1949. The influence of diethylstilbestrol on the progress and outcome of pregnancy as based on a comparison of treated and untreated primigravidas. *American Journal of Obstetrics and Gynecology* 58: 994–1009.

Smith, G. V., O. W. Smith and D. Hurwitz. 1946. Increased excretion of pregnanediol in pregnancy from diethylstilbestrol with special reference to the prevention of late pregnancy accidents. *American Journal of Obstetrics and Gynecology* 51: 411–15.

Smith, O. W. 1948. Diethylstilbestrol in the prevention and treatment of complications of pregnancy. *American Journal of Obstetrics and Gynecology* 56: 821–34. Quoted in R. Meyers, *DES: The Bitter Pill* (New York: Seaview/Putnam, 1983), 65.

Sobol, R. 1991. *Bending the Law: The Story of the Dalkon Shield Bankruptcy.* Chicago: University of Chicago Press.

Steinman, J. 1992. Women, medical care, and mass tort litigation. *Chicago-Kent Law Review* 68: 409–29.

Tietze, C. and S. Levitt, eds. 1962. *Proceedings of the First Conference on the IUCD.* April 30–May 1, New York: Excerpta Medica, 3. Quoted in K. Hicks, *Surviving the Dalkon Shield IUD: Women v. The Pharmaceutical Industry* (New York: Teachers College Press, 1994), 19.

WOMEN IN THE MARKETPLACE

Targets of Corporate Greed

Joan Claybrook

As long as there is money to be made, someone will provide products to buy. Bad buys lurk at every turn. Women, first as managers of the home and now as independent wage earners, are no strangers to the dangers of the marketplace. Oddly, the unequal pay ratio between men and women is reversed in the marketplace, where women actually pay more than men for products and services such as cars and car repairs, dry cleaning, and haircuts. In the area of fashion and beauty, women have been particularly vulnerable, pushed to buy rapidly changing and often uncomfortable clothing and footwear.

Bad buys must, however, be distinguished from bad products. Bad buys involve the unfortunate waste of money; bad products compound financial waste with injury to well-being. Sometimes a bad buy is also a bad product. For centuries women have bought and worn high-heeled shoes that place enormous strain on ankles, legs, and hips and distort normal posture. Corsets, also de rigueur for centuries, squeezed women's bodies into unnatural shapes; in fact the corset placed such a strain on the internal organs of women's bodies that it created a collateral market for a second device, the pessary, designed to prevent the prolapse of the uterus that corset wearing sometimes prompted.[1] And in 1994 the Consumer Product Safety Commission (CPSC) issued a recall on sheer chiffon skirts that burned faster than newspaper; approximately 250,000 of the skirts were in circulation, having entered the marketplace at prices ranging from $6 to $80. These skirts, largely imported from India, failed to comply with the federal Flammable Fabrics Act.[2]

Women pay for bad products in three ways. First, many products are manufactured exclusively for, or marketed mainly to, women. In the area of cosmetics, cosmetic devices, and contraceptives, where manufacturers have been largely unregulated, or regulated only unsuccessfully, women have been unsuspecting guinea pigs, testing silicone breast implants, the Dalkon Shield, lactation suppressants, and other products with clinical trials at great personal injury.

Women also pay the price for bad products when, as chief purchasing agents for their households, they unwittingly bring dangerous products home to family members, who are subsequently injured. Such products include infant formula, which until the 1980s was not regulated by the government, and became so only after a series of disasters in which nutritionally deficient formula caused serious developmental problems in hundreds of infants. When members of a family are injured, the resulting stress may destroy the family unit; women, as primary caregivers, are also forced to deal with injury recovery.

The third way in which women pay for bad products is when they seek compensation, as only one in ten injured women does, for harm suffered. Undertaking a lawsuit forces the survivor to relive the trauma of injury. Further, the compensation system is biased against women, awarding economic damages based on earning power and, conversely, trivializing noneconomic damages such as pain, suffering, and loss of fertility. The tort system has been under attack for the past fifteen years, with manufacturers fighting to eliminate or severely restrict the availability of compensation for noneconomic damages.

Women understand the full costs that dangerous products exact and have made clear their safety bias in making purchasing decisions. Many manufacturers have been quick to capitalize on this purchasing preference with ads that advertise the safety of their products, even if they don't put much effort into really improving the design of these products. But even if women want to buy safe products, how can they be certain that they are safe? Many people assume that the government protects citizens from dangerous and unsafe products. To some extent, this is true. Regulatory agencies, some independent and some under the umbrella of the executive branch of the federal government, issue performance standards for many consumer products: children's toys, cars, infant formula, and so on. But these agencies cannot be everywhere, and they are often forced to rely upon the good faith of the manufacturers for assurances that products are safe. Furthermore, such agencies are susceptible to political machinations, and for the last fifteen years they have been cast as scapegoats responsible for economic ills. The courts have consistently provided a safety net and have sometimes even acted as a catalyst, forcing manufacturers to take due care in designing products. Information from lawsuits often filters to government agencies and is used to force the recall or redesign of products that manufacturers refuse to fix.

But this after-the-fact process takes time—often years—during which people are needlessly injured. This chapter describes some products that have caused great harm. Some have been removed from the market because of revelations during litigation initiated by women who had been harmed and by public interest groups like Public Citizen; others remain un- or underregulated. The chapter then explains the product liability system, so instrumental in product safety but often unfairly maligned by detractors in the business community, in the hope that better understanding will foster use and support of a crucial underpinning of our democracy: access to the courts to enforce our health and safety rights.

BREAST IMPLANTS

In December 1991, a jury of citizens seated in a courtroom of the United States District Court for the Northern District of California handed down a startling verdict. Awarding $840,000 in compensatory damages and $6.5 million in punitive damages to Mariann Hopkins, they found Dow Corning, a *Fortune* 500 corporation liable for fraud, malice, and oppression in manufacturing and selling defective and dangerous silicone-gel breast implants. Hopkins, who had the prostheses implanted following a double mastectomy in 1976, suffered from mixed-tissue disease, a debilitating immune disorder, resulting from her exposure to silicone gel.[3]

As Hopkins's attorney, Dan Bolton, would write to David Kessler, the commissioner of the FDA, the federal agency that regulates medical devices,

> The jury found that Dow's silicone breast implants were defectively designed and manufactured, that Dow had failed to warn of the risks associated with implants, that Dow had breached implied and expressed warranties relating to its product and that Dow had committed fraud. The jury also found by "clear and convincing evidence" that Dow's fraud, in addition to its "malice" and "oppression" warranted the imposition of punitive damages. Under California law, "malice" means conduct that is "intended by the defendant to cause injury to the plaintiff or despicable conduct which is carried on by the defendant with a willful and conscious disregard of the rights and

safety of others." "Oppression" requires a finding by the jury that the defendant has engaged in "despicable conduct that subjects a person to cruel and unjust hardship in conscious disregard of that person's rights."[4]

Bolton enclosed with his letter to Kessler a copy of the trial transcript, a public document, to familiarize the commissioner with the discoveries that had come to light during the trial. But Bolton could not provide the FDA with any of this evidence, which included eighty internal memos from Dow Corning providing a road map of the company's decisions that led to the verdict, because they were sealed by a court-issued protective order.

Mariann Hopkins was not the first client Dan Bolton had represented in a product liability lawsuit against Dow Corning. In 1984 he represented Maria Stern and won the first breast implant product liability case to go to trial.[5] In that case the jury ordered Dow Corning to pay $1.5 million in punitive damages to Stern. The presiding judge condemned Dow Corning for "corporate malice" in marketing the silicone implants without informing consumers of their risk. The documents produced by and used against Dow Corning in *Stern v. Dow Corning* were placed under court seal.

By the time that Mariann Hopkins and Dan Bolton defeated Dow Corning in the courts, the Department of Health and Human Services estimated that one million women nationwide had had silicone-gel breast prostheses implanted, at a rate rising by 1991 to approximately 150,000 women electing to have breast implants each year. Roughly 80 percent of those women underwent breast implant surgery for purposes of augmentation; only 20 percent chose reconstructive surgery following mastectomies.[6]

The implants are associated with a number of medical problems attributed to exposure to silicone, which may infiltrate surrounding tissue or the bloodstream and migrate through the body following a rupture of the implant or by seeping through an intact implant. A variety of connective-tissue diseases are associated with silicone, including Raynaud's phenomenon and chronic arthropathy as well as autoimmune disorders including lupus and systemic sclerosis or scleroderma. Any of these complications may cause disability and disfigurement.

Another frequent complication arising after implantation is capsular contraction. Capsular contraction is the body's natural reaction to the presence of a foreign substance; scar tissue develops around the implant as the body attempts to isolate the foreign substance from organic mass. The result for the implant wearer is discomfort and the sensation of hard, unnatural breasts. The clinical remedy for this complaint is breaking up the scar tissue. This procedure, which is performed manually without any anesthetic, sometimes breaks the implants as well as breaking up scar tissue, allowing silicone to escape and migrate.

Further, the implants interfere with mammography. Implants obscure the tissue images that need to be read and make the breast harder to compress, compromising the clarity of the x ray. Even worse, compression of the augmented breast can cause the implants to rupture or fracture, creating another opportunity for silicone migration.

Silicone was first discovered during the 1930s by laboratory scientists.[7] Without a socially productive or commercially advantageous use, silicone remained a laboratory curiosity until World War II, when Dow Chemical and Corning Glass collaborated at the government's request to find a use for the material. Silicone's ability to withstand extreme temperatures made the material suitable for construction, particularly as a lubricant, sealant, and coolant. It was not until the early 1960s that company researchers for Dow Corning invented the earliest silicone breast implants, a solid silicone prosthesis. The product entered the marketplace without government scrutiny because at that time the FDA did not have the authority to require premarket approval of medical devices.

In the early 1970s, Dow Corning and other implant manufacturers "improved" the prosthesis by filling a silicone envelope with liquid-gel silicone rather than using a solid, rubbery piece of silicone; to the touch, the gel closely simulated a real breast. The gel would shortly prove troublesome. While product literature touted the implants as safe, physiologically compatible with the body, and capable of lasting a lifetime, Dow Corning knew by 1972 that silicone could migrate to the lymphatic system and to various organs of the immune system.[8] Furthermore, Dow Corning had conducted no tests that might have substantiated its broad claim about the longevity of the product. The longest test Dow Corning had conducted before marketing the liquid-gel implant lasted eighty days and, significantly, showed "a chronic inflammatory response to silicone and evidence of granuloma [benign tumor] formation which can be a potential indicator of an immune response."[9]

In 1976 Congress enacted the Medical Device Act, requiring that all medical devices, from tongue depressors to heart valves, be classified in one of three categories and meet the safety standards established for that classification. Category I required labeling; Category II required satisfaction of performance standards; and Category III required FDA premarket approval based on submission of data proving the safety and efficacy of the product.[10] The Panel on Review of General and Plastic Surgery Devices convened by the Department of Health, Education, and Welfare (the forerunner to the Department of Health and Human Services) initially recommended that breast implants, given their fifteen-year history of use, be classified as the less rigorous Category II.[11]

As early as 1978, the panel had received independent reports and data chronicling a number of complications associated with silicone-gel breast implants and the accompanying phenomenon known as "gel-bleed."[12] Despite these findings and FDA staff recommendations to classify breast implants as Class III devices that would require a premarket showing of safety and efficacy, the panel, comprising many plastic surgeons, resisted the more restrictive classification. It was not until 1982 that the FDA officially proposed that silicone-filled breast prostheses be classified into Class III, thus requiring premarket approval.[13] No further action was taken on this proposal, however, until June 1988.

During the years in which the FDA failed to move forward, despite evidence that silicone implanted in the human body could cause considerable damage to the host, injured women took the implants, and their manufacturers, to court. Maria Stern, represented by Dan Bolton, filed and won the first breast implant product liability suit to go to trial.[14] Although Stern was awarded financial compensation, the public could not benefit from the discoveries she and her attorney made. The internal company documents that prompted the jury and judge to condemn Dow Corning for "corporate malice" were obtained by the plaintiff's attorney on the strict condition that they remain under court seal. These findings were neither turned over to the FDA nor disseminated to the public, even though as many as 150,000 women were undergoing implant surgery each year. Because of the secrecy orders that Dow Corning persuaded judges to grant, each of the early challenges the company faced in court remained isolated. Though later lawsuits helped individual women, the company continued to net profits on implant sales, despite occasional payouts following adverse decisions.

While Dow Corning was beginning to face challenges in the courts, the company continued to test the safety of its implants, with discouraging results. A company study conducted between 1985 and 1987 found alarming incidences of malignant tumors forming in the bodies of rats exposed to silicone. Dow Corning tested three groups of one hundred rats, half male and half female. In the group implanted with the silicone gel used before 1976, 20 percent of the female rats and 22 percent of the male rats developed fibrosarcomas at the site of the injection; further, 21 percent of these rats had evidence of metastases spreading to organs including the kidney, liver, lungs, and skin. In the second group, implanted with the silicone gel currently used in implants, 23 percent of the females and 26 percent of the males developed fibrosarcomas associated with the silicone gel; 18 percent of those rats showed metastases in distant organs. The third cohort, the control group, showed no corresponding fibrosarcoma tumors. The tumors caused death in 85 percent of the animals afflicted with gel-associated fibrosarcomas.[15]

FDA staff, later evaluating the Dow Corning study, concluded that silicone could cause cancer in rats. Summarizing the concern expressed in several internal FDA memoranda, the acting chief of the Health Sciences Branch at the FDA Center for Devices and Radiological Health warned that "while there is no direct proof that silicone causes cancers in humans, there is considerable reason to suspect that it can do so."[16]

Dow Corning responded to the lawsuits, its own tests, and negative reports by rewriting its product inserts to warn with quiet understatement of certain risks that could be associated with the implants: the possibility of immune system sensitivity and possible silicone migration following rupture.[17] Given the risks documented in laboratories and courtrooms, the warning was inadequate.

When the FDA finally acted on the January 1982 proposal and reclassified mammary prostheses as Class III medical devices in June 1988, the agency cut the industry some slack. To soften the blow of this rule, manufacturers of silicone breast implants were granted thirty months to develop data and conduct investigations necessary to support their applications for premarket approval (PMAs), giving them until January 1991 to submit data on the safety and efficacy of these devices.[18]

Shortly after the ruling was issued, Public Citizen petitioned the FDA to ban silicone breast prostheses for implantation into the human body.[19] Citing internal Dow Corning and FDA documents, Public Citizen stated that evidence of carcinogenicity and other adverse effects justified the proposed ban. Despite the Public Citizen petition and the recommendations of its own staff, the FDA stuck to its schedule and received PMAs until July 1991.

The applications submitted by major manufacturers of breast implants, including Dow Corning, defending the safety and efficacy of a product that had been on the market for approximately fifteen years, were dismal. Shortly after reviewing the applications, the FDA issued a notice requiring complete patient risk information explaining the complications associated with the implants to be distributed to any consumer considering implantation. The notice stated that the FDA had "identified significant deficiencies in premarket approval applications for these devices."[20] Further, the FDA stated that any implant not carrying an adequate and comprehensible warning would be considered misbranded under the Federal Food, Drug and Cosmetic Act. By law, the FDA was required to review and either approve or deny the applications within 180 days; the agency offered manufacturers the opportunity to produce more promising data, if any could be marshaled to support their applications, during the review period.[21]

In November the FDA convened the General and Plastic Surgery Devices Panel to consider and make recommendations on whether or not the agency should exercise its authority to extend the review period; the panel recommended that the agency extend the review period. After openly acknowledging the failure of any applicant to show safety and efficacy, the panel determined that the "public health need" for breast implants was too great to warrant removal of the product from the market without gathering further data on the risks and benefits of its use. The "public health need" discussion distorted a legitimate concern—that women facing radical surgery to arrest cancer growth might be less likely to undergo surgery without the availability of implants—to justify cosmetic surgery as fulfilling a "public health need," despite the fact that four out of five implantees were undergoing surgery for augmentation, rather than reconstruction.[22] This logic deftly appropriated feminist rhetoric of self-determination for the purpose of empowering women to undergo unnecessary, risky surgery. This advisory panel recommendation, though solicited by the FDA, was not binding.

With the clock winding down on the time left for the FDA to approve or deny the PMAs, the *Hopkins* decision in California was announced in December 1991. Following the court decision, attorney Dan Bolton wrote to FDA Commissioner David Kessler. Days later, Dr. Kessler announced a voluntary forty-five-day moratorium on the use of silicone-gel breast implants on January 6, 1992. The FDA announced that a final decision, following a meeting of the General and Plastic Surgery Devices Panel to reevaluate the implants, would be reached before the end of February.[23]

The following day, the FDA urged an *indefinite*, voluntary moratorium, which both Dow Corning and the American Society of Plastic and

Reconstructive Surgeons agreed to support. The breadth and gravity of the FDA's announcement prompted consumers, reporters, plastic surgeons, and many others to demand disclosure of the internal Dow Corning documents produced during the *Hopkins* litigation, but remaining under protective order. The clamor led to a protracted struggle between the FDA and Dow Corning over the release of the documents. While Dow Corning claimed a desire to cooperate with these requests, company executives drew a stark distinction between studies, which they were willing to release, and internal memoranda and other documents produced during litigation, which they characterized as conjecture, not fact, and were therefore not willing to make public. Dow Corning officials said they would release scientific information but were "inclined to withhold" documents in which the company officials debated the adequacy of safety studies. Robert Rylee, chief of Dow's Health Care Businesses, said release of all documents would paint on inaccurate, one-sided picture of what went on inside the company.[24] On January 22, 1992, under intense pressure from the FDA and the public, Dow Corning made public materials including ten scientific studies on the safety of implants and eighty company memoranda. The company released an additional eight hundred pages of documents (both studies and internal company papers) the following month.

The real issue for Dow Corning was not the possibility of lost profits should the FDA decide to ban or severely restrict the uses for silicone breast implants. Dow Corning reported that implant sales represented less than 1 percent of the company's total sales of $1.85 billion in 1991.[25] Dow Corning faced more threatening prospects: a damaged reputation and enormous liability.

On February 20, 1992, after two days of discussion, the FDA Advisory Panel on General and Plastic Surgery recommended significant restrictions on the use of silicone breast implants for cosmetic purposes, while allowing them to be used with some limitations for reconstructive surgery. Any recipient of the implants, the panel recommended, should be enrolled in a carefully controlled study. The FDA accepted this recommendation.

Shortly after the FDA ruling on silicone breast implant PMA applications, Dow Corning revealed that the company had $250 million in insurance to cover potential losses in any product liability suits that might arise.[26] At the time, attorneys representing plaintiffs injured by their breast implants predicted that the amount would not begin to

120   cover the legal costs Dow Corning could expect to accumulate, which they speculated could run as high as $1 or $2 billion.

In 1993 so many suits were in the works against the manufacturers of breast implants that it was no longer judicially efficient to adjudicate each claim separately; all claims against American and some overseas manufacturers were consolidated into a class action suit. Defendant companies pledged approximately $4.25 billion to pay present and future claims from women and their families injured by breast implants.[27]

WEIGHT LOSS PRODUCTS

The medical and scientific communities agree that a complex combination of factors determines weight: food intake, activity, size and body type, metabolism, and genetics. Conventional wisdom holds that the best way to lose weight, and maintain that weight loss, is to reduce calorie consumption, modify dietary habits, and increase physical activity.

Carrying excessive surplus weight is not healthy and can lead to serious medical problems, among them heart disease, high blood pressure, diabetes, various cancers, gallstones, and varicose veins.[28] In a survey published in 1984, of more than 30,000 women between the ages of eighteen and thirty-five, 75 percent considered themselves fat, though only 25 percent actually met the medical standard for being overweight.[29] And according to a study conducted during the late 1980s, approximately 25 percent of American women, on any given day, are "on a diet"; 50 percent are breaking, finishing, or starting a diet.[30] Clearly, many women diet not so much for health reasons but to achieve a beauty ideal promoted through a commercial barrage of thin, and even emaciated, female images. The chase for unnatural shapes pushes many women to diet unnecessarily and to use services and products of questionable efficacy and safety in their pursuit.

Nevertheless, commercial products that largely emphasize calorie reduction continue to be sold at alarming rates. In 1993 approximately fifty million Americans were dieting; they invested $30 billion at weight loss centers and on diet products trying to shed weight. For all their money and effort, approximately 5 percent are projected to maintain their weight loss.[31]

Very low calorie diets are rarely recommended, and only for obese patients under the close supervision of a doctor. People aiming to lose small amounts of weight through liquid diets risk very damaging loss of lean body mass, which threatens many organs, including the heart.[32] During the 1970s and 1980s, inadequately supervised liquid protein diets caused approximately thirty-five deaths. Today these diets have supposedly improved, both in terms of nutritional content and supervision; however, they are guardedly recommended only for the severely obese. Among these liquid protein diets are Medifast, Health Management Resources (HMR), and Optifast.

Other programs, like Weight Watchers, Jenny Craig, Diet Center, Nutri/System, and Physicians Weight Loss Center facilitate weight loss through different combinations of controlled diet, counseling, and exercise. Most of these programs encourage participants to purchase "company food" in addition to paying enrollment and meeting fees. In 1993 *Consumer Reports* published a rating of eight commercial weight loss programs based on the experiences of its readers. Of the 95,000 readers who responded, 19,000 had entered commercial programs at some point between 1989 and 1992. The *Consumer Reports* survey ultimately found that weight loss products produced, at best, short-term results; "respondents reported that they stayed on the programs for about half a year and lost about 10 to 20 percent of their starting weight. But the average dieter gained back almost half of that weight just six months after ending the program, and more than two-thirds of it after two years."[33] Interestingly, many of the respondents who tried these programs—more than 25 percent—did not meet the medical definition for even moderate obesity.

In addition to liquid diets and diet programs, the marketplace offers a considerable array of over-the-counter (OTC) diet pills, sold in the average drugstore or supermarket. In 1988 consumers—the majority of them women—paid more than $300 million for these pills.[34] The active ingredient found in many OTC diet pills is phenylpropanolamine hydrochloride (PPA). Although an FDA advisory panel has approved this substance as an anorectic (appetite suppressant) for weight control, many scientists and health activists believe that PPA is neither safe nor effective in the long term.

PPA essentially acts like an amphetamine and suppresses appetite, leading to quick weight loss, but it does not help the user achieve the changes in eating habits needed to sustain weight loss in the long term. Further, PPA usage has been linked to hypertension among young, healthy adults consuming the recommended dosages;[35] it has also been associated with amphetaminelike reactions including "accelerated

122   pulse rate, tremor, restlessness, agitation, anxiety, dizziness and hallucinations."[36]

OTC pills are examples of products that are underregulated. Indeed, the medical safety of many OTC diet pills has been underexamined. The FDA has rated PPA safe and effective, despite skepticism in some scientific quarters and a lack of any well-controlled studies showing its long-term efficacy. In an effort to combat deceptive and fraudulent claims,[37] however, the Federal Trade Commission has launched investigations into both nationally advertised diet products and programs.

LACTATION SUPPRESSANTS

Soon after delivery, new mothers begin to produce milk. If they choose not to breast-feed, milk production ceases within seven to fourteen days; most women cease to lactate within a week. While lactating, women not breast-feeding may experience postpartum breast engorgement—the accumulation of unreleased breast milk—which in a small percentage of women is accompanied by swelling, discomfort, and mild fever. The simplest, safest, and most effective treatment for such symptoms is to use cold compresses, take a low dose of acetaminophen, and wrap the breasts securely against the chest. Nevertheless, a significant financial interest developed around this temporary, benign condition after drugs that affect hormonal activity were first prescribed to suppress lactation. Parlodel (generic name: bromocriptine) was first approved for use as a lactation suppressant in 1980, and before the end of the decade the drug had captured more than 80 percent of the market share, with its competitors TACE (chlorotrianisene) and DES (diethylstilbestrol) splitting the remaining sales.[38] Despite adverse reactions ranging from mild (vomiting, headaches, nausea, and diarrhea) to severe (dramatic blood pressure changes, blood clots, strokes, seizures, and heart attacks), total sales for Parlodel, prescribed to at least 300,000 women annually, were estimated at $12.5 million each year.[39]

In 1988 Public Citizen filed a petition with the FDA requesting that the agency revoke approval of these drugs for the purpose of lactation suppression. The petition was based upon the benign, self-resolving nature of postpartum lactation and the increased incidence of side effects caused by lactation-suppressing drugs. During the summer of 1994, Public Citizen filed a lawsuit to compel the FDA to initiate the process for banning Parlodel. The basis of the lawsuit was the rising toll of serious injuries and deaths occurring among healthy women for whom this drug had been prescribed, as well as significant data indicating that the drug was not effective for its recommended use.

The FDA, after sitting for six years on the 1988 petition, responded quickly to the lawsuit with an announcement of plans to initiate hearings on the drug. The manufacturer of Parlodel, Sandoz Pharmaceuticals, a subsidiary of the larger Swiss company Sandoz Ltd., trumped the FDA's response with an announcement of its own: that "unwarranted criticism" had prompted the company voluntarily to withdraw its product for use as a lactation suppressant in U.S markets.[40]

Like many unsafe pharmaceutical products, Parlodel presented a two-fold threat to consumers. First, its effectiveness was dubious. Second, and far worse, the product was associated with alarming, life-threatening, and undisclosed side effects.

According to the FDA's own analyses, between 18 and 40 percent of the women who take Parlodel will experience a phenomenon known as "rebound lactation," that is, they will experience delayed lactation as soon as drug treatment ends. Further, one study used in the FDA's evaluation of bromocriptine for approval showed that 31 percent of the women using bromocriptine remained symptomatic.[41] Essentially, the drug does not prevent lactation; at best, it postpones the process among a high percentage of users.[42]

By the time Sandoz announced its intention to remove Parlodel from the market in 1994, the FDA had received 531 reports of adverse reactions submitted by consumers and health care professionals.[43] Of these reported reactions, thirty-two resulted in death, mostly from heart attacks, strokes, and hypertension. In addition to these deaths, more than 250 of the adverse reactions reported also led to heart attacks, strokes, hypertension, and seizures, some of which were permanently disabling events.[44]

GUNS

According to recent data from the CDC (Centers for Disease Control), firearms killed 38,317 people in 1991. Firearms are the fastest-growing source of injuries in America; gun violence is escalating at a rate that, if unabated, will surpass motor vehicle crashes as the leading cause of death from injuries in America by the year 2003.[45] In several states, including New York and Texas, and in the District of Columbia, the

124 number of firearm deaths exceeded the number of traffic fatalities occurring in 1991. The other costs of gun violence are staggering as well; firearm injuries now cost the United States approximately $20 billion annually, according to researchers at the University of California at San Francisco.[46]

The Bureau of Alcohol, Tobacco and Firearms (ATF) estimates that two hundred million guns are currently in private circulation in the United States—nearly enough to arm every man, woman, and child in our country. Approximately one-third of these guns, or seventy million, are handguns.[47] Approximately two million new handguns enter the market each year.[48]

Despite the superfluity of guns in America and the well-documented damage they inflict upon the population, guns are one of the least-regulated products in the American marketplace. Access to guns is minimally controlled by new federal statutes imposing a brief waiting period on potential gun purchases and banning the manufacture of assault weapons. And while food, medicine, automobiles, and children's toys must all conform to some minimal safety standards issued by executive agencies, no federal body has authority to regulate design and performance safety standards for firearms. The ATF regulates only the commercial aspects of the firearms industry, such as dealer licensing and importation practices.

Despite the absence of a regulatory presence requiring (or prohibiting) any design features in the gun industry, manufacturers showed remarkably little innovation and imagination in their product line for many decades.[49] Eventually, and inevitably, the market reached saturation in 1986 when handgun production, according to the ATF, hit a low of 1.4 million pieces manufactured; only four years earlier, production had peaked at more than 2.5 million handguns. Reduced production could only mean reduced sales and profits for manufacturers; that diminished sales base was weakened by the recession of the late 1980s, when many repeat and potential customers lost significant discretionary income. To compete for consumer dollars, manufacturers diversified their product lines and invested in efforts to expand their market appeal. To protect their livelihood, they looked to a large segment of the population they had only marginally considered before: women.

The groundwork for establishing a female customer base was laid before the gun industry developed a marketing approach to attract women. During the early 1980s the National Rifle Association, the de facto trade association representing the gun industry in Washington,

D.C., struggled to refine its image and position itself politically and socially for difficult gun-control battles ahead. Polls on issues related to gun violence and gun control have consistently shown that women are more likely than men to favor control measures. By aggressively recruiting female members, the NRA increased not only its revenue but also its political base. In 1982 it began to soften, and subsequently strengthen, its image with a public relations campaign tagged "I'm the NRA." To illustrate the diversity of the gun-owning public, this campaign used print ads to profile individual members of the NRA: celebrities, people of color, and—very prominently—women.

The "I'm the NRA" campaign showed women as independent, confident gun owners. The text accompanying photographs of female NRA members in these ads appropriated the language that had fueled the women's and reproductive freedom movements: the language of choice. An ad featuring smiling, off-duty Detective Jeanne Bray ran, "A gun is a choice women need to know more about and be free to make. And the NRA is working to ensure the freedom of that choice always exists."[50] Although the NRA found some success in borrowing feminist rhetoric, later ad campaigns developed a more salient selling point: fear.

In the late 1980s the NRA unveiled its "Self-Defense" ad campaign, premised not so much on teaching self-defense as on exploiting public fears of escalating crime. The campaign began with a series of print ads that ran in major daily newspapers, among them *USA Today*, the *New York Times*, the *Washington Post*, and the *Los Angeles Times*. By the start of the 1990s, the NRA had fused the messages of its earlier ad campaigns—empowerment and fear—into one refined message and was ready to unveil the "Refuse to Be a Victim" campaign, targeted exclusively at women. The cornerstone of the campaign was an ad featuring a photograph of a woman and her young daughter walking through a dark parking garage. The woman is looking back over her shoulder, alarmed, while her daughter, holding her mother's hand, looks apprehensively forward. The text, in enormous letters, blares "How to Choose to Refuse to Be a Victim." The ad ran in regional editions of popular, mainstream women's magazines, including *People, Family Circle, Ladies' Home Journal, Redbook,* and *Woman's Day.*

The NRA claims that its motive in conducting the ad campaign was public education, not a call to arms. Nevertheless, the campaign caused a remarkable stir. A group of twenty-five female members of the U.S. House of Representatives publicly asked the NRA to recall the ads. Representative Nita Lowey of New York called the ads "a veiled attempt by the NRA to add new members and promote gun ownership by preying on women's legitimate fears of violence."[51]

While the NRA courted women, gun manufacturers labored to fulfill new market demands by designing guns and related accessories for women. After two years of research and development, Smith and Wesson introduced the LadySmith line. The company used warranty cards to track and contact six thousand women who provided the data for initial research; the company incorporated this information into designs and prototypes, which were then tested on focus groups composed of female gun owners and nonowners. The end result was a product line comprising four models of a .38 caliber, five-shot revolver. The models varied in barrel length and color.[52]

Smith and Wesson ads, many of which never mentioned the Lady-Smith product, used fear and the Smith and Wesson name to suggest that gun ownership could soothe anxieties about personal safety. One Smith and Wesson ad that ran in *Ladies' Home Journal* in 1989 showed a woman sitting straight up in bed, alarm obvious in her features. The text above her head read, "Things that go bump in the night aren't always your imagination." The ad did not mention guns, but it was signed "Smith and Wesson. Because we care about your safety."

Smith and Wesson was not the only manufacturer to realize the potential profit in cultivating a market of female consumers. Colt, New Detonics, Lorcin Engineering, and American Derringer all produced guns specifically for women. Size and handling adjustments, for instance reducing the trigger tension, made these guns easier for women (and incidentally children) to fire; these design modifications actually made an inherently unsafe product more dangerous. Otherwise, these products differed from their "male" counterparts only in the range of available colors, which included pinks, blues, and purples as well as frosted and pearlized finishes.

When compared with ads of competitors, Smith and Wesson's scare tactics seem tame. Lorcin Engineering ran an ad showing a telephone and a handgun side by side under text that read, "911 is a great way of summoning help fast but . . . Occasionally the best response time in assault situations is not fast enough. The Lady Lorcin L-25 was designed and built to be a comforting companion, to accommodate the time between the call and the arrival of help."

One of the most disturbing ads was produced by Colt Manufacturing Company. Showing a photograph of a mother tucking her daughter, holding Raggedy Ann, into bed at night, the text above chided, "Self-protection is more than your right . . . it's your responsibility." This ad ran in *Ladies' Home Journal*,[53] among other publications.

The NRA and the gun industry enlisted two popular myths to encourage women to buy guns. The first myth is that shadowy strangers present grave threats to women's personal safety. According to the FBI, rates for violent crime per one hundred thousand people rose 19 percent between 1988 and 1992.[54] Despite this rise in street crime, domestic violence remains the leading cause of injury to women. As noted in the *Journal of the American Medical Association*, "women in the United States are more likely to be victimized, through assault, battery, rape or homicide, by a current or former male partner than by all other assailants combined."[55] And when guns are added to an atmosphere of domestic violence, the violence will often end with a fatal conclusion. Studying family and intimate assaults in Atlanta, Georgia, CDC researchers found that when a gun was involved in domestic violence, death was twelve times more likely.[56] These data are supported by another CDC-supported study, in which researchers studied FBI reports of gun homicide in the most populous counties of Tennessee, Washington, and Ohio to produce a risk-benefit analysis of gun ownership. They found that three-quarters of the victims in their survey were murdered by relatives or acquaintances.[57]

The second damaging myth used to promote gun ownership is that a gun is an effective self-defense tool. Again, facts do not support this assertion. In 1992 the FBI reported 262 justifiable homicides by private citizens nationwide; that number is insignificant when compared with the 4.9 million occurrences of murder, rape, robbery, assault, and burglary committed the same year.[58] Simply weighing justifiable homicides (committed with a handgun) against the number of handgun homicides occurring in 1992 (12,489), roughly forty-eight murders occurred for every justified homicide. Furthermore, a CDC study published in the *New England Journal of Medicine* in 1993 found that "keeping a gun in the home was strongly and independently associated with an increased risk of homicide."[59]

Even more alarming was the connection, established in another CDC study, between the presence of a gun in the home and suicide. Approximately 29,000 Americans kill themselves each year; firearms are used more often than all other weapons and methods combined to commit suicide, according to the CDC. Of the 38,000 people killed with firearms in 1991, more than half were cases of suicide. In a study based in Shelby County, Tennessee, and King County, Washington, research revealed that "keeping one or more firearms was strongly associated with a [4.8-fold] increased risk of suicide in the home."[60] Adolescents and young adults are particularly vulnerable to suicidal impulses, and the rates of firearms suicide among both groups doubled between 1968 and 1985.[61]

While the NRA and the gun industry are selling guns to American women, suggesting that a gun can guarantee safety, medical professionals and epidemiologists have published evidence to the contrary. Guns are an example of a harmful product that is virtually unregulated.

PRODUCT LIABILITY LAW

Bad products have always been and will always be available in the marketplace. In 1988 the CPSC reported that consumer products are involved in 29,000 deaths and 33 million injuries each year.[62] And as women command greater earning power, manufacturers and advertisers will increasingly target women's money for consumption. While regulatory agencies have contributed significantly to improving the safety of the marketplace, their powers are limited by constrained budgets, limited jurisdiction, and political whims. The courts—where citizens harmed by dangerous products can confront and expose negligent manufacturers while seeking redress—have truly shaped the landscape of our markets and deserve credit for the withdrawal of some of the most lethal products from the market—notably the Ford Pinto, asbestos, the Dalkon Shield, and silicone-gel breast implants.

In an industrial society like the United States, the likelihood of injury is often beyond the control of the individual. Most citizens agree, on a visceral level, that a person injured by a defective or poorly designed product should be allowed to seek compensation from the manufacturer; commonly accepted values of responsibility dictate fair distribution of costs incurred. This belief is animated in our common law and in state statutes administered by the courts.

A full appreciation of the value of product liability law, however, requires an analysis of its purpose and full benefits. The law continually adapts to emerging hazards posed by modern technologies and new products through rulings by juries and judges, reflecting community values, which are driven by the evidence on a case-by-case basis. This law serves five fundamental functions: compensation, deterrence, prevention, disclosure, and authority on health and safety rights.

Compensation The product liability system compensates victims. For the individual, its purpose is to compensate those who are wrongfully injured both for specific economic costs and for pain and suffering. For many injured Americans, liability damages are the only or the primary source of help for covering costs and losses associated with injury. Because more than forty million Americans have no health insurance and many more are inadequately covered, the opportunity to secure liability damages is particularly important.

Deterrence The product liability system deters misconduct and punishes wrongdoers. The deterrent effect of the liability system is both individual and general. For the defendant, it provides a hard lesson in responsibility, inflicting unbudgeted costs to pay damages and raising the possibility of more lawsuits by others similarly harmed. For intentional acts, such as designing a motor vehicle not equipped with known safety technology, liability law imposes punitive damages that can amount to millions of dollars. Even though such sanctions are not frequent, the possibility generally acts as a powerful deterrent to misbehavior that could injure or kill innocent people.

Injury prevention The product liability system prevents death and injury by removing dangerous products and practices from the marketplace and by spurring safety innovation. Liability law places manufacturers and service providers on notice to take precautions against foreseeable harm and often leads to immediate, specific action to protect against the danger identified in a lawsuit by recall and correction of the product, removal from the market, or redesign.

The preventive role was documented in 1983 by the RAND Institute for Civil Justice, which reported that of all the external social pressures influencing product design decisions, product liability seems to be the most fundamental.[63] This little-discussed effect of liability law was documented by the industry-financed Conference Board of New York in a 1987 report, "Product Liability: The Corporate Response." After surveying the risk managers of 232 U.S. corporations with annual revenues of at least $100 million, the Board reached the following conclusion:

> Where product liability has had a notable impact—where it has most significantly affected management decision-making—has been in the quality of the products themselves. Managers say products have be-

come safer, manufacturing procedures have been improved, and labels and use instructions have become more explicit.[64]

Almost one-third of the manufacturers surveyed admitted that product liability had led them to improve the safety design of their products.

Disclosure of public safety information The product liability system forces public disclosure of information about dangerous practices and defective products. Government agencies learn of product defects through information discovered during lawsuits. The public can be spared injury because the disclosure itself often gives agencies sufficient information to force manufacturers and others to take corrective action. Even if companies or service providers refuse to act, consumers can protect themselves by acquiring knowledge of safety defects, poor medical practices, toxic waste dumps, improper road design, and other dangers.

Defendants are acutely aware of the powerful impact of disclosure. In recent years they have sought to prevent both discovery and release of information in liability cases. To prevent disclosure of information and documents that could be revealed during litigation, defendants increasingly are requesting protective, or secrecy, orders from the court. These court orders prohibit injured plaintiffs from publicly disclosing information to interested consumers, government agencies, and reporters. Defendants also frequently insist on secrecy for all documents and information about the case as a condition of settlement, despite recent unfavorable publicity about court secrecy. However, if plaintiff attorneys with good cases assert serious resistance, defendants will relinquish this demand. Recently, some courts and state legislatures have reacted adversely to the incessant requests of defendants for secrecy, requiring them to disclose information that affects public health and safety.

Authority on health and safety rights The product liability system provides authoritative judicial forums for the ethical growth of the law where the responsibility of perpetrators of trauma and disease can be established. The liability system accords the respect of law to the physical integrity of human beings and permits victims to confront their assailants. In doing so, liability law expands human rights and basic values as society advances and technologies change.

Despite the clear and compelling benefits of product liability law, manufacturers dislike it. Their major concern is not the cost of product

liability lawsuits, which are modest, but the embarrassment following 131
disclosures about the decisions behind the sale of defective products
that maim and kill. Prompted by the election of President Reagan in
1980, manufacturers, backed by retailers and insurers, launched a campaign in the early 1980s to limit citizens' rights under product liability
law. Over the last fifteen years, bills designed to reduce corporate accountability and restrict consumers' rights have been introduced regularly in Congress.

To persuade legislators of the need to restrict citizens' access to justice, this campaign promoted the myth of a "litigation crisis" and found
enthusiastic, high-profile spokesmen in Ronald Reagan, George Bush,
and Dan Quayle. While the "litigation crisis" found short-term cur-
rency and retains residual credibility purely through the wide exposure
it achieved during the 1980s, numerous studies and analyses have since
shown that, in fact, there is no litigation crisis. To the contrary, if there
is a flaw in the civil justice system, it is that too few injured people ever
enter the system at all and that of those who do, many are undercompensated.

It is now clear from work published in 1991 by the RAND Institute
for Civil Justice and the 1990 Harvard Medical School study of medical
malpractice in New York state that between one and seven[65] and one in
ten people[66] who are injured through the negligence of others file suit.
Furthermore, the RAND report found that people suffering from permanent injuries recover only 20 percent of their losses in court—80 percent
of the costs of devastating injuries are borne by the victims themselves.
Other studies by the National Center for State Courts and Jury Verdicts
Research show a stable curve of lawsuits and awards comparable to the
growth of population and inflation.

In 1992 product liability suits comprised only .36 percent of the approximately ten million civil case filings in state courts. It was other
types of litigation that were responsible for clogging the courts: Domestic claims constituted 35 percent and contract disputes 11 percent of all
civil case filings.[67]

According to data published by A. M. Best based upon figures reported
by insurance companies to the state insurance commissions, the total
cost of product liability verdicts and settlements for insured and uninsured manufacturers was $4.1 billion in 1993.[68] To put this amount in
perspective, consider that according to the Pet Food Institute, Americans spend $5 billion on dog food each year. For every one hundred dol-
lars spent on retail products in the United States over the last decade,

twenty-six cents went toward product liability insurance; in 1993 less than fourteen cents per one hundred dollars of retail sales was spent on product liability insurance.[69] Product liability premiums have dropped almost 50 percent since 1987.[70]

Contrary to the business lobby's propaganda, product liability awards are not a windfall for "lucky" Americans. An extensive study of product liability verdicts by the U.S. Government Accounting Office in 1989 found compensatory awards to be neither excessive nor erratic; and the size of the awards generally correlated with the severity of the injury suffered and the amount of actual economic loss incurred.[71] This finding is supported by a Consumer Federation of America study showing that between 1984 and 1993, the average payment for all product liability claims closed by insurance companies was $5,948.[72]

Punitive damages, which receive tremendous press coverage when they are awarded, are rarely awarded in product liability cases. Most are awarded in intentional tort and business liability cases.[73] Only 355 punitive awards were made in product liability cases over a twenty-five year period ending in 1990, and about 25 percent of these awards were reversed or remitted on appeal.[74] Seventy-five percent of these product liability punitive awards involved the failure of a company to publicize well-known dangers or the failure to remedy known and serious dangers after marketing or regulatory approval.[75] Despite juries' sparing use of punitive damages to send strong messages to negligent manufacturers, punitive damages are already highly restricted by the states. A few states do not permit punitive damages at all, and many others have taken action to reduce the frequency and size of punitive damages awards.

A federal product liability law being pushed by manufacturers would impose federal limits on a body of law that has traditionally been developed and administered by state courts and citizen juries. Aside from the significant procedural implications of a federal law, substantive elements of the proposed changes are a one-way street designed to benefit manufacturers at the expense of consumers. The following types of provisions in the legislative proposals would protect corporate interests while exposing consumers to threats:

- shortening the statute of limitations for filing lawsuits after the discovery of injury and cause, which is particularly damaging for children
- eliminating liability for products more than fifteen years old, in-

cluding cars, farm equipment, and other consumer durables that
are supposed to last longer than fifteen years
- abolishing joint and several liability for noneconomic damages, effectively reducing the compensation of a victim who is injured by more than one party if one of the parties cannot pay its share of the damages
- capping punitive damages for all products at $250,000 or twice the economic damages assessed, whichever is greater, and additionally barring punitive damages in the case of FDA-approved drugs and medical devices (unless fraud was involved), no matter how egregious the wrongdoing of the manufacturer

These provisions, if passed, would downgrade the rights of injured consumers and erode the deterrent effect of product liability law by reducing the financial incentive for manufacturers to produce safe products. Foreseeable results include more injuries and deaths, more uncompensated victims, and greater costs to society (through programs like Medicare, Medicaid, welfare, unemployment compensation) that should be paid by the manufacturers of defective products responsible for injuries.

Most disturbing, the proposals to limit joint and several liability and indemnify FDA-approved products against punitive damages would have a disproportionately damaging effect on women, denying them fair compensation for terrible injuries. The long-standing doctrine of joint and several liability provides that when more than one defendant is responsible for causing injury, but not all of the defendants can contribute to the award, the plaintiff is allowed to recover fully from the solvent wrongdoers. The following example illustrates how this doctrine operates. A woman driving her car is hit from the rear at a low speed by another driver, traveling slowly. Her car explodes in flames because her fuel tank was defectively designed and poorly located, causing it to rupture on impact and spill gasoline, which is then ignited by a spark from the crash. Both the driver of the other car and the manufacturer of the fuel tank contributed to the circumstances that injured the woman and should share responsibility for compensating her. If the driver of the other car is uninsured and indigent, joint and several liability would require the manufacturer to compensate this injured woman fully. Joint and several liability aims to make the innocent victim "whole" again.

"Noneconomic" damages compensate for losses other than out-of-pocket expenses like medical bills and lost wages. "Noneconomic" damages include pain and suffering for victims who suffer horrible dis-

134   figurement or loss of fertility. The ability to recover these types of damages is particularly important to women for two reasons. First, women have been used as unsuspecting guinea pigs for untested products like DES, the Dalkon Shield, Copper-7 IUDs, and silicone breast implants, suffering injuries whose costs, such as loss of fertility and miscarriage, are noneconomic but take a tremendous toll on mental health and quality of life. These losses are real even if they cannot be easily quantified. Second, if women are forced to recover for injuries solely on the basis of economic damages, they are disadvantaged by the fact that *if* they work they generally earn less money than men, even men performing the same work. If recovery were limited to economic damages, women and men suffering from the same injuries would likely be entitled to different levels of compensation.

If punitive damage awards for defective FDA-approved products are barred or capped, an important deterrent discouraging manufacturers from marketing dangerous products like DES, the Dalkon Shield, the Copper-7 IUD, and breast implants will be removed. As the breast implant case study illustrates clearly, government "approval" does not guarantee safety. When implants were invented, the FDA lacked the authority to require manufacturers to prove the safety of their new product. And when the FDA was granted the authority to require pre-market approval of medical devices in 1976, the implants had the benefit of an established marketplace position. As a result, more than one million women received silicone breast implants without knowing the serious health threats they posed. Public disclosure of these risks and the FDA's response occurred only after a citizen jury sitting in a northern California courthouse decided that a company had no right to run roughshod over one woman's health and well-being.

Although punitive damages are seldom awarded, they serve an important public health function. The $6.5 million punitive damage award in *Hopkins v. Dow Corning* grabbed public and government attention and led to tough new restrictions on the availability of that product and an aggressive FDA investigation into the product's safety and the manufacturer's conduct concerning disclosure of health risks to women who had put their trust in its product. Manufacturers continue to sell thousands of other defective products that harm and kill thousands of Americans each year.

NOTES

1. H. Green, *The Light of the Home: An Intimate View of the Lives of Women in Victorian America* (New York: Pantheon, 1983), 124.

2. U.S. Consumer Product Safety Commission, "News from the CPSC: CPSC Recalls Dangerously Flammable Imported Chiffon Skirts," *Press Release*, Washington, DC, August 12, 1994.

3. *Hopkins v. Dow Corning*, No. C88 4703 TEH (N.D. Cal. 1991).

4. D. Bolton, letter to FDA Commissioner David Kessler, Washington, DC, December 30, 1991.

5. *Stern v. Dow Corning*, No. C83 2348 MHP (N.D. Cal. 1984).

6. U.S. Department of Health and Human Services, "HHS News," *Press Release*, Washington, DC, January 6, 1992.

7. P. J. Hilts, "Silicone: Assessing the Risks," *New York Times* (January 13, 1992): B10.

8. Bolton, letter to David Kessler.

9. Ibid.

10. *Medical Device Amendments of 1976*, Public Law 94-295, 90 Stat. 539, 21 U.S.C. Sections 360c–360k.

11. U.S. Food and Drug Administration. Panel on Review of General and Plastic Surgery Devices, *Summary Minutes*, Washington, DC, June 24, 1976.

12. U.S. Food and Drug Administration. Panel on Review of General and Plastic Surgery Devices, presentation by Dr. H. Jenny, *Transcript of Meeting*, Washington, DC, March 24, 1978; U.S. Food and Drug Administration. General and Plastic Surgery Section, Surgical and Rehabilitation Device Panel, *Transcript of Meeting*, Washington, DC, July 6, 1978.

13. 47 Fed. Reg. 2810 (1982).

14. *Stern v. Dow Corning*.

15. U.S Food and Drug Administration, Dr. H. M. D. Luu, *Memorandum to the File*, Washington, DC, August 15, 1988. Dr. Luu is an FDA pharmacologist and member of the FDA task force that has analyzed the evidence concerning the carcinogenicity of silicone gels.

16. U.S. Food and Drug Administration, Dr. M. E. Stratmeyer, "Analysis of Dow Corning Data Regarding Carcinogenicity of Silicone Gels," *Memo*, Washington, DC, August 9, 1988.

17. Dow Corning, Silastic II Brand Mammary Implant H.P., *Product Insert*, 1985.

18. 53 Fed. Reg. 23856 (1988).

19. S. Wolfe, letter to FDA Commissioner Frank Young, Washington, DC, November 9, 1988.

20. 56 Fed. Reg. 49098 (1991).

21. U.S. Food and Drug Administration, "Important Information on Breast Implants," *Backgrounder*, Washington, DC, August 1991: 3.

22. U.S. Food and Drug Administration, "Panel Issues Breast Implant Recommendation," *Talk Paper*, Washington, DC, November 15, 1991.

23. U.S. Department of Health and Human Services, "HHS News."

136

24. P. J. Hilts, "FDA Tells Company to Release Implant Data," *New York Times* (January 21, 1992): C7.

25. M. L. Wald, "An Ex-Chemist's Formula for Dow Corning," *New York Times* (February 17, 1992): D3.

26. S. McMurray, "Dow Corning Discloses It Has Insurance of $250 Million to Cover Possible Claims," *Wall Street Journal* (March 9, 1992): B5.

27. "Questions and Answers," Breast Implant Litigation Settlement Agreement, N.D. Ala., So. Div., in *Silicone Gel Breast Implants Products Liability Litigation* MDL 926, Case No. CV-94-P-11558-S (1993), 1.

28. S. Wolfe, *Women's Health Alert* (Reading, MA: Addison-Wesley, 1991): 233.

29. W. Wooley and S. Wooley, "33,000 Women Tell How They Really Feel About Their Bodies," *Glamour* (February 1984): 198–201, 251–52.

30. R. P. Seid, *Never Too Thin: Why Women Are at War with Their Bodies* (New York: Prentice Hall, 1989), 3.

31. U.S. Federal Trade Commission, "The Facts About Weight Loss Products and Programs," *Brochure*, Washington, DC, 1995.

32. Wolfe, *Women's Health Alert*, 248.

33. "Rating the Diets," *Consumer Reports* (June 1993): 353.

34. "What's Ahead? The Weight Loss Market," *Obesity and Health* 3 (1989): 51–54.

35. J. D. Horowitz et al., "Hypertensive Responses Induced by Phenylpropanolamine in Anorectic and Decongestant Preparations," *Lancet* 1 (1980): 60–61.

36. A. J. Dietz, "Amphetamine-like Reactions to Phenylpropanolamine," *Journal of the American Medical Association* 245 (1981): 601–2.

37. U.S. Federal Trade Commission, "FTC Chairman Testifies Before House Subcommittee on FTC Regulation of Weight-Loss Products and Plans," *Press Release*, Washington, DC, March 27, 1990.

38. Wolfe, *Women's Health Alert*, 181–82.

39. U.S. Food and Drug Administration. Fertility and Maternal Health Drugs Advisory Committee, testimony by D. L. Kennedy on drug use for lactation suppression, *Hearings*, June 1, 1989; S. Wolfe, letter to David Kessler, Commissioner of the FDA, Washington, DC, August 16, 1994.

40. A. Gerlin, "Sandoz Is to Stop Marketing Parlodel as a Drug for Suppression of Lactation," *Wall Street Journal* (August 19, 1994): B6.

41. S. Wolfe, L. Silver and V. Leonard, letter to FDA Commissioner Frank Young, Washington, DC, November 18, 1988.

42. A. C. Turnbull, "Puerpal Thrombo-Embolism and Suppression of Lactation," *Journal of Obstetrics and Gynecology of the British Commonwealth* 75 (1968): 1321–23; summary basis for approval for bromocriptine mesylate to FDA, October 27, 1978.

43. U.S. Food and Drug Administration. Adverse Drug Reporting System   137
data, Washington, DC.

44. Wolfe, letter to David Kessler.

45. U.S. Department of Health and Human Services. Public Health Service. Centers for Disease Control, "Deaths Resulting from Firearm—and Motor Vehicle-Related Injuries—United States, 1968–1991," *Morbidity and Mortality Weekly Report* 43, no. 3 (January 28, 1994): 37.

46. W. Max and D. Rice, "Shooting in the Dark: Estimating the Cost of Firearm Injuries," *Health Affairs* (Winter 1993): 171.

47. U.S. Bureau of Alcohol, Tobacco and Firearms, "How Many Guns?" *Press Release,* Washington, DC, May 1991.

48. U.S. Bureau of Alcohol, Tobacco and Firearms, "Civilian Firearms: Domestic Production, Importation, and Exportation, 1899–1994," *Annual Data,* Washington, DC, 1995.

49. J. Sugarmann, *National Rifle Association: Money, Firepower, Fear* (Washington, DC: National Press, 1992), 94–95.

50. Ibid., 154.

51. "NRA Crime Ad Irks 25 Congresswomen," *Chicago Tribune* (October 17, 1993): C29.

52. T. Attlee, "A Way to Establish a New Customer Base," *American Firearms Industry* (December 1989): 20.

53. *Ladies' Home Journal,* July 1992.

54. U.S. Department of Justice. Federal Bureau of Investigation, *Uniform Crime Reports* (Washington, DC: Government Printing Office, 1992), 12.

55. Council on Ethical and Judicial Affairs, "Physicians and Domestic Violence: Ethical Considerations," *Journal of the American Medical Association* 267, no. 23 (1992): 3190–93.

56. L. E. Saltzman et al., "Weapon Involvement and Injury Outcomes in Family and Intimate Assaults," *Journal of the American Medical Association* 267, no. 22 (1192): 3043–47.

57. A. L. Kellerman et al., "Gun Ownership as a Risk Factor for Homicide in the Home," *New England Journal of Medicine* 329, no. 15 (1993): 1084–91.

58. U.S. Department of Justice, *Uniform Crime Reports.*

59. Kellerman et al., "Gun Ownership as a Risk Factor."

60. A. L. Kellerman et al., "Suicide in the Home in Relation to Gun Ownership," *New England Journal of Medicine* 327, no. 7 (1992): 467–72.

61. Ibid.

62. U.S. Consumer Product Safety Commission, *Who We Are and What We Do* (Washington, DC: Government Printing Office, 1988).

63. G. Eads and P. Reuter, *Designing Safer Products: Corporate Responses to Product Liability and Regulation* (Santa Monica, CA: RAND Institute for Civil Justice, 1983), viii.

138   64. Conference Board of New York, *Product Liability: The Corporate Response* (New York: Conference Board of New York, 1987), 2.

65. U.S. House. Committee on Energy and Commerce. Subcommittee on Health and the Environment, testimony of T. A. Brennan, Professor of Law and Public Health, Harvard School of Public Health, *Medical Malpractice and Health Care Reform Hearings*, November 10, 1993, 7.

66. D. R. Hensler et al., *Compensation for Accidental Injuries in the United States* (Santa Monica, CA: RAND Institute for Civil Justice, 1991), 19.

67. National Center for State Courts, *Conference of Chief Justices Statement on S.565, the Product Liability Fairness Act of 1995*, submitted to the U.S. Senate, Committee on Commerce, Science and Transportation, 1995, 8–9.

68. Cited in J. R. Hunter, *Product Liability Insurance Experience 1984–1993* (Washington, DC: Consumer Federation of America, 1995).

69. Ibid., 2.

70. Ibid., 1.

71. U.S. General Accounting Office, *Product Liability: Verdicts and Case Resolution in Five States*, Report to the Chair, Subcommittee on Commerce, Consumer Protection and Competitiveness, Committee on Energy and Commerce, U.S. House, 1989, 31.

72. Hunter, *Product Liability Insurance Experience 1984–1993*, 5.

73. E. Moller, *Trends in Punitive Damages: Preliminary Data from California* (Santa Monica, CA: RAND Institute for Civil Justice, 1995), 4–7.

74. M. Rustad, *Demystifying Punitive Damages in Product Liability Cases: A Survey of a Quarter Century of Trial Verdicts* (Washington, DC: Roscoe Pound Foundation, 1991), 23, 27.

75. Ibid., 28.

REFERENCES

Attlee, T. 1989. A way to establish a new customer base. *American Firearms Industry*, December: 20–21.

Conference Board of New York. 1987. *Product Liability: The Corporate Response*. New York: Conference Board of New York.

Council on Ethical and Judicial Affairs. 1992. Physicians and domestic violence: Ethical considerations. *Journal of the American Medical Association* 267(23): 3190–93.

Dietz, A. J. 1981. Amphetamine-like reactions to phenylpropanolamine. *Journal of the American Medical Association* 245: 601–2.

Eads, G. and P. Reuter. 1983. *Designing Safer Products: Corporate Re-*

sponses to Product Liability and Regulation. Santa Monica, CA: RAND Institute for Civil Justice.

Gerlin, A. 1994. Sandoz is to stop marketing Parlodel as a drug for suppression of lactation. *Wall Street Journal,* August 19: B6.

Green, H. 1983. *The Light of the Home: An Intimate View of the Lives of Women in Victorian America.* New York: Pantheon.

Hensler, D. R., M. S. Marquis, A. F. Abrahamse, S. H. Berry, P. A. Ebener, E. G. Lewis, E. A. Lind, R. J. MacCoun, W. G. Manning, J. A. Rogowski and M. E. Vaiana. 1991. *Compensation for Accidental Injuries in the United States.* Santa Monica, CA: RAND Institute for Civil Justice.

Hilts, P. J. 1992. FDA tells company to release implant data. *New York Times,* January 21: C7.

———. 1992. Silicone: Assessing the risks. *New York Times,* January 13: B10.

Horowitz, J. D., J. W. Lang, L. G. Howles, M. R. Fennessy, N. M. Christophidis and M. J. Rand. 1980. Hypertensive responses induced by phenylpropanolamine in anorectic and decongestant preparations. *Lancet* 1: 60–61.

Hunter, J. R. 1995. *Product Liability Insurance Experience 1984–1993.* Washington, DC: Consumer Federation of America.

Kellerman, A. L., F. P. Rivara, N. B. Rushforth, J. G. Banton, D. T. Reay, J. T. Francisco, A. B. Locci, J. Prodzinski, B. B. Hackman and G. Somes. 1993. Gun ownership as a risk factor for homicide in the home. *New England Journal of Medicine* 329(15): 1084–1091.

Kellerman, A. L., F. P. Rivara, G. Somes, D. T. Reay, J. T. Francisco, J. G. Banton, J. Prodzinski, C. Fligner and B. B. Hackman. 1992. Suicide in the home in relation to gun ownership. *New England Journal of Medicine* 327(7): 467–72.

Max, W. and D. Rice. 1993. Shooting in the dark: Estimating the cost of firearm injuries. *Health Affairs,* Winter: 171.

McMurray, S. 1992. Dow Corning discloses it has insurance of $250 million to cover possible claims. *Wall Street Journal,* March 9: B5.

Moller, E. 1995. *Trends in Punitive Damages: Preliminary Data from California.* Santa Monica, CA: RAND Institute for Civil Justice.

National Center for State Courts. 1995. *Conference of Chief Justices Statement on S.565, the Product Liability Fairness Act of 1995.* Submitted to the U.S. Senate. Committee on Commerce, Science and Transportation. Washington, DC.

NRA crime ad irks 25 Congresswomen. 1993. *Chicago Tribune,* October 17: C29.

Rating the diets. 1993. *Consumer Reports.* June: 353.

Rustad, M. 1991. *Demystifying Punitive Damages in Product Liability*

140   *Cases: A Survey of a Quarter Century of Trial Verdicts.* Washington,
DC: Roscoe Pound Foundation.

Saltzman, L. E., J. A. Mercy, P. W. O'Carroll, M. L. Rosenberg and P. H.
Rhodes. 1992. Weapon involvement and injury outcomes in family and
intimate assaults. *Journal of the American Medical Association*
267(22): 3043–47.

Seid, R. 1989. *Never Too Thin: Why Women Are at War with Their Bodies.*
New York: Prentice Hall.

Sugarmann, J. 1992 *National Rifle Association: Money, Firepower, Fear.*
Washington, DC: National Press.

Turnbull, A. C. 1968. Puerpal thrombo-embolism and suppression of lactation. *Journal of Obstetrics and Gynecology of the British Commonwealth* 75: 1321–23.

U.S. Bureau of Alcohol, Tobacco and Firearms. 1991. How many guns? *Press
Release,* May. Washington, DC.

———. 1995. Civilian firearms: Domestic production, importation, and exportation, 1899–1994. *Annual Data.* Washington, DC.

U.S. Consumer Product Safety Commission. 1988. *Who We Are and What
We Do.* Washington, DC: Government Printing Office.

———. 1994. News from the CPSC: CPSC recalls dangerously flammable
imported chiffon skirts. *Press Release,* August 12. Washington, DC.

U.S. Department of Health and Human Services. Public Health Service,
Centers for Disease Control. 1994. Deaths resulting from firearm—and
motor vehicle-related injuries—United States, 1968–1991. *Morbidity
and Mortality Weekly Report* 43(3): 37.

U.S. Department of Justice. Federal Bureau of Investigation. 1992. *Uniform
Crime Reports.* Washington, DC: Government Printing Office.

U.S. Federal Trade Commission. 1995. The facts about weight loss products
and programs. *Brochure.* Washington, DC.

———. 1990. FTC chairman testifies before House Subcommittee on FTC
regulation of weight-loss products and plans. *Press Release,* March 27.
Washington, DC.

———. 1988. Analysis of Dow Corning data regarding carcinogenicity of
silicone gels. *Memo,* August 9. Washington, DC.

———. 1991. Important information on breast implants. *Backgrounder,* August. Washington, DC.

U.S. General Accounting Office. 1989. *Product Liability: Verdicts and Case
Resolution in Five States.* Report to the chair, Subcommittee on Commerce, Consumer Protection and Competitiveness. Committee on Energy and Commerce. U.S. House of Representatives. Washington, DC.

———. 1991. Panel issues breast implant recommendation. *Talk Paper,* November 15. Washington, DC.

U.S. Food and Drug Administration. Fertility and Maternal Health Drugs Advisory Committee. 1989. *Hearings,* June 1.

U.S. Food and Drug Administration. General and Plastic Surgery Section, Surgical and Rehabilitation Device Panel. 1978. *Transcript of Meeting,* July 6.

U.S. Food and Drug Administration. Panel on Review of General and Plastic Surgery Devices. 1976. *Summary Minutes,* June 24.

———. 1978. *Transcript of Meeting,* March 24.

U.S. Food and Drug Administration. 1988. *Memorandum to the File.* August 15. Washington, DC.

U.S. House. Committee on Energy and Commerce. Subcommittee on Health and the Environment. 1993. *Medical Malpractice and Health Care Reform Hearings.* November 10.

Wald, M. L. 1992. An ex-chemist's formula for Dow Corning. *New York Times,* February 17: D3.

What's ahead? The weight loss market. 1989. *Obesity and Health* 3: 51–54.

Wolfe, S. 1991. *Women's Health Alert.* Reading, MA: Addison-Wesley.

Wooley, W. and S. Wooley. 1984. 33,000 women tell how they really feel about their bodies. *Glamour,* February: 198–201, 251–52.

EMPLOYMENT DISCRIMINATION

Susan M. Davis

 Women are victimized economically when employers discriminate against them in compensation or employment opportunity. Whether such discrimination stems from prejudice, stereotyping, or merely taking advantage of market conditions in which women's skills are undervalued, the resulting limits to women's employment and earnings potential inflict social harm on women, their dependents, and ultimately society at large. The market mechanism is notoriously unable to correct injustice and inequality and in fact may build on and contribute to perpetuating such features. For example, an individual employer may acknowledge that the services of female workers are undervalued (relative to their contribution to the firm or to male workers), but unilaterally to increase the compensation to female workers would put this company at a competitive disadvantage with other firms that continue to pay the lower rate, allowing them to bring their product or service to the market at a lower price. Similarly, an individual employer may believe that a woman could perform as well as a man selling cars or practicing law, but if the customers expect to see a man in those roles, the employer may be reluctant to buck the norm and risk losing business. The point is, once inequality has become established, it is difficult for the system to right itself. This is why antidiscrimination laws are so important: They level the playing field. They hold *all* employers up to the same scrutiny and expectations, making it possible to change the trend—something an individual employer, despite good intentions, could not do.

One might think that three decades after equal opportunity became law, we could at least agree on what employer practices constitute discrimination. Yet this is precisely one of the most bitter controversies in law and in theory. Is discriminatory intent the only unlawful employer

144 practice, or is adverse impact also subject to scrutiny under the law? In what cases should discriminatory hiring and compensation be excused on the grounds of "business necessity," and at what point should the law be used to overturn the status quo, even though it imposes costs on some groups in the economy? As we shall see, the tentacles of discrimination are both subtle and tenacious. They permeate the economy, the culture, the socialization process, and consciousness of both the victims and the beneficiaries of inequality. Thus, our definition of discrimination and recognition of it in its various guises is an evolving process. We might conclude that while much has been achieved in the last thirty years, much remains to be done.

This chapter presents evidence on discriminatory outcomes in the labor market, summarizes the theories that have contributed important insights into the causes of discrimination and mechanisms enforcing it, and discusses the evolution in the interpretation and enforcement of U.S. antidiscrimination laws. In conclusion, the chapter examines how other advanced industrial countries have addressed the issue and suggests policy prescriptions that might be appropriate for the United States.

EVIDENCE OF DISCRIMINATION

If we start from the premise that most people are "normal"—that is, that they fall within a defined range in terms of ability; motivation; and desire for income, satisfying work, status, and upward mobility—then there is no objective reason for women to be overwhelmingly concentrated in occupations where wages, benefits, satisfaction, and status are relatively low and upward mobility is difficult to achieve. Yet since women *are* concentrated in these areas of the labor market, should we conclude that they choose to be there because their primary focus is on their roles as mothers and wives and not their position in the labor force; or that their personal characteristics (availability for work, skills, aptitudes, or motivation) confine them there? There is, in fact, considerable variation in both women's and men's characteristics and job preferences. In the United States there has been, and continues to be, a considerable amount of occupational segregation by gender. There is an ongoing debate about why this is the case. Are women fundamentally different from men in terms of the characteristics they bring to the market or in the types of jobs they prefer?

Gender typing, that is, the monopolization of particular occupations by one sex or the other, would appear to be unnatural. Yet as Table 1 shows, it exists in many areas of the labor market. There are many other occupational fields, particularly those with more lucrative jobs, in which women are virtually absent: from airline pilots and auto mechanics (less than 1 percent female) to carpenters, plumbers, and electricians (less than 2 percent female).[1] The question is, how much of this underrepresentation exists because women choose not to compete in these areas, how much is the residue of past discrimination—which limited women's aspirations and access to apprenticeships, training, and educational programs relevant to these fields—and how much is attributable to employer discrimination?

Patterns of occupational segregation by gender are remarkably similar across the advanced industrialized nations as well as in the developing countries' economies: Women are concentrated in clerical, retail trade, and health and educational services.[2] It is tempting to conclude that women prefer or excel in certain areas and not others. Otherwise, we

Table 1   Proportion of Females in Selected Professional Specialty Occupations

Occupation	1970 (%)	1989 (%)
Architects	4.0	20.6
Chemists	11.7	27.8
Clergy	2.9	7.8
Computer systems analysts and scientists	13.6	32.4
Dentists	3.5	8.6
Dietitians	92.0	90.8
Editors and reporters	41.6	49.2
Engineers	4.9	22.2
Lawyers	4.9	22.2
Librarians	82.1	87.3
Pharmacists	12.1	32.3
Physicians	9.7	17.9
Registered nurses	97.3	94.2
Teachers		
Pre-K and K	97.9	97.8
Elementary	83.9	84.7
Secondary	49.6	52.6
College and university	29.1	38.7

Source: U.S. Bureau of the Census, *Detailed Occupation of the Experienced Civilian Labor Force by Sex for the United States and Regions* (Washington, DC: Government Printing Office, 1970); U.S. Bureau of Labor Statistics, *Employment and Earnings* (Washington, DC: Government Printing Office, 1990).

146   would have to suspect a global conspiracy among male employers, employees, and customers to keep women in their place. Another commonality across cultures and economies is women's role in the domestic sphere: Women bear the primary responsibility for child care and housework, even when they work full-time outside the home. But does this in and of itself explain why women type instead of installing electrical outlets or become nurses rather than doctors?

The rapid movement of women into predominantly male professions since the educational amendments to the Civil Rights Act[3] were passed indicates that artificial barriers, rather than choice or aptitude, kept women out of many areas of the labor market. Table 2 illustrates this succinctly.

Since the 1960s, economists have tried to explain the observed patterns of occupational segregation by gender, focusing on measurable differences between men and women in their human capital characteristics (that is, their levels of education, experience, specific skills, and labor force commitment). A famous early study by Corcoran and Duncan—notable because of its detailed information on work history compared with other studies of the time—showed precisely how women differed from men in these human capital factors, and how much of the earnings difference by gender they explained.[4] It illustrated several things that encapsulate what we now "know" about differences by gender. The findings are presented in Table 3.

First, notice that in fact women were not markedly different from men in terms of levels of formal education. A common assumption at the time was that women's subordinate status in the labor market could be explained because men were better educated and therefore better qualified for the higher-paying jobs. Second, the data showed that women were more likely than men to miss work and to have a more casual attachment to the labor force (entering and leaving more fre-

Table 2 **Proportion of Degrees Conferred on Women in Four Selected Professions**

	1960 (%)	1982 (%)
Medicine (M.D.)	5.5	25.0
Dentistry (D.D.S. or D.M.D.)	0.8	15.4
Law (LL.B. or J.D.)	2.5	33.4
Engineering	0.4	10.8

Source: U.S. Bureau of the Census, *Statistical Abstract of the United States* (Washington, DC: Government Printing Office, 1985), 159.

Table 3   Accounting for the Wage Gap Between Men and Women

	Average Values		Percentage of Wage Gap Explained by Gender
Factor	Men	Women	Differences
Education (in years)	12.9	12.7	2%
Years of work experience			
Before present employer	11.3	8.1	3
With present employer	8.7	5.7	11
Training (years of training in current job)	1.7	0.7	11
Indicators of labor force attachment			
Years out of labor force since leaving school	0.5	5.8	6
Percentage of years working part-time	10.0%	21.0%	8
Hours of work per year missed due to:			
own illness	36.5	43.5	0
illness of others	4.0	12.5	0
Percentage that placed limits on hours or location of job	14.5%	34.5%	2
Percentage planning to stop work	3.0%	8.6%	2
Percentage of wage gap explained			45%
Percentage not explained			55%

Source: M. Corcoran and G. J. Duncan, "Work History, Labor-Force Attachment, and Earnings Differences Between the Races and Sexes," *Journal of Human Resources* 14 (Winter 1979): 3–20. This table was adapted from the information in the journal article and refers to whites in the sample only.

quently, having fewer years of experience since leaving school, and more likely to work part-time). Thus, the study supports the premise that women's domestic role is the most important factor in explaining their lower wages: Work experience and indicators of labor force attachment together explained 32 percent of the wage gap by gender. Undoubtedly this is a choice many women make: to provide primary care for their families and, therefore, be less able to compete in the labor market. The fact that women's domestic constraints account for such a large portion of the explained earnings difference is quite important in terms of developing policies to ease the incompatibility between work outside the home and family life. It is unfortunate that this conflict is still seen as primarily a women's issue instead of a "family issue," since in most families both spouses are now engaged in market work.

Another significant finding of this study is that differential access to job training (which is a decision made by the employer) accounts for 11 percent of the earnings gap. Women's groups have been maintaining for some time that women are locked out of training slots that would allow them to advance further within the firm and, therefore, earn more over time. The employers, predictably, respond that training women represents a poor investment, since women are more likely than their male counterparts to quit (the feedback mechanism of the division of labor within the family).

Finally, this study was important because it was able to *explain* more of the wage gap by gender than any study to date (primarily because of the detailed information on work history)—and yet it explains only 45 percent of the gap! A common interpretation was that the 55 percent of the gap that was still unaccounted for was attributable to discrimination.

Chalking up the residual (unexplained differential) to discrimination was, admittedly, simplistic. Data limitations, for example, would not capture differences by gender in majors among college graduates, in demeanor, motivation, or preferences for different types of work—such as the desire to give rather than take orders; the acceptance of long, demanding workloads versus simple, nine-to-five jobs that require no continuing burden after office hours; the need to find esteem or status on the job; preferences for work that does not get one dirty or does not have to be done outdoors in inclement weather; the ability to perform jobs requiring physical strength and endurance; and so on.

Some researchers took another tack to try to explain earnings differences by gender. Instead of focusing on the human capital characteristics of the employee, they examined the skills required on the job. Using objective measures of verbal, math, physical strength, analytic, interpersonal, and other skills required in 900-odd job categories, England found that women and men were not compensated equally for performing these skills (particularly in the areas of literacy, math, and manual dexterity). Treiman and Hartmann discovered that the level of compensation awarded for those skills was determined to a significant degree by whether they were performed primarily by men or primarily by women.[5]

Why would women be systematically underpaid for their skills compared to men? Bergmann said it was because the "crowding" of women into a relatively narrow range of employment opportunities had depressed wages in predominantly female job categories.[6] In the long run, she suggested, antidiscrimination laws will solve the problem; once this "crowding" is relaxed (as women move into nontraditional, formerly all-male jobs), then wages in currently female-dominated job markets will rise to their real, appropriate levels.

Table 4 verifies that in contrast to men, women are "crowded" into certain areas of the labor market and, significantly, that these areas include the lowest-paid jobs in the economy. In 1989, 57 percent of all women in the labor force were employed in just three areas: retail sales, clerical, and service jobs. Male workers, on the other hand, were more evenly distributed across the major occupational areas, but even where they tended to be concentrated (for examples, as crafts workers and laborers) wages were substantially higher than in the areas of female concentration.

Table 4 also illustrates that, while women's share of managerial positions increased substantially from 1972 to 1989, there was not much change elsewhere in the employment structure. Sizable differences still exist in weekly earnings by gender within the same categories. We might surmise that some of this wage disparity is due to the fact that women are newer (less experienced) in some of these fields—a residue of past discrimination—or that it is an indication of continued discrimination.

So far, we have discussed attempts to explain differences in earnings and occupational distribution that focused on differences by gender in educational attainment, experience, commitment to the labor force, and other personal characteristics (what economists call the "supply side" of the labor market). If educational and training barriers were eliminated, presumably *some* women would rush to these new opportunities.[7] We will now examine unequal employment opportunities (what economists call the "demand side" of the labor market) because this has been the focus of legal attempts to dismantle unequal opportunity and artificial barriers to women (and other "protected" groups).

Understanding the employers' role in the labor market is critical in identifying the mechanisms and motivation for employment discrimination. We cannot mandate that women compete in all areas of the labor market, only that the barriers preventing them from doing so be eliminated. Since women earn less than men, it would seem that a profit-maximizing employer would actually prefer women over equally qualified men. Obviously, more complex factors are at work.

Employers must find a means of evaluating job applicants, particularly if there are many applicants for a single position. The most obvious

Table 4 Occupational Distribution and Median Weekly Earnings by Gender

| | Occupational Distribution | | | | Median Weekly Earnings 1985* | | |
| | 1972 | | 1989 | | | | |
	Men	Women	Men	Women	Men ($)	Women ($)	W/M**
Executive, administrative and management	11.5%	4.6%	13.9%	11.1%	593	383	.68
Professional specialty	9.7	12.4	12.0	14.8	571	408	.71
Technicians and related support	2.3	2.4	2.9	3.3	472	331	.70
Sales occupations	10.0	11.1	11.1	13.1	431	226	.52
Administrative support, including clerical	6.4	31.5	5.7	27.8	391	270	.69
Service occupations	8.3	21.2	9.6	17.7	272	185	.68
Precision prod., craft and repair	19.4	1.6	19.6	2.2	408	268	.66
Operators, fabricators and laborers	25.9	13.4	20.7	8.9	325	216	.66
Farming, forestry and fishing	6.4	1.9	4.4	1.1	216	185	.86
Total	100	100	100	100			

Source: U.S. Bureau of Labor Statistics, *Employment and Earnings* (Washington, DC: Government Printing Office, Jan. 1984 and 1990). Data include civilian workers aged 16 and over; U.S. Bureau of Labor Statistics, *Weekly Earnings of Wage and Salary Workers, 4th Qtr., 1985* (Washington, DC: Government Printing Office, Feb. 3, 1986).

*Median earnings of full-time workers.

**Women's weekly earnings divided by men's.

screening device is job-related educational, training, or experience requirements. But what if several applicants meet all these requirements? The next criterion might be letters of recommendation or other indicators of success. In the end, the employer may choose the best-qualified person willing to work for the least pay.[8]

Beyond these obvious and legitimate means of choosing among job applicants (bona fide occupational qualifications) we may encounter the phenomenon of discrimination. For example, employers may eschew hiring women for positions where some employer-financed training is required in the belief that women are likely to quit sooner than men. Employers may pass over women because they think that their current work force will not accept them in certain positions or that their customers will react negatively. In fact prejudice (on the part of the employer, current employees, or customers) and statistical discrimination (judging applicants based on stereotypical views of what individuals will be like because they are members of a particular demographic group) have now been recognized as major sources of discriminatory practice among employers. Furthermore, this framework of prejudice and stereotyping helps explain patterns of occupational segregation in the majority of job categories in which bona fide occupational qualifications are not involved.

DISCRIMINATION IN EMPLOYMENT OPPORTUNITIES

Employer Discrimination

Employers may practice discrimination for several reasons. The first, and most obviously illegal, reason is personal animus against a particular group or a disposition against hiring people from certain groups for certain jobs within the firm. The same employer who would not consider a woman for a managerial position may prefer women as secretaries. In theory, the employer who passes over a qualified woman in favor of a less-qualified man (or an equally qualified woman who could be hired at a lower rate of pay) must "pay" to indulge this taste for discrimination; the price is losing the more productive (and cheaper) worker. Also in theory, employers who indulge in this expensive taste or preference will, in the long run, be eliminated from their respective markets: Their competitors (who do not incur these costs) can bring their product to market at a lower cost and capture market share. In other words, discrimination will be eliminated through the forces of market competition.[9] But this theory obviously has a major flaw: Two hundred years (at least) of employment discrimination of this type have not been eliminated through the market mechanism. In fact, markets tend to coexist quite comfortably with inequality.

Employers with a personal prejudice against hiring women for certain jobs may attempt to circumvent the law by establishing hiring standards (or screening devices) designed to eliminate women from the applicant pool. The first case to go to the U.S. Supreme Court after Title VII of the 1964 Civil Rights Act became law concerned the issue of using a screening mechanism to discriminate. In *Griggs v. Duke Power Co.*[10] (discussed more fully in the next section), the Court found both that the hiring standard had an adverse impact on a protected group (in this case minorities) *and* that the standard was not job-related. These intentionally discriminatory tactics may be the easiest to identify and root out.

Statistical Discrimination

A second attempt to understand employer discrimination came from Phelps, who suggested that employers may have an economic motive for discriminating against women (or other groups) for particular positions within the firm.[11] Specifically, because information is costly, the employer may judge an individual job applicant on the basis of the (real or perceived) average attributes of the group to which the applicant belongs. So if women, on average, are more likely to exhibit discontinuous labor force attachment patterns, for example, then the individual woman applying for the job is assumed to have that attribute. This approach is referred to as statistical discrimination. It is consistent with profit maximization and thus with the persistence of discrimination in the short run. Statistical discrimination is now illegal, even if based on real statistical averages for the group. Individuals must be evaluated on their personal characteristics, rather than on averages for their group, even if individual evaluations are more costly to the employer.

Employer discrimination on the demand side of the labor market has pernicious implications for the supply side of the labor market. As Arrow noted, if discrimination has led employers to pass over women for training that would lead to promotion within the firm, or if it has led employers to assign women to jobs where the costs of turnover are minimized, then women have little incentive to stay on the job. Women may respond by exhibiting exactly the unstable behavior that employ-ers expected.[12] As employers' expectations are confirmed, they continue their discriminatory employment practices, and so the cycle is perpetu-ated over time.

Blau and Kahn have shown that most of the differences in male and female "quitting" behavior can in fact be explained by the types of jobs women hold within the firm.[13] Women in jobs with better pay and pro-motional opportunities tend to be as stable as men. It is the women (and men) who occupy jobs with "built-in turnover," that is, low-paying, dead-end jobs, who exhibit unstable commitment to those jobs.

This cycle of self-fulfilling prophecy with respect to the stability of women's employment commitment may be one of the hardest to break, because it has set in motion so many adjustments in the private sphere. Higher-earning and more upwardly mobile male spouses have priority in determining both where the family locates (the "tied mover–tied stayer" syndrome) and who stays home or works part-time to care for children, sick parents, and the like. Women's erratic labor force behav-ior is, thus, reinforcing employers' unwillingness to train or promote them. This may be why women's greatest gains have occurred in those areas of the labor market where self-financed training and education are the primary criteria for being hired.

Employee Discrimination

Discrimination practiced by other employees may pressure employ-ers to discriminate. Again, we can explain this form of prejudice on eco-nomic grounds. To the extent that male employees have benefited from restricted competition in their occupations (artificially high pay due to limited entry, relatively easy access for those belonging to the "pre-ferred group") they do have something to lose from equal opportunity initiatives. Once the doors are opened wider to admit women (or minor-ities), the benefits of entry barriers are eroded. Ironically, the same man who would benefit from his wife's higher earning ability (higher house-hold income) in another field has a vested interest in excluding women from his own line of work.

Current employees may impose costs on the employer who tries to integrate the labor force. Since current employees usually train new workers, they may purposely do a poor job. If employee morale suffers, productivity may be lost. In short, the "adjustment costs" of integration may be high.[14] Firms have brought this issue up in defending their traditional hiring practices as a "business necessity." Over time, the courts have been less willing to accept this defense. Furthermore, employers who have long wanted to integrate their labor force now have a potent response to disgruntled workers: "It's the law!"

In the meantime, there have been many instances in which the first or lone woman in an occupational category or industry has been literally hounded out of the job because of the harassment or outright intimidation of her male coworkers. This makes "tokenism"—the hiring of one of a kind—both cruel and unproductive when integration is the long-term goal.[15]

The feedback mechanism of past discrimination is relevant here as well. Since women are the newest hires in many nontraditional areas of employment, they are also the most junior. Consequently, they are disproportionately vulnerable to cyclical downturns or structural changes in the workplace. The "adverse impact" of seniority rules on women (and other protected groups) is well known, but the U.S. Supreme Court has ruled that where legally negotiated and ratified seniority systems exist, they supersede the goals of affirmative action.[16] This decision implies that women will gain a strong foothold in nontraditional sectors of the labor market only after a long, sustained, stable period of economic prosperity—something lacking in the U.S. economy for some time now. Without that, the effects of past discrimination will be felt well into the future.

Customer Discrimination

Customers may also play a role in perpetuating past patterns of occupational segregation or employer discrimination. For example, people who feel quite comfortable entrusting their children to a female daycare worker may not be willing to trust their auto repairs or maintenance to a woman. The consumer who accepts the ministration of a female registered nurse without qualms may be less confident about having a woman administer anesthesia before surgery. Profit-maximizing employers must meet their customers' expectations (bowing to their prejudices) or risk losing business. Again, the firm may claim "business necessity" as a defense in explaining particular hiring practices.

But how significant is the prospect that customers will actually come face-to-face with the workers who produce a product or provide a service? It does not happen in most jobs in manufacturing, mining, agriculture, wholesale trade, or public utilities. Yet the service sector (in which customers are more likely to come into direct contact with service providers) now accounts for roughly 77 percent of all jobs in the U.S. economy.[17] Thus, if consumers are prejudiced in this area, it will have an impact on employer hiring patterns.

The fact is that women are relatively new (and, therefore, inexperienced) in some areas of the economy. A rational consumer may prefer an experienced dentist, for example, to perform a root canal. On the other hand, as the "face" of consumers themselves changes, so might expectations for the work force. A prominent example is car dealerships. Women buy nearly half the cars sold nowadays. Yet women complain that when they enter a dealership they are frequently patronized or, if they have brought along a husband or boyfriend, ignored—even though they are paying for the car.

Discrimination against women by employers, fellow employees, or customers is not always—or even usually—conscious and overt. The subtle barriers limiting women's access to formal schooling and on-the-job training, together with their different patterns of labor or experience in general, contribute to the perception that women are different from men in regard to their productivity and expertise, and the resulting statistical discrimination kicks in to reinforce or reproduce the differences.

WAGE DISCRIMINATION

Many economists would argue that past discrimination—and especially the resulting occupational segregation, with its crowded female labor markets—has dramatically skewed the wage structure. If, before passage of the Equal Pay Act[18] in 1963, firms could, and did, pay women less than men for doing the same work, then it is logical to assume that the entire wage structure has been affected by discrimination.

Blau looked at wage patterns in white-collar occupations and found that the firms that hired only women in a particular occupation paid lower wages than other firms that hired only men for that occupation.[19] This finding suggests that the wages for a particular job are set by virtue of whether the employer decides those jobs will be held by men or by women. If the firm decides to hire men for the job, then the "market rate" for men in that job prevails. But if it decides to hire women, then the standard is women's alternative (lower) wages. When women are employed in nontraditional occupations, their wages are still pegged to

156 female wage rates. One can see why men would be so opposed to seeing their occupations "integrated" by sex: Women's traditionally low-wage status can drive down the market wage in a traditionally male occupation. In fact, Treiman and Hartmann showed that in integrated areas of the labor market, men earn less than, and women more than, their gender cohorts with comparable human capital characteristics.[20] This illustrates why in the long run, men were ill advised to promote gender segregation, since the resulting wage differentials by sex could come back to haunt them.

Blau's findings suggest that when employers discriminate in favor of women for traditionally male jobs, they will be able to take advantage of the existing segregation to lower their own labor costs vis-à-vis the employer who hires from the traditional male group.[21] This will increase the resistance to integration by entrenched interests. Thus, we see how the effect of past discrimination will continue to bedevil attempts to undo it.

We should note, however, that the reverse is true when men take jobs in traditionally female labor markets. In this case men are paid wages commensurate with the relatively high pay set in male labor markets (for example, male secretaries and general office clerks earn more than their female counterparts).[22] If integration continues, this trend should raise wages in these female areas of the labor market.

What is more likely to happen within a firm is a clustering of jobs by sex. Often, to get around the Equal Pay Act, certain positions are filled by either men or women but not both. Some theorists suggest that the Equal Pay Act and Title VII have actually increased this practice within firms.[23]

Wage discrimination is illegal, but how can we ensure economic justice when the labor market remains segregated by gender within firms and across occupations. Bergmann's speculation that compensation for skills will eventually equalize in competitive labor markets is a long-term proposition.[24] It provides little hope for older women in the labor force who will find it particularly difficult either to change their human capital attributes—to compete in nontraditional jobs—or to wait until the market works its magic. These older female workers' education, training, and experience will continue to justify discrimination against them in the market. In the next section we will see how the courts and the EEOC have grappled with these residual inequalities. Older female members of the work force will bear the brunt of residual wage discrimination for the rest of their working lives. For them the only hope is the pay equity, or "comparable worth," approach to correcting wage rates.

Past discrimination will play havoc for years with efforts to establish competitive labor markets, simply because the labor market is a social environment. People have friends, acquaintances, networks in which information is passed regarding job opportunities, possible candidates, the mentoring process, and so on. Women, however, will have fewer of these networks, especially if they are alone and as long as they occupy distinctly different jobs within the firm. This disadvantage is one of the subtle barriers that is not amenable to legal recourse, and it explains why many successful women have made a conscious effort to establish beneficial mentor-protégé relationships with younger women. Yet they have to be in a position to do that. In the short run, then, even tokenism is better than continued exclusion.

Still another subtle barrier for women stemming from past discrimination is the prevalence of a male culture at the top of most corporations. While corporations report that women often add another dimension to the traditional management style (for example, leading by consensus rather than force), some men still may simply not feel comfortable around women. This unease would tend to limit women's opportunities to socialize and otherwise engage in out-of-office encounters where deals are made. Again, legal remedies are not practical; the situation merely reinforces the point that continued pursuit of affirmative action strategies (over sufficient time to allow the establishment of a critical mass of women in the corporate world) is needed.

Employment discrimination violates civil law and is therefore subject to prosecution. It is important that Congress has passed legislation making employment discrimination unlawful because, as we have shown, there is nothing inherent in the market process that automatically rights discrimination wrongs. We now turn to the passage, evolutionary interpretation, and practical application of laws against employment discrimination.

THE LAW ON EMPLOYMENT DISCRIMINATION

As the foregoing suggests, the forces contributing to and reproducing discriminatory employment practices and outcomes over time are complex. Not only are there unsavory prejudices among some employers, employees, and customers, but stereotypical thinking and pernicious

158   feedback mechanisms are at work as well. Finally, in the case of employment discrimination against women, there is the complicating factor of women's dual role in the market and domestic spheres.

Our understanding of the operation of discrimination is evolving. Important insights have emerged since 1964, when passage of Title VII of the Civil Rights Act and scholarly work focused attention on the issue. Title VII was vague on what constitutes discrimination. It specified, for example, that failure to hire because of gender or other noneconomic factors (race, religion, color, or national origin) was discriminatory and thus prohibited. But it then went on to state that it shall be an "unlawful employment practice to otherwise discriminate," without specifying what that meant.

For a time, the language of Title VII was interpreted as prohibiting discriminatory *intent* only, for example, making employment decisions motivated by animus or stereotyped thinking, as a result of which protected groups were judged and treated less favorably than otherwise. But even the narrow focus on "discriminatory intent" engendered disagreement. For example, is it discrimination to treat pregnant women differently from other workers? The U.S. Supreme Court in 1976 said that it was not. The employer was not distinguishing between men and women, but between "pregnant women and nonpregnant persons."[25] In response, Congress adopted the Pregnancy Discrimination Act of 1978, which defined differential treatment based on pregnancy to be sex discrimination.

But by far the most serious disagreement about what constitutes discrimination has occurred in assessing employment practices that have an adverse *impact* (or disparate impact) on protected groups. In *Griggs v. Duke Power Co.*[26] the U.S. Supreme Court expanded the definition of discrimination to encompass not only intent but impact. In *Griggs*, the Court found *both* that the hiring standard used by Duke Power had an adverse impact on a protected group *and* that its requirements were not job-related. In its defense, the Duke Power Company argued for the use of tests that measured "general abilities and aptitudes." However, the Court concluded that tests must bear a more intimate relationship to the necessities of the work. In effect, the employer had attempted to circumvent Title VII by using the ruse of "business necessity," which under Title VII justifies screening employees.

Many criticized the change from the traditional definition of discriminatory intent to one of discriminatory impact as opening the door to preferential treatment for women and minorities—leading to quotas, a concern for group representation in the workplace rather than justice for individuals, and a new form of reverse discrimination.[27] For those who support the disparate impact approach, however, insistence on finding evidence of discriminatory intent seems quite irrelevant. The history and complexity of employment practices are such that practices harming specific groups can be institutionalized without there being any way to attribute discriminatory intent to any one employer. For those supporting the impact approach, the only way to break the patterns of employment practices is to approach the problem from the result, rather than the original intent.

The Business Necessity Defense

The *Griggs* case concluded that barriers to employment that had an adverse impact on protected groups were allowed only when justified by business necessity. In other words, in the Court's view, Congress had placed on "the employer the burden of showing that any given requirement must have a manifest relationship to the employment in question."[28] Once it is found that the consequences of the employer's conduct (with respect to the requirements of certificates, diplomas, or test results) have an adverse effect on minorities, the burden of proof shifts to the employer (that is, the employer must prove business necessity in imposing the hiring standards).

This shift was important because certain groups may perform more poorly on some types of test instruments. The crucial question is whether these test results are pertinent to job performance. If the screening devices disproportionately remove members of protected groups from the competition, *then* the onus is on the employer to show that they are job-related. The *Griggs* decision made it clear that the defense of business necessity under Title VII would not be permitted simply because it would be more convenient for the employer.

**Bona Fide Occupational Qualifications and
Statistical Discrimination**

Title VII, which generally prohibits employers from classifying people according to noneconomic factors such as sex, race, religion, national origin, or age, does make an exception. The framers of the act recognized that these factors (except race) might, in special circumstances, be a legitimate concern of an employer. For example, Congress

160   did not want to force a Catholic school preparing young men for the priesthood to hire Protestants as teachers. The interpretation of bona fide occupational qualification (BFOQ) was clearly crucial to the application of the act.

Whether employers were using a BFOQ as a pretext for continuing their discriminatory practices or out of legitimate concern for the welfare of their employees (perhaps out of fear of future litigation, as is considered in Chapter 5's discussion of the exclusion of women of reproductive age from certain jobs), the issue in law became what stood the test of a BFOQ. In a landmark case, *Cheatwood v. South Central Bell Telephone*, Cheatwood charged that her employer discriminated against her by refusing to consider her, or any women, for the post of commercial representative.[29] Her employer's defense was that being male was a BFOQ because, in the course of the representative's work, the representative would occasionally have to collect coin boxes weighing sixty to ninety pounds; possibly have to enter bars, poolrooms, and other such locations to deal with financial matters, complaints, and delinquencies; and occasionally might have to change a tire on the company car. The court rejected the BFOQ defense, ruling that the company had discriminated in failing to consider Cheatwood's application. The court reasoned that though it might be rational for the employer to discriminate against women as a class because

> on average, men can perform these tasks somewhat more efficiently and perhaps somewhat more safely than women . . . it appears . . . it will not impose a hardship on this Employer to determine on an individual basis whether a person is qualified for the position. . . . It is manifest that the use of this class distinction deprives some women of what they regard as a lucrative and otherwise desirable position.[30]

The importance of *Cheatwood* was that it required the company to consider candidates individually, rather than relying on its view—with which the court concurred—that women on average were less qualified than men.

In other words, it was a ruling against statistical discrimination. The employer was penalizing an individual for belonging to a group rather than judging that individual's characteristics or actual performance. Despite the fact that acquiring information about individuals may be costly, it is illegal to exclude someone for this reason.[31] It is not relevant whether the employer's assumptions about women's abilities are true, on average. People have the right to be considered on their own merits and not disadvantaged by their sex.

Affirmative Action

Title VII allowed for the use of affirmative action to redress the effects of past discrimination. Although affirmative action plans are mandatory only for federal agencies and contractors, most large private firms have voluntarily undertaken such plans in the past thirty years.

Affirmative action plans consist of a set of goals and timetables developed by the firm and the EEOC. These plans are tailored to the individual firm and demography of the region. For example, if the firm estimates that it will need to hire a hundred employees over the next two years, and 30 percent of the labor force in the hiring area are women, the goal would be that 30 percent of the new hires would be women. If affirmative action plans are not fulfilled, the EEOC can challenge the employer. When courts have found a willful negligence on the part of the employer (for example, qualified members of the protected group applied and the employment projections were correct yet minority hiring goals were not met) in some cases they have imposed hiring quotas on the employer. This has happened most frequently in regard to public employers such as school districts, law enforcement agencies, and fire departments—all of whom receive some portion of their funding from the federal government.[32]

Affirmative action plans and hiring quotas have frequently been conflated in the public perception. As such they have generated considerable political backlash, especially as conditions in the labor market deteriorated after 1973.

A variety of views are held about affirmative action.[33] There are those who argue that there is no conclusive evidence of past discrimination and that, even if there had been, making it illegal (as Title VII did) is sufficient to end the problem. According to this view, affirmative action is not needed. Others accept the need for limited affirmative action but oppose the use of goals and timetables for fear that they will constitute de facto quotas. Even among those who support affirmative action more broadly, opinions differ as to whether it should take the form of sincere efforts to find and encourage fully qualified candidates from the protected groups or should extend to preferential treatment to overcome the effects of past discrimination.

162   The U.S. Supreme Court has found, amid much controversy, that employment preferences are legal under certain circumstances. Specifically, employers can voluntarily give preference to women and minorities as a temporary measure to remedy manifest imbalances in traditionally segregated jobs.[34]

Most affirmative action programs have not required such preferences. Virtually all the employers included in a sample of government contractors, for example, stated that no lowering of employment standards was necessary to achieve the company's affirmative action objectives.[35] Furthermore, it has been found that affirmative action programs caused many firms to implement wider and more systematic search procedures and to develop more objective criteria and procedures for hiring and promotion. In a survey reported by *Fortune* magazine, 90 percent of firms claimed that they had established numerical objectives for affirmative action, in part to satisfy corporate objectives unrelated to government regulations. Perhaps most impressive, 95 percent stated that they planned to continue to use numerical objectives regardless of government requirements. In May 1985, the directors of the National Association of Manufacturers adopted a policy statement supporting affirmative action as "good business policy," adding that "goals, not quotas, are the standards to be followed."[36]

All this evidence suggests that the backlash against affirmative action is coming not so much from employers but from those in the work force who see their prospects dimmed by increased competition. The backlash will necessarily be stronger when unemployment and underemployment are generally high, and the gains of one group may actually come at the expense of another.

If the 1970s and early 1980s were watershed years for attempts to integrate blue-collar areas of the labor market in unfavorable economic conditions, the late 1980s and early 1990s were equally difficult in the white-collar world. By this time corporate downsizing, outsourcing, and computerization of tasks had begun to affect lower and middle management as well as an entire range of clerical occupations, often referred to as "pink collar" (filing, data entry, billing, and accounting). The move to reclassify previous full-time positions as part-time and to subcontract out work has had a dramatic effect on the labor market. In 1993 the largest employer in the United States was Manpower, Inc., a temporary services agency.[37] In this context the struggle of women to gain access to positions within a firm that provides training and access to career ladders has become even more difficult.

As conditions for wage earners in general have deteriorated, the backlash against affirmative action has increased. During Reagan's first term, the EEOC announced that henceforth, rather than employers having to prove that they were not practicing unlawful discrimination, the claimant had to prove that they were.[38] This policy change made it difficult for individuals with limited access to the firm's internal documents and restricted financial resources. In fact, the major cases considered during the 1980s tended to be suits filed by employees already working in the firm who had been relegated to lower rungs of the corporate hierarchy.[39] The Civil Rights Act of 1991 subsequently shifted the burden of proof back to the employer and raised the costs of (penalties for) intentional discrimination.

Comparable Worth

Comparable worth or pay equity entails "equal pay for jobs of comparable worth." Proponents start from the position that labor markets are segmented (by sex and race) and that this segmentation has artificially lowered earnings for some occupations and inflated earnings in others.[40] Sixty percent of the women in the U.S. labor force would have to move into "male" occupations in order to create a completely integrated work force and thereby eliminate the effects of segregation on the wage structure.[41] Ergo, unless we are willing to wait until occupational integration occurs (a very long-term strategy), we should examine the current pay structure to identify the earnings disparities that are the result of this segmentation. Pay equity strategies identify the compensable factors associated with a job (that is, the skills required to perform the job) and estimate its worth to the firm. In some instances, for example, physical strength may be needed; in others math or writing skills are essential. The point is to be able to compare *different* jobs in terms of their worth to the firm.

Despite the fact that the pay equity movement has been much criticized, historically many firms have used such job evaluation systems. They are common in unionized establishments, for example, where employees have demanded an accounting for pay differentials among workers.

The best-known "pay equity" case is *AFSCME v. State of Washington*.[42] In the early 1970s, the Washington Federation of State Employees, a union affiliated with AFSCME (the American Federation of State, County and Municipal Employees, AFL-CIO), and the Washington State

Women's Council pressed the state government in Washington to look at differences in the salaries it assigned its employees in male- and female-dominated jobs. In the ensuing comparable worth study, performed in 1974, the personnel consultants hired by the state government used four "compensable factors" (knowledge and skills, mental demands, accountability, and work conditions) and rated jobs by assigning points to each factor. For example, secretarial jobs were rated modestly higher than those of auto mechanics and considerably ahead of delivery truck drivers on the knowledge and skill factor. On the other hand, the jobs of both mechanics and truck drivers were rated higher on the working conditions factor because of the lifting and occasional danger inherent in those jobs. Similarly, a registered nurse's job was evaluated as higher than that of a civil engineer but lower than that of a senior computer analyst on the knowledge and skills factor. The nurse's job was judged to make higher mental demands on the worker than the engineer's because the former required analysis that is less cut-and-dried than the latter. In this way, all the job titles in the employment structure of the state of Washington were evaluated, and each job was assigned a total number of points. The results were as the unions had surmised: The existing pay structure could not be justified on the basis of the skills required for the job but correlated closely with whether or not the job was held primarily by men or by women (for examples see Table 5).

The study made clear that in jobs held primarily by men relative wages did correspond to relative point scores. But the pay for jobs performed primarily by women was out of line with their point scores. Nurses were paid less than auto mechanics, and secretaries less than

Table 5 Comparable Worth Ratings for Selected Occupations

Job Title	Total Points Awarded	1985 Salary/Week ($)
Sr. computer systems analyst	372	553
Registered nurse	341	411
Civil engineer	287	513
Secretary III (highest level)	197	306
Auto mechanic	175	465
Delivery truck driver	97	382

Source: Adapted from data presented in *AFSCME v. State of Washington*, 770 F.2d 1401 (9th Cir. 1985).

delivery truck drivers. The state of Washington claims to have paid attention to market rates in each occupation. However, the market had assigned job skills in predominantly female occupations a lower value than the same skills in jobs done mainly by men.

Now the nub of the argument against pay equity strategies is that employers (whether in the private or public and nonprofit sectors) should pay the prevailing rate for a certain type of labor, because to pay more than is necessary is economic suicide (or fiscal irresponsibility). The idea that the market rate must be forcibly altered is, in this view, anathema to the free-market system.

After the Washington state study was published, the advocates of comparable worth urged the governor and the state legislature to raise salary levels in women's jobs in accordance with its results. Almost ten years later, however, little had been accomplished. In 1983, therefore, the union filed suit in *AFSCME v. State of Washington*. The judge in the case ruled that not only should salaries in women's occupations be raised immediately but that back wages should also be paid, since the state had known of the disparities since 1973.

In 1985, however, an appeals court reversed the judge's ruling. The political climate was hostile to such a precedent-setting ruling, which, if allowed to stand, would set the stage for massive litigation by unions or other employee organizations.

Ultimately, in 1986, the state and the union agreed to raise women's salaries gradually to achieve pay equity based on point scores by 1993—twenty-five years after the case was initiated and without back pay.

At present, the comparable worth approach to improving pay in predominantly female occupations in the United States has been used successfully only in the public sector, for example, the City of New York, the State of New York, and the City of San Jose, California.[43] Not surprisingly, the private sector has eschewed undertaking such studies and confronting the probable pay adjustments that would ensue. However, if enough change were achieved in the public sectors, the private sector—especially the largest firms—would feel "market pressure" to follow suit and pay the "new" prevailing wage. Meanwhile, the province of Ontario in Canada passed a bill in 1988 requiring *public and private* sector employers to pay the same wages to women performing jobs different from, but of equal value to, those performed by men in the same unit.[44]

We have now discussed the three major concepts guiding the determi-

166   nation of discrimination: evil motive (animus on the part of employers or current employees), disparate impact (hiring standards or work rules that negatively affect women), and unequal treatment through pay disparities. The movement from proof of "intent to discriminate" to proof of "discriminatory impact" has been particularly important in expanding the scope of our antidiscrimination laws to confront the status quo. This is so because the feedback mechanisms of past discrimination will continue to affect women's human capital attributes (education, training, labor force experiences, and the division of labor within the family) for years. Equal access *alone*, therefore, will not change women's prospects greatly. For this reason affirmative action has been a linchpin in the effort to break the cycle of inequality.

Indeed, women's relative earnings and occupational distribution did not change noticeably over time prior to 1964, but notable progress has been made since the 1964 law was passed. While for the first six decades of this century women's earnings were 59 percent of men's, in the last three decades this proportion increased to 70 percent. Unfortunately, it has been estimated that 75 percent of the shift was due to a fall in men's wages, not growth in female wages.[45] Similarly, women have made significant gains since 1960 in the professional and managerial ranks. But these represent less than 0.5 percent of all employed women.[46]

An area less amenable to change through legal means is, of course, women's domestic constraints: the unequal division of labor in the home by gender. Here the policies of the other advanced industrial nations have much to teach us. In Europe especially, policies to reduce the negative labor market consequences of the decision to have children, have been in place—in some cases for generations.

OTHER ADVANCED INDUSTRIAL NATIONS

A higher percentage of single mothers participate in market work in other industrial nations than in the United States, partly because they have access to publicly provided services (day care, health benefits, and other subsidies), which are absent for that population in this country.[47] There is no political dissent in Europe over providing these subsidies, because they are universally available. In France, for example, child and family allowances are paid to all, regardless of income. In Germany, "kinder care," including summer camps, is universally available. Health care is provided for all, regardless of income, in Canada, Germany, and the United Kingdom. Some of these policies have been in place for many decades. France instituted *paid* maternity leaves in 1911 and state-sponsored child care in the early 1950s.[48] The cost of child care and job interruptions caused by childbearing falls on the state, not on the parents themselves.

Table 6 presents the maternity protection, benefits, length of leave, and year of their enactment in eight industrialized countries. It is notable that *only* in the United States did the leave come so late (1993) and is the leave *unpaid*. For all families in Europe and Canada, the loss of income due to the decision to have a child is greatly mitigated. As Table 6 shows, *paid* leaves replace from 60 percent to 100 percent of prior pay during the leave in Europe and Canada, whereas in the United States the decision to take a leave entails the loss of the entire income.

The upshot of the various policies is that in Canada and Europe, while the inherent rate of poverty (that is, the rate of poverty due to economic conditions) is no lower than in the United States (and in some countries, such as Sweden, is actually much higher), the *effective* rate of poverty is much lower. In other words, government policies in Europe and Canada are much more effective in reducing poverty than they are in the United States. For example, in Sweden, which has about the same proportion of female-headed households as exist in the United States, the combination of labor market and social policies pursued for four decades has produced a lower rate of poverty in single-parent families than in the United States. In 1988 American single parents were six times as likely to be poor as their Swedish counterparts.[49]

In sum, there are three noticeable differences between the United States and the other industrial nations stemming from their array of programs and subsidies: lower rates of poverty, higher rates of labor force participation among female household heads, and protection of household incomes in connection with the decision to have children.

On the other hand, it is clear that the European policies have focused more on subsidies than on achieving equality of employment opportunity. The similarity in the patterns of occupational segregation across the national boundaries is striking. As in the United States, women in Europe and Canada tend to be concentrated in the "caring occupations" (health care, education, child care, elderly care) and in clerical services. A commonly used measure of occupational segregation is the Index of Segregation, which is arrived at by calculating the percentage of one group that would have to change jobs in order for the occupational distribution of the sexes to be the same. As Table 7 shows, the United

Table 6   Maternity Protection, Benefits, and Year of Enactment in Eight Industrialized Countries

Country	Year Enacted	Reemployment and Protection of Acquired Job Rights	Length of *Paid* Leave	Pay During Leave as % of Prior Pay
Canada	1971	Yes	15 weeks	60%
France	1975	Yes	16 weeks	90
Italy	1971	Yes, job must be held for one year	20 weeks	80
The Netherlands	1976	Yes	12 weeks	100
Sweden	1976	Yes	36 weeks	90% for first 8 months, $16 a day for last month
U.K.	1975	Yes, provided worker returns within 29 weeks after childbirth	6 weeks	90
U.S.A.	1993	Yes	0 12 weeks *unpaid*	0
West Germany	1972	Yes	14 weeks	100

Source: Adapted from the following information: Six Western European Countries: T. Kennedy, *European Labor Relations* (Lexington, MA: D. C. Heath, 1980); Canada: G. S. Goldberg and E. Kremen, eds. *The Feminization of Poverty* (NY: Praeger, 1990); U.S.A.: N. Woloch, *Women and the American Experience*, 2nd ed. (NY: McGraw-Hill, 1994).

States scores better than the other industrial nations in this respect. In the United States the index stands at 36.6, suggesting that roughly one out of three women would have to move into male-dominated occupations for an equal distribution to occur. In Japan, the inequality is greatest on this measure.

Laws exist in all the countries to promote equal employment opportunity and equal pay, yet the gains appear to be greatest in the United States. In the long run, real gains for women are achieved by equal opportunity. If income inequalities are smoothed by government subsidies, then the need to pursue higher-paying employment may not be as urgent in these other countries. Yet what government gives, government can later take away. Western Europe and Canada face the same global competitive pressures as U.S. businesses. Movements are already under way to chip away at the social services as budget deficits become common in the other advanced industrial countries. For example, in Sweden there is a move to reduce parental leave benefits from 90 percent of prior pay to 80 percent.[50] Thus, in the long run, the U.S. model—using market-based strategies to promote gender equality—may be a more lasting means of improving women's economic status.

POLICY PRESCRIPTIONS FOR THE UNITED STATES

Thirty years after passage of our equal employment opportunity laws we know several things without question. One is that positive action

Table 7   Index of Segregation, Selected Countries

Country	Index (%)
Austria	44.5
Belgium	38.5
Canada	39.8
Denmark	48.0
France	38.4
Germany (FR)	36.9
Japan	48.9
Netherlands	38.5
Norway	46.3
Sweden	39.3
U.K.	44.5
U.S.A.	36.6

Source: International Labor Organization, *Yearbook of Labor Statistics, 1989–90* (New York: Oxford University Press, 1991).

170   to break the cycle of educational and employment barriers for women has achieved more in three decades than two hundred years of free-market activity. Affirmative action in particular, by imposing compliance targets and timetables, effectively disrupted a long-standing equilibrium and thus has begun to break down barriers. As the barriers in education, training, and employment were reduced, women demonstrated their desire to compete in many formerly male bastions of the labor market. But until equality is much closer and the barriers permanently removed, we must ensure that affirmative action continues.

Another thing we know is that women's parental role—unlike men's—continues to constrain their time and, therefore, their ability to compete at the educational, training, and experience levels. Particularly for poorer women, child-care costs may make it a rational choice not to compete at all. As long as we have a social safety net, and inadequate support services, this phenomenon will continue. If the safety net disappears, the consequence for low-earning women and their children may be disastrous: children left alone while the single parent works, loss of health care, and food stamps. Because women as a group are poorer than men, public subsidies to higher education are particularly important for women. In short, public subsidies to education and support services are desirable for both men and women but crucial for women, given that the latter are more likely to be poor in their own right.

Finally, a strong commitment to full employment is the only way to defuse the backlash against women (and minorities) from white men, whose positions are being threatened primarily by structural changes in the economy but who may regard their plight as caused by affirmative action, antipoverty programs, and the like. The record shows that competition over scarce employment has led to battles drawn along racial, ethnic, and gender lines. Rather than redistributing access to a limited number of preferred jobs, it is preferable to ensure employment for all groups. To the extent that a philosophy of full employment operates in this country, it is of the "trickle down" variety. This has proven woefully inadequate. It also has the undesirable social effect of polarizing different demographic groups in pursuit of scarce employment.

It is immediately obvious that affirmative action, public subsidies, and a strengthened safety net are not current priorities in this country. In fact the GOP's "Contract with America" would clearly set us back on all three. Affirmative action is under attack, public subsidies are under attack, and dismantling the social safety net will only exacerbate competition for jobs—thus driving down wages, increasing tensions among groups, and so on. While we know what works to improve women's status, present policy is clearly moving in the opposite direction.

What is the employer likely to do in an environment where there is no pressure to alter traditional hiring patterns; where hiring, training, and promotion decisions are still overwhelmingly in the hands of white males; and where subsidies that might enable women to compete no longer exist? If history is a guide to the future, the small gains made from the momentum built up in the past thirty years may not survive the backlash, much less enable us to move forward. We are truly at a crossroads. We can go forward, or we can go back. Do we have confidence that the corporate world—still dominated by a white male elite—will continue to move in a progressive direction without being pushed? Are there enough women with sufficient leverage to ensure that they do? It will be ten years before we know whether the past thirty years were enough to break the age-old patterns permanently. Should we be "cautiously optimistic," or should we prepare our daughters to fight the old battles once again?

NOTES

1. U.S. Bureau of Labor Statistics, *Employment and Earnings* (Washington, DC: Government Printing Office, January 1990).

2. G. S. Goldberg and E. Kremen, eds. *The Feminization of Poverty, Only in America?* (New York: Praeger, 1990), 205.

3. Title IX, 1972, which prohibits discrimination on the basis of sex in educational programs.

4. M. Corcoran and G. J. Duncan, "Work History, Labor-Force Attachment, and Earnings Differences Between the Races and Sexes," *Journal of Human Resources* 14 (Winter 1979): 3–20.

5. P. England, "The Failure of Human Capital Theory to Explain Occupational Sex Segregation," *Journal of Human Resources* 17 (1982): 358–370; D. Treiman and H. Hartmann, eds. *Women, Work and Wages: Equal Pay for Jobs of Equal Value* (Washington, DC: National Academy Press, 1981).

6. B. R. Bergmann, "Occupational Segregation, Wages and Profits When Employers Discriminate by Race or Sex," *Eastern Economic Journal* 1 (1974): 561–73.

7. The implicit assumption is that once barriers on the demand side of the market are removed, women (and minorities) will make adjustments in their supply-side characteristics to take advantage of the new opportunities. We should just note here that for women in particular, the dual role will still impose constraints. In the short run, unless there is a cultural revolu-

172 tion in which child rearing and housework is shared equally, women's ability to compete in the new environment will depend on access to affordable day care, formal leave policies that protect acquired seniority rights in jobs and benefits, and the like—such as are routine in some other advanced industrial countries.

8. However this last is not always applicable; in government, unionized jobs, and professional specialty occupations starting rates are set and are not negotiable.

9. G. S. Becker, *The Economics of Discrimination* (Chicago: University of Chicago Press, 1971).

10. *Griggs v. Duke Power Co.*, 401 U.S. 424 (1971).

11. E. Phelps, "The Statistical Theory of Racism and Sexism," *American Economic Review* 62 (1972): 659–61.

12. K. Arrow, "The Theory of Discrimination," in *Discrimination in Labor Markets*, ed. O. Ashenfelter and A. Rees (Princeton, NJ: Princeton University Press, 1973), 23–33.

13. F. D. Blau and L. M. Kahn, "Race and Sex Differences in Quits by Young Workers," *Industrial and Labor Relations Review* 34, no. 4 (1981): 563–77.

14. Arrow, "The Theory of Discrimination."

15. R. Kanter, *Men and Women of the Corporation* (New York: Basic Books, 1977).

16. *Firefighters Local 1784 v. Stotts*, 467 U.S. 561 (1984).

17. U.S. Bureau of Labor Statistics, *Employment and Earnings* (Washington, DC: Government Printing Office, July 1993), 6–8.

18. 29 U.S.C. 206(d).

19. F. D. Blau, *Equal Pay in the Office* (Lexington, MA: Lexington Books, 1977).

20. Treiman and Hartmann, eds. *Women, Work and Wages.*

21. Blau, *Equal Pay in the Office.*

22. Ibid.

23. C. Lloyd, ed. *Sex, Discrimination and the Division of Labor* (New York: Columbia University Press, 1975).

24. Bergmann, "Occupational Segregation, Wages and Profits."

25. *General Electric Co. v. Gilbert*, 429 U.S. 125, 138 (1976).

26. *Griggs.*

27. P. Burstein, ed. *Equal Employment Opportunity, Labor Market Discrimination and Public Policy* (New York: Walter De Gruyter, 1994).

28. *Griggs*, 432.

29. *Cheatwood v. South Central Bell Telephone*, 303 F. Supp. 54 (M.D. Ala. 1969).

30. Ibid., 54.

31. Phelps, "The Statistical Theory of Racism."

32. D. Wise, ed. *Public Sector Payrolls* (Chicago: University of Chicago Press, 1987), 243–88; "Courts Change Course," *New York Times* (March 27, 1987): 1.

33. See F. D. Blau and M. A. Ferber, *The Economics of Women, Men and Work*, 2nd ed. (Englewood Cliffs, NJ: Prentice Hall, 1992).

34. *Steel Workers v. Weber*, 443 U.S. 193 (1979) and *Johnson v. Santa Clara County Transportation Agency*, 480 U.S. 616 (1987).

35. Center for National Policy Review, *Employee Relations Weekly* 1, no. 2 (September 12, 1983): 45.

36. A. B. Fisher, "Businessmen Like to Hire by the Numbers," *Fortune* 112, no. 6 (September 1985): 26–30.

37. "Use of Disposable Workers on the Rise," *Buffalo News* (April 17, 1994): F1.

38. *Wards Cove Packing Co. v. Atonio*, 109 S.Ct. 2115 (1989).

39. See, for example, *Morgan v. Hertz Corporation*, 542 F. Supp. 123 (1981). This case involved the denial of promotion to two female car rental agents who had applied for promotion to station manager on four occasions when vacancies had arisen. They were turned down and the vacancies were filled by men, some of whom had less experience. Though most Hertz rental agents are women and experience as a rental agent qualifies a person to become station manager, Hertz had promoted very few women. Those who had been promoted were forced to struggle or file charges to get the promotions. The court found that the firm mobilized its resources to back managers known to be discriminating against women in regard to promotions. The Hertz case would have been nearly impossible for the plaintiffs to lose, given the circumstances. The city manager for Hertz in Memphis—who was directly responsible for denying the promotions—had been known to voice his opinion that a woman should not be station manager. Further, high-level company officials had induced an employee to sign a false statement denying that the city manager had made sexist statements. They also induced one the previously promoted female managers to sign a statement condemning the female plaintiffs' abilities (these false statements were later recanted under oath). In other words, the firm supported discriminatory policies.

40. See, for example, Treiman and Hartmann, eds. *Women, Work and Wages*.

41. Goldberg and Kremen, eds. *The Feminization of Poverty*, 25.

42. *AFSCME v. State of Washington*, 770 F.2d 1410 (9th Cir. 1985).

43. R. Steinberg, L. Hagner et al., *New York State Pay Equity Study*, Research Report (Albany, NY: The Center for Women in Government, March 1986).

44. Goldberg and Kremen, eds. *The Feminization of Poverty*, 72.

45. "The Truth About Women's Pay," *Working Woman* (April 1993): 52.

174   46. Goldberg and Kremen, eds. *The Feminization of Poverty,* 25.
47. Ibid.
48. Ibid., 117.
49. Ibid., 202.
50. "Swedish Plan Cuts Family, Worker Benefits," *Buffalo News* (Jan. 11, 1995): A3.

REFERENCES

Arrow, K. 1973. The theory of discrimination. In *Discrimination in Labor Markets,* ed. O. Ashenfelter and A. Rees, 23–33. Princeton, NJ: Princeton University Press.

Becker, G. S. 1971. *The Economics of Discrimination.* Chicago: University of Chicago Press.

Bergmann, B. R. 1974. Occupational segregation, wages and profits when employers discriminate by race or sex. *Eastern Economic Journal* 1: 561–73.

Blau, F. D. 1977. *Equal Pay in the Office.* Lexington, MA: Lexington Books.

Blau, F. D. and L. M. Kahn. 1981. Race and sex differences in quits by young workers. *Industrial and Labor Relations Review* 34(4): 563–77.

Center for National Policy Review. 1983. *Employee Relations Weekly* 1(September 12): 45.

Corcoran, M. and G. J. Duncan. 1979. Work history, labor-force attachment, and earnings differences between races and sexes. *Journal of Human Resources* 14 (Winter): 3–20.

Courts change course. 1987. *New York Times* March 27: 1.

England, P. 1982. The failure of human capital theory to explain occupational sex segregation. *Journal of Human Resources* 17: 358–70.

Feiner, S. F. 1994. *Race and Gender in the American Economy.* Englewood Cliffs, NJ: Prentice Hall.

Fisher, A. B. 1985. Businessmen like to hire by the numbers. *Fortune* 112(September): 26–30.

Goldberg, G. S. and E. Kremen, eds. 1990. *The Feminization of Poverty, Only in America?* New York: Praeger.

International Labor Organization. 1991. *Yearbook of Labor Statistics, 1989–90.* New York: Oxford University Press.

Kanter, R. 1977. *Men and Women of the Corporation.* New York: Basic Books.

Kennedy, T. 1980. *European Labor Relations.* Lexington, MA: D. C. Heath.

Lloyd, C., ed. 1975. *Sex, Discrimination and the Division of Labor.* New York: Columbia University Press.

Phelps, E. S. 1972. The statistical theory of racism and sexism. *American Economic Review* 62: 559–66.

Steinberg, R., L. Hagner, L. Possin, A. Chertos and D. Trieman. 1986. *New York State Pay Equity Study*, Research Report, March. Albany, NY: Center for Women in Government.

Swedish plan cuts family, worker benefits. 1995. *Buffalo News* January 11: A3.

Treiman, D. and H. Hartmann, eds. 1981. *Women, Work and Wages: Equal Pay for Jobs of Equal Value.* Washington, DC: National Academy Press.

The truth about women's pay. 1993. *Working Woman* April: 52.

U.S. Bureau of the Census. 1970. *Detailed Occupations of the Experienced Civilian Labor Force by Sex for the United States and Regions.* Washington, DC: Government Printing Office.

———. 1985. *Statistical Abstract of the United States.* Washington, DC: Government Printing Office.

U.S. Bureau of Labor Statistics. 1984. *Employment and Earnings* January. Washington, DC: Government Printing Office.

———. 1986. *Weekly Earnings of Wage and Salary Workers, 4th Qtr. 1985* February 3. Washington, DC: Government Printing Office.

———. 1990. *Employment and Earnings* January. Washington, DC: Government Printing Office.

Use of disposable workers on the rise. 1994. *Buffalo News* April 17: F1.

Wise, D., ed. 1987. *Public Sector Payrolls.* Chicago: University of Chicago Press.

Woloch, N. 1994. *Women and the American Experience,* 2nd ed. New York: McGraw-Hill.

EXCLUSIONARY POLICIES IN THE WORKPLACE

A Corporate Response to the Threat of Reproductive Risk

Donna M. Randall

Over the last several decades, the number of women in the work force has increased significantly. By 1990 women constituted 45 percent of the U.S. labor force,[1] and this accelerated growth of women into the labor pool is expected to continue over the next decade. Of the 26 million net increase in the civilian labor force anticipated between 1990 and 2005, women will account for 15 million, or 62 percent, of net growth.

Women have not only moved in greater numbers into the work force; more significant, since the late 1970s they have moved in greater numbers into traditionally male-dominated jobs.[2] In the past women were denied entry into certain unionized, blue-collar jobs. Due to considerable pressure exerted by the EEOC and the Office of Federal Contract Compliance, barriers into these professions have been largely removed. Many firms have now established, voluntarily or by court order, affirmative action programs to recruit and retain female employees at all levels.[3]

Accompanying the expanding numbers of women entering the workplace has been a growing concern about the potential effects of toxic exposure on the female reproductive system. Such concern has coalesced into corporate policies that prevent fertile women from working around toxic substances. Such policies are, paradoxically, at the same time overinclusive and underinclusive in their concern for the reproductive health of workers.

The following sections outline the nature of occupational hazards facing employees, describe the corporate response to such threats (exclusionary policies), and discuss the consequences of these corporate restrictions. Exclusionary policies maintained by three companies—Bunker Hill, American Cyanamid, and Johnson Controls—are then ex-

178   plored in more depth. Finally, the chapter addresses several troubling issues raised by the development and implementation of those exclusionary policies and offers suggestions for coping with the threat of reproductive risk.

HAZARDS FACING WOMEN IN THE WORKPLACE

Of the nearly 3.5 million known chemicals, 65,000 are in commercial use. Approximately 5,000 new chemicals are introduced each year; the plastics industry alone uses approximately 2,500 different chemicals or mixtures. Due to the tremendous number of chemicals currently in use and under development, scientific information is lacking on the toxic effects of approximately 80 percent of chemicals in commercial use in the United States.[4]

The limited data that exist reveal that an occupational exposure to toxic chemicals could very well affect a worker's capacity to produce normal children. Over fifty years ago, the U.S. Department of Labor recommended that pregnant women should avoid workplace exposure to specified toxic substances. However, the issue came to public prominence in the mid-1970s with the publication of a U.S. Department of Health, Education, and Welfare report on occupational health problems of pregnant women.[5]

Despite the long-standing public concern expressed over potential reproductive hazards, the toxic effects on the human reproductive system, using animal or human data, have been estimated in only 1 percent of chemicals.[6] Although only 30 to 40 of the 79,000 chemicals on the National Institute of Occupational Safety and Health (NIOSH) registry are proven human teratogens, over 1,000 exhibit some teratogenic potential in animal studies.[7] As a consequence, there are no reliable estimates of the extent of reproductive risk in the workplace.[8] Yet while the exact number of workplace hazards is unknown and the precise manner in which many chemicals affect the development of the fetus is unclear, a growing body of evidence from both animal and human studies strongly suggests that workplace exposures are clearly linked to fetal harm.[9]

Moreover, the consequences of reproductive hazards can be devastating. Research evidence reveals that reproductive hazards can serve as mutagens (causing irreparable changes in the DNA of the chromosomes of either parent), teratogens (causing damage to the embryo in the first eight weeks of pregnancy or to the fetus from eight weeks to birth), or as gametotoxins (causing damage to egg and sperm cells before fertilization). Other reproductive hazards may cause impotence, reduced sexual drive, or irregular periods.

Women involved in the metal, chemical, wood, textile, and farm industries and medical technicians are at increased reproductive risk.[10] To illustrate, a Finnish study revealed that female textile workers experienced one of the highest rates in their country of spontaneous abortion.[11] Similarly, a Swedish study found an increased rate of spontaneous abortion among both female employees and wives of male workers in rayon textile jobs.[12] Peters et al. found that the highest rates of stillbirth and neonatal deaths correlated with women working in the glass and pottery industry, hospitals, laundry/dry cleaning, the chemical industry, woodworking, and furniture manufacturing.[13] An increase in miscarriages among women involved in sterilizing instruments in hospitals has also been noted, most likely due to exposure to ethylene oxide.[14]

In addition to these health concerns, corporations have perceived the economic consequences of fetal damage due to workplace exposure to be potentially devastating. A child born with defects or diseases caused by parental exposure to toxic chemicals might bring personal injury action against the company. Even though no lawsuit on behalf of a child born with occupationally induced birth defects has been won, Katz argued that employers' fear of future tort liability is legitimate, because of the economic ramifications of huge damage claims and the resulting negative publicity.[15] Workers' compensation laws do not cover claims by children with injuries resulting from their parents' employment in a toxic work environment. The parents cannot legally waive the right of the fetus to sue for damages in the future.

COPING WITH HAZARDS IN THE WORKPLACE: EXCLUSIONARY POLICIES

The growing number of women entering the workplace, the rising concern about the possibility and consequences of reproductive damage, and employers' increasing fear of legal liability for such damage caused in the workplace have led to the development of corporate "fetal protection" or "exclusionary" policies. Such policies are typically im-

180 plemented in workplaces where employees may be exposed to such substances as lead, radiation, vinyl chloride, and benzene.

Instead of eliminating hazards that might cause reproductive damage, exclusionary policies generally seek to remove all women of childbearing age from workplaces deemed hazardous to the health of the fetus. The exclusionary policies are implemented not necessarily for the health of the female worker but rather for the health of the potential unborn child.

According to an Office of Technology Assessment report, tremendous diversity exists among company exclusionary policies.[16] More specifically,

> Some of these policies are strongly grounded in epidemiological and toxicological research findings with respect to particular substances, while others are more speculative about potential reproductive health hazards. Some policies are carefully written and documented, while others are unwritten, making them more flexible and ambiguous. In large manufacturing companies, policies are generally announced to employees and their unions prior to implementation, while smaller organizations appear to formulate and apply policies as a perceived problem arises. Some policies recognize that a fetal hazard may be mediated through either the male or female workers, while others apply only to women.[17]

Even though the policies clearly vary in scope and substance, in most cases they exclude from certain work environments any woman of childbearing age who cannot prove that she is infertile.[18]

IMPACT OF EXCLUSIONARY POLICIES

Estimates of the number of women affected by corporate exclusionary policies also vary widely, with some as high as twenty million.[19] On the low end, others estimate that a minimum of one hundred thousand jobs have been closed to women through the use of exclusionary policies, predominantly in large corporations in the automobile, chemical, steel, oil, rubber, and pharmaceutical industries.

Paul, Daniels, and Rosofsky found that a much larger proportion of companies with over five hundred employees (57 percent) had restrictive policies than was the case in firms with fewer than five hundred employees (13 percent). The Office of Technology Assessment reported that at least fifteen *Fortune* 500 companies, as well as numerous hospitals, excluded fertile and/or pregnant women from some jobs. Some of the large firms that have adopted exclusionary policies include General Motors, St. Joe's Minerals, Allied-Signal, Olin, Gulf Oil, Exxon, Firestone, Dow Chemical, Sun Oil, Goodyear, BASF, Eastman Kodak, Union Carbide, and Monsanto.[20]

The most extensive survey on corporate exclusionary practices was conducted by Paul, Daniels, and Rosofsky.[21] Their study focused on 198 chemical and electronics manufacturing industries in Massachusetts. Paul and her associates found that thirty-seven companies (approximately 20 percent of those sampled) excluded certain types of workers from handling specific substances, working in certain areas, or holding certain positions on the basis of reproductive health concerns. All but one of the fifty-eight collective restrictions imposed by these companies applied uniquely to female employees.

In brief, the number of exclusionary policies in effect is unknown, the identity of companies adopting them is not publicized, and data on how they are enforced are sketchy. Given the limited data on the extensiveness of exclusionary policies, the study by Paul and associates is particularly revealing: Nearly one in five companies in the study had an exclusionary policy, and such policies tended to be used more by larger companies. Furthermore, Paul and associates warned that their study might reflect a "cautious underreporting" by firms due to the timing of the survey.[22]

ALTERNATIVES TO EXCLUSIONARY POLICIES

In defending exclusionary policies, corporations have maintained that feasible alternatives are simply not available. For instance, industry representatives contend that the elimination of hazards is not technically feasible and that many toxic workplaces, such as lead smelters, can never be made completely safe for a developing fetus.[23] Whereas firms can attempt to establish safe handling procedures, impose engineering controls, and remove toxins through technological controls, the environment still cannot be made completely safe for the fetus.

Furthermore, industry contends that even if technological changes were completely effective in reducing reproductive hazards, such modifications would not be financially feasible. According to Dr. Robert Cline, American Cyanamid's medical director, making the workplace

182   safe for everyone is an "ideal . . . that's totally unachievable without emasculating the chemical industry."[24] Sor concurred: Although cleaning up the workplace is, "the most attractive resolution of the problem . . . it is the least achievable."[25]

Rather than implementing technological changes, reproductive rights groups argue that firms should provide alternative employment opportunities to those workers planning a family. In large companies, temporary removal to a safe area at comparable pay and benefits may be feasible, but that is not the case in small firms. Furthermore, even in large firms, such a "temporary removal" might be needed throughout the worker's childbearing years. Waiting until the female worker is pregnant before temporary removal does not constitute an effective alternative, because if she is temporarily rotated out of a job in a hazardous area only upon notification of pregnancy, severe damage to the health of the fetus may have already occurred. In addition, some toxicants such as lead are retained in the body long after exposure. Even if the female worker is not exposed to toxins after she becomes pregnant, the fetus could still be harmed by the woman's preconception exposure.[26]

Thus, due to a perceived lack of alternatives, a number of firms over the past two decades have implemented exclusionary policies. The decision-making process that led to the adoption of a fetal protection policy in each of three companies is explored in more detail below.

THREE CORPORATE EXCLUSIONARY POLICIES

Bunker Hill

One of the first companies to adopt an exclusionary policy was the Bunker Hill Mining Company in Kellogg, Idaho. Bunker Hill, founded in 1897, maintained a zinc refinery, fertilizer plant, and lead smelter. In 1972 Bunker Hill opened production jobs to women in response to pressure from the EEOC. Between 1972 and 1976, forty-five women were hired as production workers in the lead smelter and zinc plant.

In April 1975, the physician on contract with Bunker Hill returned from a lead industries conference and advised the company president that no fertile women should be allowed to work in jobs that entailed lead exposure because such exposure potentially harms the growing fetus.

After meeting with the union, the president of the company informed all twenty-nine women working in the lead smelter and zinc plant that they could no longer work in lead operations and that they would have to show proof of sterilization (no other form of birth control was acceptable) in the form of a note from their physician before they could return to their original jobs.

The women were immediately removed from their jobs and told to report to the mine yard crew the next day (where they were to perform general yard work) until permanent jobs could be found for them in nonleaded areas. As they were transferred out of their departments, they lost their departmental seniority.

Six of the women, who had undergone a sterilization operation and could provide documentation, returned immediately to the smelter. Some women consented to a sterilization procedure in order to keep their jobs. The other women protested the policy in various ways: Some contacted a civil rights lawyer (though never formally retained the lawyer), some protested the policy to the United Steelworkers of America (who were not able to provide sufficient guidance), some complained to the Idaho Human Rights Commission (which drew up a "Memorandum of Understanding" that Bunker Hill reportedly refused to sign), and others filed a complaint with the EEOC.

After an investigation by the EEOC, women affected by the policy were individually reimbursed for wages lost due to the transfer. An individual monetary settlement was negotiated, and the women agreed to drop sex discrimination charges filed with the EEOC. Despite the settlement, these women did not feel satisfied with the outcome; some felt that they had been "bought out" and would have preferred the EEOC to make a decision about the legality of the policy rather than individually negotiating a settlement.

The controversy was reopened four years later when OSHA conducted an investigation into health and safety conditions at Bunker Hill. In September 1980, Bunker Hill was cited for the maintenance of a "sterilization policy" and fined $10,000. OSHA had previously cited American Cyanamid for a similar policy. When OSHA lost the case against American Cyanamid in April 1981 (the matter was held to lie outside OSHA's jurisdiction), OSHA lawyers decided to drop the citation for a sterilization policy against Bunker Hill.

In 1981 Gulf Resources, the owner of Bunker Hill, announced its intention to close the plant. Those women who had consented to a sterilization operation only a few years earlier solely to keep their jobs joined the ranks of the unemployed.

American Cyanamid

Although Bunker Hill's exclusionary policy raised concern among many advocacy groups, the policy instituted by American Cyanamid garnered a much greater public outcry. American Cyanamid manufactures and sells a highly diversified line of agricultural, medical, specialty chemical, and consumer products. At the plant in Willow Island, West Virginia, company officials announced that beginning May 1, 1978, all women who were not sterilized would be excluded from eight of the plant's ten departments. The women were told that they might transfer to the two other departments or to janitorial work subject to openings and that most transfers would result in lower wages.

In announcing the policy, a company official told women that hundreds of chemicals were harmful to the fetus, that the company would no longer employ women between the ages of sixteen and fifty in production jobs in the lead pigments department, that similar sterilization policies were being implemented by a number of other chemical companies, that in the near future no women of childbearing age would be allowed to work for any U.S. chemical company, and that the plant would provide only seven jobs for the thirty fertile women affected by the policy—the rest would be dismissed.[27]

Between February and July 1978, five women at American Cyanamid underwent sterilization in compliance with the policy. Two other women who did not consent to sterilization were demoted to lower-paying jobs. One woman who consented to the sterilization procedure explained that she was supporting a disabled husband and said, "I did it because I was scared and I have to have the income." Another woman explained her perception of lack of choice, "They don't have to hold a hammer to your head . . . all they have to do is tell you that it's the only way you can keep your job."[28]

These women, in consenting to the sterilization requirement, did not know that the company had actually decided to delay implementation of the policy pending a more detailed review. The subsequent review resulted in a significant change in policy.[29]

As mentioned above, OSHA cited American Cyanamid in October 1979 for maintenance of a fetal protection policy. In April 1981, the Federal Occupational Safety and Health Review Commission dismissed the case. The commission maintained that the matter did not lie within OSHA's jurisdiction, that OSHA could not use the general duty clause to cite employers for exclusionary policies, and that the impact of the company's policy was outside the reach of the Occupational Safety and Health Act.

As happened at Bunker Hill, restricted departments at American Cyanamid were closed in 1979—one year after American Cyanamid announced its exclusionary policy and after five women had consented to a sterilization procedure to secure their employment.

Johnson Controls

The most recent and, clearly, the most widely publicized fetal protection policy was that maintained by Johnson Controls, the leading manufacturer of automotive batteries in the United States. Before the Civil Rights Act of 1964, Johnson Controls did not employ women in its battery-manufacturing jobs. In June 1977, however, it announced its first official policy regarding employment of women in jobs that involved lead exposure. Johnson Controls advised women who expected to have children not to take jobs involving exposure to lead, warned women who took such jobs of the reproductive risks associated with lead exposure, and recommended that workers consult their family doctors for advice. The company also required a woman who wished to be considered for employment to sign a statement that she had been advised of the risk of becoming pregnant while she was exposed to lead.[30]

Between 1979 and 1983, eight employees became pregnant while maintaining blood levels in excess of 30 micrograms per deciliter, the critical level noted by OSHA for a worker planning to have a family. Due to this finding, in 1982 Johnson Controls shifted from a policy of warning to a policy of exclusion. The company announced a broad exclusion of women from jobs that exposed them to lead. The new policy read:

> Women who are pregnant or who are capable of bearing children will not be placed into jobs involving lead exposure or which could expose them to lead through the exercise of job bidding, bumping, transfer, or promotion rights.

The policy defined women capable of bearing children as all women except those who had medical confirmation that they could not bear children.[31]

In 1984 the policy was examined in the federal district court in Milwaukee. The class action suit challenged the policy as a violation of

Title VII of the Civil Rights Act of 1964. The court ruled in favor of Johnson Controls, and in 1989 the U.S. Court of Appeals for the Seventh Circuit upheld the policy in a 7–4 vote. The case was then appealed to the U.S. Supreme Court.

On March 20, 1991, the Court issued its ruling in *International Union v. Johnson Controls, Inc.*[32] In a unanimous decision (with two concurring opinions) the Court reversed the appeals court decision, ruling Johnson Controls' fetal protection policy discriminatory on the grounds that it classified workers on the basis of sex and childbearing capacity rather than fertility alone. Federal law prohibits employers from excluding women from job categories because they are, or might become, pregnant. Thus, the Court stated that the bias in Johnson Controls' policy was obvious, "because fertile men, but not fertile women, are given a choice as to whether they want to risk their reproductive health by holding a particular job."[33]

The policy did not seek to protect the unconceived children of its male employees, despite evidence that lead exposure can also have a debilitating effect on the male reproductive system. The Court concluded that the language of the BFOQ exception, the Pregnancy Discrimination Act, and legislative history and case law prohibit an employer from discriminating against a woman because of her capacity to become pregnant unless her reproductive potential prevents her from performing the duties of her job.[34]

Although the Court was divided on the issue of whether any fetal protection policy could ever conceivably be justified under the BFOQ defense, all nine justices agreed that Johnson Controls' policy could not be justified. Johnson Controls could not show that substantially all of its fertile women employees were incapable of doing their jobs. The implications of the Supreme Court decision are far-reaching, being applicable to all employers engaged in interstate commerce, including hospitals and clinics.[35]

THE IMPLICATIONS OF EXCLUSION

The development and implementation of exclusionary policies at Bunker Hill, American Cyanamid, and Johnson Controls raise a host of complex, interrelated issues: Are these policies overinclusive? Are the policies underinclusive? Who, ultimately, should make decisions about reproductive issues in the workplace: the company, the mother, the father, both parents, the government?

Overinclusiveness of Exclusionary Policies

Not all women of childbearing age are going to become pregnant. However, exclusionary policies assume that every woman of childbearing age may become pregnant and that women are not capable of planning pregnancies. As Becker stated, "Such polices assume that the probability that any given fertile woman will become pregnant is sufficiently high to justify excluding her from a job for which she is otherwise qualified. Yet, only one out of 5000 women aged 45 to 59 has a child in a given year, and for blue-collar women over age thirty the birth rate may be less than 2%."[36]

Exclusionary policies restrict all female employees' choices regarding reproduction. In requiring sterilization, the woman may be viewed as either incompetent or untrustworthy in making choices that affect her potential offspring. Exclusionary policies ignore the fact that a woman can control many aspects that affect her fertility, for example, contraceptive practice, sexual activity, and marital status.[37] Furthermore, as Becker pointed out, it is only the female employee, not the employer, who can fully consider the advantages and the disadvantages of a particular course of action for herself and her dependents.[38]

Underinclusiveness of Exclusionary Policies

Exclusionary policies ignore potential risk to men and assume that only the exposure of the fertile female employee puts a child at risk. To illustrate, Paul, Daniels, and Rosofsky's study of large chemical and electronics companies in Massachusetts determined that fifty-four of the companies surveyed used glycol ethers.[39] In very low doses, glycol ethers can produce toxic effects on sperm. While none of these fifty-four companies excluded men from exposure, thirty-seven restricted women's employment opportunities on the basis of reproductive risk.

Gender-based exclusion is not warranted on the basis of available medical and scientific evidence. As the Office of Technology Assessment concluded, "There is no biological basis for assuming that either the embryo/fetus or the female is more susceptible [to reproductive toxicants] than the male."[40] Indeed, the criteria used for exclusion of female employees reported in Paul, Daniels, and Rosofsky's study, "bore

188   little relationship to current scientific knowledge about the effects of
particular substances or about the categories of workers truly at risk."[41]

The underinclusive nature of exclusionary policies—reflected by the
lack of concern for male risk—may relate more to legal issues than to
medical or scientific issues. A male employee who alleges that workplace exposure to lead caused a deformed child would have to prove
paternity. According to Dr. Nicholas Ashford, this extra burden of proof
would make it unlikely that a lawsuit would succeed.[42] The House
Committee on Education and Labor states that exclusionary policies
often "constitute a pretext for a new form of arbitrary gender stereotyping in which employers incorrectly assert that fetal health risks are primarily or exclusively traceable to women."[43]

Exclusionary policies are also underinclusive in that they ignore risk
to women in female-dominated industries. Interestingly, exclusionary
policies are rarely implemented in industries that depend heavily on
a female work force. While reproductive hazards in nursing, dentistry,
textiles, clothing, laundry, dry cleaning, food processing, and electronics are well established, exclusionary policies for workers in those occupations are uncommon. As Blank stated, exclusionary policies "have
been adopted almost exclusively in unionized industries with rigid pay
scales where increased costs of hiring women cannot be offset by paying
women less. The conspicuous absence of [exclusionary policies] in occupations that are highly dependent on women to supply relatively low-
cost labor raises serious questions concerning the motivation for such
policies."[44]

RESPONSIBILITY FOR PROTECTING FETAL HEALTH
IN THE WORKPLACE

Many have argued that the health of the fetus must be protected even
at the expense of maternal rights.[45] Corporations adopting exclusionary
policies contend that they have a humanitarian interest in protecting
the reproductive health of female employees. The matter of fetal health
"is clearly of great and increasing importance to current generations
and to the well-being of future generations."[46]

For instance, Johnson Controls argued that its policy was ethical and
socially responsible and that it was designed only to prevent exposing
the fetus to avoidable risk.[47] Similarly, the president of Bunker Hill ada-

mantly stated that for humanitarian reasons he did not want Bunker Hill to contribute to fetal damage.[48]

Unfortunately, such concerns are not consistent across the full spectrum of occupational safety and health issues. As Blank observed, "Although some companies defend [exclusionary policies] on the ground that any risk of harm to the fetus no matter how remote is unacceptable and therefore ground for exclusion of all fertile women, they do not set the same stringent standards to protect the workers themselves. Of course, if they did . . . many industries would have to close."[49]

In reality, corporations appear to have adopted exclusionary policies more from a concern for the economic costs of possible liability suits brought by children whose mothers were exposed to toxic substances than from humanitarian concerns. However, this fear of employer liability appears to be unfounded.

Blank maintained that there has been only one recorded case of a child bringing a lawsuit for injuries suffered while the mother was pregnant and continued to work.[50] In this case the jury found in favor of the employer, even though there was evidence that the employer had violated OSHA safety standards. Although Becker argued that it is impossible to state with certainty the standard for employer liability in tort for injuries to workers' children, under general tort principles there "would seem to be no basis for holding an employer liable for fetal harm if Title VII bans sex-specific fetal vulnerability policies, the employer fully informs the woman of the risks, and the employer has not acted in a negligent manner."[51] Annas argued that, in addition to this, there is the extraordinarily difficult issue of causation, even if the employer is negligent.[52]

In the Johnson Controls case, the Supreme Court addressed the issue of potential tort liability should a fetus be injured by the mother's occupational exposure. The Court indicated that if the employer followed OSHA guidelines and fully informed its workers of the risks involved, liability would be "remote at best."[53]

As it is apparent that corporations will not be assuming responsibility for decisions about female employees' reproductive status in the future, questions can be raised about what role the state should play in the regulation of reproductive health. The state clearly has a major interest in fetal health. As Zielinski stated,

an employee's impaired reproductive health is personal and catastrophic. It may be irreversible and affect the health of many generations. The cost of such health impairments isn't covered by workers' compensation, and health insurance isn't offered by all companies. Yet, the physical or mental disabilities of the worker's children may require a lifetime of medical, educational or other special attention.[54]

Unfortunately, the government's response over the past two decades to the threat of reproductive risk in the workplace has been inconsistent, haphazard, and often contradictory. The overall effectiveness of the three federal agencies involved in the assessment or regulation of reproductive toxins—OSHA, the Environmental Protection Agency, and NIOSH—is questionable.[55]

For instance, the incompatibility between requirements set forth by OSHA and Title VII is well noted. The Occupational Safety and Health Act of 1970 charges employers with the responsibility of providing a safe and healthy workplace. Employers maintain that the only way to guarantee a safe workplace for the fetus is through the exclusion of female workers from hazardous work environments. Yet Title VII makes employers responsible for ensuring equal employment opportunities for women.[56] Exclusionary policies represent a corporate judgment, only recently subjected to U.S. Supreme Court review, that "the goal of equal employment is secondary to that of worker safety and that a trade-off can be made between the two."[57] Until the Supreme Court decision, federal agencies were unwilling, or perhaps unable, to deal aggressively with the thorny issue of reproductive risk in the workplace.

The regulatory situation should improve over the next decade now that the U.S. Supreme Court has concluded that Congress left the welfare of the next generation to the parents, not the employers.[58] The Court also clearly stated that companies cannot use a concern for fetal health to limit job opportunities for women. Such a definitive statement should help guide the actions and policies of regulatory agencies and reduce the regulatory ambiguity and conflict that has existed for decades.

SUMMARY

Exclusionary policies threaten many of the significant professional advancements made by women in the workplace since the 1960s. They limit equal employment opportunities, they deprive women of the opportunity to make choices regarding their reproductive status, they are conspiciously absent in female-dominated industries, they protect neither the reproductive health of males nor their potential progeny, and they are largely based on a legal threat that may be nonexistent. Moreover,

> Women of color and poor women are especially at risk for reproductive injury or disease. Not only do they often have the most hazardous jobs (most of which were never covered by [exclusionary policies]) but also their low income forces them to live in inadequate housing and in neighborhoods contaminated by an array of environmental pollutants.[59]

With the U.S. Supreme Court's prohibition of exclusionary policies in the Johnson Controls case, exclusionary policies will not be as frequently implemented. The Court clarified the lack of legal grounds for exclusionary policies and restated the preeminence of women's rights to employment in male-dominated industries.

However, the issue of how to safeguard fetal health effectively remains unaddressed. Some work simply is, and will remain, high risk. While the prohibition of Johnson Controls' policy sends a strong and clear message to industry regarding the utility of fetal protection policies, the Supreme Court's decision did not address the issue of how best to minimize occupational hazards and how those workers and their children who suffer injury due to workplace exposures ought to be compensated.[60]

Equal treatment of male and female workers may be a good start, but it is not the answer. Whereas men and women both should be given the choice to assume risk related to their reproductive ability, all negative consequences of the decision should not be shifted from the corporation directly onto the shoulders of the employees. As a result of the Supreme Court decision, it is critical that employees not be forced to assume all financial, social, and medical costs of their choice to work in a toxic workplace. Indeed, as a result of the Johnson Controls decision, some companies are insisting that if women work with hazardous substances, they must accept responsibility for any damage that may result.[61] "Because of possible economic concerns, geographic constraints or limited employment opportunities of the worker, allowing workers the choice of fertility or employment would present them with no choice at all."[62]

The real challenge for public policy remains to turn industry's focus away from new methods of sex discrimination and toward new ways to

192   reduce workplace hazards.[63] To handle the threat of reproductive risk in the workplace effectively, shared responsibility among workers, industry, government, unions, and consumers is needed. As Blank observed, "Other Western democracies have made a societal commitment to children and families and have backed up this high priority with varying degrees of public funding."[64]

In potentially hazardous workplaces, safeguards should be maintained by industry. Organizations within a specific industry, rather than workers, are in a better position to assess risks. They have access to research data coming from government regulatory agencies and trade groups, and they are more likely to have professional safety and health staffs who can understand the research data and relate it to the manufacturing process.[65] Industry can encourage the identification and monitoring of hazards, hire risk-assessment consultants, provide adequate employee training, provide extensive education and counseling programs, fully disclose potential risks presented by toxic substances to allow workers to make informed decisions about their reproductive health, and support research to identify less harmful substitutes.[66] Various engineering controls can be implemented, such as improved ventilation systems or closed systems for chemical processing.[67]

To support industry efforts fully, some of the costs must necessarily be passed back to consumers. Direct government involvement, tax incentives, and financial investment from government are necessary.[68] Greater federal resources should be directed toward research into reproductive risks. The effects of all known or suspected hazards present in the workplace need to be investigated. Such research should extend beyond fertile women to include nonfertile women, men in general, and men with pregnant wives; and it should seek to differentiate between individuals who are and those who are not susceptible to occupational hazards.

Further, disquieting as the question is, we need to ask ourselves whether we really need products whose manufacture involves toxic substances. For some products, the social cost may simply be too high.

NOTES

1. U.S. Department of Labor, *Women Workers: Outlook to 2005* (Washington, DC: Government Printing Office, 1992).
2. R. H. Blank, *Fetal Protection in the Workplace: Women's Right, Busi-*

ness Interests, and the Unborn (New York: Columbia University Press,
1993).

3. Office of Technology Assessment, *Reproductive Health Hazards in the Workplace* (Washington, DC: Government Printing Office, 1985).

4. S. Sexton, "The Reproductive Hazards of Industrial Chemicals: The Politics of Protection," *Ecologist* 23, no. 6 (1993): 212–18.

5. Blank, *Fetal Protection in the Workplace*.

6. Sexton, "The Reproductive Hazards of Industrial Chemicals."

7. NIOSH, *Proposed National Strategies for the Prevention of Leading Work-Related Diseases and Injuries*. Part 2 (Washington, DC: Association of Schools of Public Health, 1988).

8. Office of Technology Assessment, *Reproductive Health Hazards in the Workplace*.

9. Blank, *Fetal Protection in the Workplace*.

10. T. L. Vaughan, J. R. Daling and P. M. Starzyk, "Fetal Death and Maternal Occupation," *Journal of Occupational Medicine* 26, no. 9 (1984): 676–78.

11. K. Hemminki et al., "Spontaneous Abortions as a Risk Indication in Metal Exposure," in *Reproductive and Developmental Toxicity of Metals*, ed. T. W. Clarkson, F. N. Gunnar and R. R. Sager (New York: Plenum, 1983), 369–80.

12. K. Hemminki and M. L. Niemi, "Community Study of Spontaneous Abortions: Relation to Occupation and Air Pollution by Sulphur Dioxide, Hydrogen Sulfide, and Carbon Disulfide," *International Archives of Occupational and Environmental Health* 51 (1982): 55–63.

13. T. Peters et al., "The Effects of Work in Pregnancy: Short- and Long-Term Associations," in *Pregnant Women at Work*, ed. G. Chamberlain (London: Royal Society of Medicine and Macmillan, 1984), 87–104.

14. Hemminki et al., "Spontaneous Abortions as a Risk."

15. J. F. Katz, "Hazardous Working Conditions and Fetal Protection Policies: Women Are Going Back to the Future," *Environmental Affairs* 17 (1989): 201–30, 213.

16. Office of Technology Assessment, *Reproductive Health Hazards in the Workplace*.

17. Ibid., 261.

18. Blank, *Fetal Protection in the Workplace*.

19. U.S. Congress. House. Committee on Education and Labor, *A Report on the EEOC, Title VII, and Workplace Fetal Protection Policies in the 1980s* (Washington, DC: Government Printing Office, 1990).

20. M. Paul, C. Daniels and R. Rosofsky, "Corporate Response to Reproductive Hazards in the Workplace: Results of the Family, Work, and Health Survey," *American Journal of Industrial Medicine* 16 (1989): 267–80; Office of Technology Assessment, *Reproductive Health Hazards in the Work-*

194   *place;* Blank, *Fetal Protection in the Workplace;* Sexton, "The Reproductive Hazards of Industrial Chemicals."

21. Ibid.

22. The study was conducted after the release of a highly publicized University of Massachusetts study commissioned by Digital Equipment Corporation (DEC), which found increased spontaneous abortion rates among female workers involved in computer chip fabrication.

23. D. M. Randall, "Protecting the Unborn," *Personnel Administrator* 32, no. 9 (1987): 88–97.

24. R. Rawls, "Reproductive Hazards in the Workplace," *Chemical and Engineering News* 11 (Feb. 1980): 28–31, 30.

25. Y. Sor, "Fertility or Unemployment: Should You Have to Choose?" *Journal of Law and Health* 1 (1986): 141–228, 222.

26. Blank, *Fetal Protection in the Workplace.*

27. S. J. Kenney, *For Whose Protection?: Reproductive Hazards and Exclusionary Policies in the United States and Britain* (Ann Arbor, MI: University of Michigan Press, 1992).

28. Sexton, "The Reproductive Hazards of Industrial Chemicals," 214.

29. Kenney, *For Whose Protection?*

30. G. J. Annas, "Fetal Protection and Employment Discrimination—The Johnson Controls Case," *New England Journal of Medicine* 325, no. 10 (1991): 740–43.

31. Ibid.

32. 111 S.Ct. 1196 (1991).

33. Ibid., 1196.

34. Blank, *Fetal Protection in the Workplace.*

35. Annas, "Fetal Protection and Employment Discrimination."

36. M. E. Becker, "From *Muller v. Oregon* to Fetal Vulnerability Policies," *University of Chicago Law Review* 53 (1986): 1219–73, 1233.

37. Sexton, "The Reproductive Hazards of Industrial Chemicals."

38. Becker, "From *Muller v. Oregon*," 1241.

39. Paul, Daniels and Rosofsky, "Corporate Response to Reproductive Hazards."

40. Office of Technology Assessment, *Reproductive Health Hazards in the Workplace,* 68.

41. Paul, Daniels and Rosofsky, "Corporate Response to Reproductive Hazards," 277.

42. R. Severo, "Should Firms Screen the Workplace or the Worker?" *New York Times* (Sept. 24, 1980): 22E.

43. U.S. Congress. House. Committee on Education and Labor, *A Report on the EEOC,* 7.

44. Blank, *Fetal Protection in the Workplace,* 100.

45. S. A. Balisy, "Maternal Substance Abuse: The Need to Provide Legal

Protection of the Fetus," *Southern California Law Review* 60 (1987): 1209–38.

46. J. C. Hyatt, "Work Safety Issue Isn't as Simple as It Sounds," *Wall Street Journal* (Aug. 1, 1977): 1.

47. Annas, "Fetal Protection and Employment Discrimination."

48. D. M. Randall, "Women in Toxic Work Environments: A Case Study and Examination of Policy Impact," in *Women and Work: An Annual Review*, vol. 1, ed. L. Larwood, A. H. Stromberg and B. A. Gutek (Beverly Hills, CA: Sage, 1987), 259–81.

49. Blank, *Fetal Protection in the Workplace*, 96.

50. Ibid.; *Security National Bank v. Chloride Inc.*, 602 F.Supp. 294 (D. Kan. 1985).

51. Becker, "From *Muller v. Oregon*," 1244.

52. Annas, "Fetal Protection and Employment Discrimination."

53. Ibid.

54. C. Zielinski, "The Toxic Trap," *Personnel Journal* (February 1990): 40–49, 43.

55. Ibid.

56. Blank, *Fetal Protection in the Workplace*.

57. V. M. Andrade, "The Toxic Workplace: Title VII Protection for the Potentially Pregnant Worker," *Harvard Women's Law Journal* 4, no. 1 (1981): 7–103, 72.

58. Annas, "Fetal Protection and Employment Discrimination."

59. Blank, *Fetal Protection in the Workplace*, 179–80.

60. Ibid.

61. Sexton, "The Reproductive Hazards of Industrial Chemicals."

62. Randall, "Protecting the Unborn," 92.

63. Annas, "Fetal Protection and Employment Discrimination."

64. Blank, *Fetal Protection in the Workplace*, 190.

65. Zielinski, "The Toxic Trap."

66. Blank, *Fetal Protection in the Workplace*.

67. Randall, "Protecting the Unborn."

68. Blank, *Fetal Protection in the Workplace*.

REFERENCES

Andrade, V. M. 1981. The toxic workplace: Title VII protection for the potentially pregnant worker. *Harvard Women's Law Journal* 4(1): 7–103.

Annas, G. J. 1991. Fetal protection and employment discrimination—The Johnson Controls case. *New England Journal of Medicine* 325(10): 740–43.

196   Balisy, S. A. 1987. Maternal substance abuse: The need to provide legal protection of the fetus. *Southern California Law Review* 60: 1209–38.

Becker, M. E. 1986. From *Muller v. Oregon* to fetal vulnerability policies. *University of Chicago Law Review* 53: 1219–73.

Blank, R. H. 1993. *Fetal Protection in the Workplace: Women's Rights, Business Interests, and the Unborn.* New York: Columbia University Press.

Hemminki, K. and M. L. Niemi. 1982. Community study of spontaneous abortions: Relation to occupation and air pollution by sulphur dioxide, hydrogen sulfide, and carbon disulfide. *International Archives of Occupational and Environmental Health* 51: 55–63.

Hemminki, K., M. L. Niemi, I. Kyyronen, I. Kilpikavi and H. Vaninio. 1983. Spontaneous abortions as a risk indication in metal exposure. In *Reproductive and Developmental Toxicity of Metals*, ed. T. W. Clarkson, F. N. Gunnar and P. R. Sager, 369–80. New York: Plenum.

Hyatt, J. C. 1977. Work safety issue isn't as simple as it sounds. *Wall Street Journal* August 1: 1.

Katz, J. F. 1989. Hazardous working conditions and fetal protection policies: Women are going back to the future. *Environmental Affairs* 17: 201–30.

Kenney, S. J. 1992. *For Whose Protection?: Reproductive Hazards and Exclusionary Policies in the United States and Britain.* Ann Arbor, MI: University of Michigan Press.

NIOSH. 1988. *Proposed National Strategies for the Prevention of Leading Work-Related Diseases and Injuries.* Part 2. Washington, DC: Association of Schools of Public Health.

Office of Technology Assessment. 1985. *Reproductive Health Hazards in the Workplace.* Washington, DC: Government Printing Office.

Paul, M., C. Daniels and R. Rosofsky. 1989. Corporate response to reproductive hazards in the workplace: Results of the family, work, and health survey. *American Journal of Industrial Medicine* 16: 267–80.

Peters, T., P. Adelstein, J. Golding and N. Butler. 1984. The effects of work in pregnancy: Short- and long-term associations. In *Pregnant Women at Work*, ed. G. Chamberlain, 87–104. London: Royal Society of Medicine and Macmillan.

Randall, D. M. 1985. Women in toxic work environments: A case study and examination of policy impact. In *Women and Work: An Annual Review.* Vol. 1, ed. L. Larwood, A. H. Stromberg and B. A. Gutek, 259–81. Beverly Hills, CA: Sage.

———. 1987. Protecting the unborn. *Personnel Administrator* 32(9): 88–97.

Rawls, R. 1980. Reproductive hazards in the workplace. *Chemical and Engineering News* February 11: 28–31.

Severo, R. 1980. Should firms screen the workplace or the worker? *New York Times* September 24: 22E.

Sexton, S. 1993. The reproductive hazards of industrial chemicals: The politics of protection. *The Ecologist* 23(6): 212–18.

Sor, Y. 1986. Fertility or unemployment: Should you have to choose? *Journal of Law and Health* 1: 141–228.

U.S. Congress. House. Committee on Education and Labor. 1990. *A Report on the EEOC, Title VII, and Workplace Fetal Protection Policies in the 1980s.* Washington, DC: Government Printing Office.

U.S. Department of Labor. 1992. *Women Workers: Outlook to 2005.* Washington, DC: Government Printing Office.

Vaughan, T. L., J. R. Daling and P. M. Starzyk. 1984. Fetal death and maternal occupation. *Journal of Occupational Medicine* 26(9): 676–78.

Zielinski, C. 1990. The toxic trap. *Personnel Journal* February: 40–49.

LAW, POLICY, AND
SOCIAL CHANGE

James G. Fox

 This chapter traces the judicial and legislative evolution of women's workplace rights. In addition, it discusses the passage and interpretation of policies related to sex discrimination in the form of employment discrimination and sexual harassment, as well as women's health and pregnancy concerns, to illustrate the relative progress women have achieved. The conclusion addresses the question of whether or not law and policy have been effective tools for social change and for restructuring the hierarchy of gendered power.

To assist the reader's understanding of these relationships, a chronology of policy and legal changes affecting women's rights and status is included in the Appendix to this volume. This material should enable the reader to examine more readily the evolution of law and policy and the effects of social change, and to conceptualize the evolution of women's rights within the context of a changing American society.

POLICY DEVELOPMENT

Policy and legal changes aimed at protecting the interests of American women have emerged from a variety of sources. They were introduced at various levels of government (presidential initiative, cabinet-level or advisory groups, legislators, heads of various governmental agencies), by the influence of social movements (organized constituent groups and other special-interest organizations), and by public reaction to highly publicized salient acts or events (the renewed public discourse about sexual abuse and victimization sparked by media coverage of sev-

200 eral high-profile sexual harassment, domestic violence, and consumer product safety cases).

One major influence on policy change has been the efforts of grass-roots organizations supporting the national women's movement, although some scholars argue that government has also played a sizable and significant role in building and strengthening the women's movement.[1] In addition, community-based women's organizations and groups have been viewed as being more responsive and effective in addressing localized concerns[2] than larger, national organizations such as the National Organization for Women (NOW). However, the contemporary women's movement has been the major force in advocating legal and policy changes that address a variety of women's needs and interests.[3]

Popular support among women against (or for) a particular corporate practice or government policy frequently stimulates efforts to increase awareness of the nature of the problem, its origin, and its impact. Special-interest groups may then conduct critical assessment and public information campaigns, which in turn strengthen organizational support from constituent members. Similarly, academic interest may stimulate research and serve to sharpen the focus of critical assessment. These efforts, along with greater media attention, are typically tied to political action campaigns aimed at modifying existing legislation, regulations, or government policy related to the practice or problem in question. As will be discussed in greater detail in the following chapter, these responses are central to the process of social change and effective political action.

WOMEN'S CIVIL RIGHTS

While contemporary women's civil rights are exemplified by changes in legal status and social policy as a result of the civil rights movement of the 1950s and 1960s, an analysis of the use of law and policy to limit, restrict, and define women's role and function or to protect women's rights and interests actually begins much earlier in American legal history.[4] That is, early feminists and reformers attempting to merge concerns for women, families, and communities with their larger social and political reform agenda[5] had a profound impact on the development of social welfare policy and were instrumental in the formation of the American welfare system. Similarly, other social policy changes during the early 1900s continued to reflect the principle that attempts to advance women's welfare were virtually inseparable from efforts to improve the general welfare of American citizens.[6]

One important historical milestone was the 1908 U.S. Supreme Court decision in *Muller v. Oregon.*[7] In this case the Court upheld the right of a state to limit the working hours of women, which illustrated the influence of gender in promoting early protective labor legislation at a time when trade unions and the National Consumers League were unable to obtain federal regulation of working conditions.[8] This decision marked a major turning point in American social policy and political theory, namely, the shift to an emerging ideology in which the denial of women's rights—for example, through the exclusion of women from juries, public universities, and certain jobs—was justified on the grounds that protecting women served the larger societal interest of regulating morality. Protective legislation eventually became transformed into an ideology that viewed gender as a valid justification for employment discrimination. Hence, this period reflected society's readiness to use protective legislation to deny women employment and educational opportunities. This attitude also established a basis for national social policy that excluded women from many economic opportunities in American society.

The Women's Bureau in the U.S. Bureau of Labor was established in 1920. The bureau was supported by the Women's Bureau coalition, a liberal and reformist group favoring protectionist legislation that emerged from an ideological division between radical and liberal interests within the suffrage movement.[9] According to one contemporary scholar examining the role of government in building the women's movement, the Women's Bureau "nurtured a coalition of groups concerned with the plight of working women" and continued to foster activism among "traditional" women's organizations.[10] However, not all policy changes of this period were favorable to women. For example, the 1933 National Industrial Recovery Act, one of the first measures in Franklin Roosevelt's economic recovery package, was passed in spite of heavy lobbying from critics—including Eleanor Roosevelt. This act legalized differences in workers' wages based on gender and further reinforced the notion that women's work was qualitatively different from work done by men.

In 1935 Congress passed the National Labor Relations Act, which was primarily intended to protect workers' rights to unionize or bargain collectively, as well as to engage in strikes, picketing, and other activities

202   aimed at protecting mutual interests and needs. This act gave women a
slightly stronger foothold once they were a part of the work force, and it
provided a conceptual foundation for declaring gender equality in labor
activities. This remained the status quo until the outbreak of World War
II, which spawned a new era of social and economic change. World War
II demonstrated how much the productivity and commitment of
women workers contributed to the national economy in general and the
war effort in particular. However, after the war the value of women's
labor dramatically diminished; women were summarily forced from the
workplace and expected to become homemakers. In spite of postwar
policies of the 1950s, which displaced most women from the formal
labor market to provide employment opportunities for returning war
veterans, new standards of equality in the work force and women's role
in the trade unions slowly began to emerge.[11]

The period beginning with the civil rights movement during the
1960s heralded a fundamental change in the definition of women's
rights in American society and brought about policy reforms that ultimately enhanced the position of many women. As has been shown historically, lower-class women and women of color did not equally share
in the benefits bestowed on majority women representing the middle
and upper classes. One policy initiative of significance during this era
was the creation of the President's Commission on the Status of
Women in 1962 during the Kennedy administration.[12] The establishment of this and other governmental bodies supporting women's issues
and concerns served to mobilize women at the national level and was
essential to the success of politically oriented social movements in the
United States.[13] Other governmental entities that served this function
were the Interdepartmental Committee on the Status of Women (established in 1963) and the Task Force on Women's Rights and Responsibilities (established in 1969). State-level governmental bodies also emerged
in response to women's issues, such as the State Commissions on the
Status of Women (established from 1962 to 1967). Generally, these organizations fell into one of two different categories: statutory bodies, created by legislation; and appointive structures, created by executive
power.[14]

Together, governmental bodies gave the women's movement a number of advantages. Some of these appointive or advisory bodies, such as
the President's Commission on the Status of Women and the Task Force
on Women's Rights and Responsibilities, had substantial discretion in
the definition of objectives, control of the policy-making agenda, and

most important, significant input into the evaluation of public policy and influence on the policy-making process.[15] Unlike statutory structures, such as the Women's Bureau, which typically had greater fiscal resources and were linked to other government bureaucracies, advisory or appointive structures were generally more dependent upon favorable political climates for achieving organizational and social change.

Overall, these early government policies, coupled with the efforts of feminists and liberal reformers, had a measurable impact on the contemporary women's movement's agenda for social change, as well as on the governmental policy-making process and the political empowerment of women in American society. As a result, women in American society were able to remove some of the major obstacles to employment and other economic opportunities. Other achievements included the definition of legal interests in credit history, retirement benefits, communal property controlled by spousal partners, access to small business grants and loans, and some protection against many forms of personal and gender-based discrimination and victimization. However, in spite of these legislative changes, the economic and social position of women in society during the 1990s still lags significantly behind that of men.

SEX DISCRIMINATION POLICY

The relationship between gender and the corporate workplace provides an illustration of changing practices in the labor market. The composition and extent of contemporary women's participation in the labor market are among the most significant areas of social and economic change over the past three decades. According to 1992 U.S. census data, the labor force was 46 percent female, with married women with young children representing the majority of new entrants.[16] These same data reveal that over 80 percent of American working women are in their prime childbearing years (between eighteen and forty-four) and that 65 percent of all women in this age group are currently in the labor force.[17] As a result of changing family structure in contemporary American society, fewer than 10 percent of all American husbands are now the sole wage earner in their family.[18]

It is clear that changes in the composition of the labor force, family structure, and the household economy place greater emphasis on protecting women's interests in the workplace. However, as employment opportunities have expanded over the past thirty years, a number of

204   other pitfalls and barriers have emerged that serve to limit equal access for women to all levels of labor market participation. Practices such as sex discrimination and sexual harassment, as well as gender-based health and safety concerns, have created obstacles to women's achievement; and corporate and governmental responses to women's victimization in the workplace have raised serious questions regarding their underlying intentions.[19]

The concept of sex discrimination encompasses a wide range of discriminatory practices and policies that have had various effects on women in American society. The material presented in this chapter will examine sex discrimination within the context of labor market participation (for example, denial of employment opportunities), limitations on wages and benefits, hazardous working conditions for pregnant workers, and sexual harassment (which emerged as a significant women's issue in the 1980s). Because Chapter 4 focused on the economic impact of sex discrimination, sex discrimination issues will be approached here from a slightly different perspective.

As stated earlier, the role and position of women in the American labor force have changed radically since the end of World War II. With rapidly changing patterns in the composition of the American family, in employment opportunities for semiskilled workers, and in the economic position of women, historically determined patriarchal structures in both government and the private sector have been challenged vigorously by contemporary women. Most important, because women participate in the labor force increasingly out of economic necessity, issues such as equality of compensation, benefits, promotion opportunities, and working conditions have become central areas of concern. Sex discrimination has selectively and systematically denied women equal access to employment and other forms of economic independence and empowerment. It has also established serious limitations to success, such as a "glass ceiling" for promotions and appointment to key decision-making positions in both the private and public sectors. It is clear that gender-based discrimination not only inflicts social and economic harm upon women but also undermines the basic foundations of democratic freedom and principles of equal justice articulated in the Constitution.

Even before the passage of the Fair Labor Standards Act in 1938,[20] women workers were perceived differently from their male counterparts. The protective nature of this early legislation established gender-based restrictions, such as limitations on hours and wages for workers in different categories, as well as standards for overtime pay rates and restricted hours for child workers.[21] The societal view that, on the one hand women required "special" treatment because of their gender, while on the other hand their labor was of less value than that of male workers, was further reinforced by most early laws and policies governing the status and position of women in the work force.

The Equal Pay Act of 1963 was the first federal law intended to prevent sex discrimination in wages and salary. This legislation was designed to forbid unequal pay for men and women who worked under similar working conditions in the same company, at jobs requiring equal skill, responsibility, and effort. Furthermore, employers were not allowed to reduce wages of any employee to resolve differences among those groups covered under the act.[22] This act resulted in the creation of many state job classification systems and prompted subsequent legislation to ensure compliance with federal standards. The act required merely that jobs be "substantially equal" rather than identical, thus fostering debate over what constitutes "equal work." Hence, qualitative distinctions among jobs emerging as a result of technological advancements in the workplace added substantially to the complexity of these interpretations. Furthermore, some employers continued to evade the intent of the Equal Pay Act by redesigning jobs and restructuring assignments and responsibilities.[23] Certainly, women's wages and salaries continued to lag behind those of men despite passage of this act. Numerous studies have shown that women still earn only a percentage of the total earnings of men, although the gap has narrowed in recent years.[24] It is commonly agreed that structurally induced conditions in the labor force, combined with the influence of stereotypes on job assignments, wage scales, and opportunity systems have perpetuated the gap between male and female wages and salaries.

From a contemporary perspective, the evolution of policy, legislation, and case law addressing gender-based discrimination is closely associated with the use of the 1964 Civil Rights Act for litigating complaints of discrimination on the basis of sex, race, color, religion, or national origin. The effort to achieve equal pay has gradually shifted toward the standard of "comparable worth" or pay equity. For example, the U.S. Supreme Court held in *County of Washington v. Gunther*[25] that female workers could sue for sex discrimination in wages under Title VII of the Civil Rights Act of 1964, even if the jobs compared did not meet the equal work standard of the Equal Pay Act. Subsequent cases, such as *AFSCME v. State of Washington*,[26] discussed in detail in Chapter 4, have further clarified the concept of sex discrimination within dissimilar job classifications.

One good starting position for understanding the slow progress toward equal status in the work force is awareness of the evolution of legal standards used by the Court in deciding whether or not women's constitutional rights have been violated. Of greatest importance were efforts to have sex discrimination and race discrimination judged by the same "strict scrutiny" test. The first case before the Court as a result of this effort was *Reed v. Reed*,[27] decided in 1971, which arose from a very blatant example of sex discrimination. The facts of the case are straightforward. Richard Reed died virtually penniless in 1967 with only his estranged parents surviving. Sally Reed, his mother, petitioned an Idaho lower court to be appointed administrator of her son's estate; his father, Cecil, filed a similar petition. The court subsequently ordered that Cecil be appointed as administrator because the state code required that where persons were related in the same manner to the deceased, *males must be preferred to females.* Sally appealed, and the state appellate court found that this section of the state code violated the Constitution's guarantee of equal protection. Cecil then appealed to the Idaho Supreme Court, which reinstated the original court's order. Sally next appealed to the U.S. Supreme Court, which held that the Idaho statute violated the equal protection clause under the "rational basis" standard. This decision surprised many legal scholars, who believed that the rational basis standard should have allowed the statute to survive intact, whereas if the Court had used the more stringent "strict scrutiny" test, the statute would have been declared unconstitutional.[28]

The central issue in this case, which was to become pivotal in future litigation, was whether or not sex was a "suspect classification" and therefore entitled to the more rigorous standard of strict scrutiny. In almost all previous cases the Court had used the less rigorous rational basis standard in deciding equal protection litigation. In 1973 the Court addressed sex discrimination in military medical and dental benefits in *Frontiero v. Richardson.*[29] As the equal protection clause does not apply to the federal statute in question, Lt. Frontiero based her challenge on the due process clause of the Fifth Amendment. At issue were provisions in a federal statute for additional allowances for dependents of military personnel. The specific section of the statute provided for spouses of male military personnel to be declared as dependent absent a showing that they were dependent upon their military spouses; male spouses of female military personnel were required to prove that they were dependent upon their spouses for more than one-half of their support. The Court, in an 8–1 opinion, upheld the contention that the provisions of the statute violated equal protection provisions of the due process clause (as articulated by previous case law decisions). However, the Court was divided on the central question of whether sex would be considered to be a "suspect classification" and therefore judged on the standard of strict scrutiny. Many legal scholars saw a "middle tier," or third standard, emerging from this opinion.[30]

Subsequent Supreme Court decisions provided little additional clarity in regard to the growing confusion about the standards of review used in sex discrimination cases.[31] Finally, in 1976 the Court issued an opinion in *Craig v. Boren*[32] that attempted to clarify equal protection questions by holding that an intermediate standard would be used in sex discrimination cases. The Court articulated this "middle tier" standard as requiring the government to "demonstrate a substantial relationship between the classification used and the goal to be achieved" in order to survive constitutional challenges.[33] After *Craig*, virtually all sex discrimination cases were attempts to provide additional clarification and refinement of the middle-tier standard.[34] Hence, sex would not readily be viewed as a suspect classification and given the same status as race under the equal protection clause, although there appears to be opportunity for further development of the middle-tier standard of evaluation.[35]

There are substantial differences between standards of review for sex discrimination cases based upon statutory violations, particularly under Title VII of the 1964 Civil Rights Act, and those based on constitutional challenges using the equal protection clause of the Fourteenth Amendment. The Court has been more consistent in deciding cases brought under challenges to equal protection than in deciding sex discrimination cases involving challenges to specific statutes. In the former instance, the nature of the discrimination and the classification involved most often determine the standard used in the review. In the latter instance, the facts of the case, the legislative history, and the specific wording of the statute serve to shape the nature of the Court's review.

From a historical perspective, it appears that the Civil Rights Act of 1964 was clearly the most influential legislation enacted to remove barriers to equality in the workplace. However, its legislative history illustrates that many lawmakers did not believe that women and men were equally suited for various jobs.[36] While Title VII contains specific provisions against discrimination on the basis of sex, race, color, religion, or

208   national origin in virtually all aspects of employment, legislation and
policy designed to eliminate sex discrimination in most aspects of the
labor market have been somewhat unresponsive to many women's issues. Furthermore, federal case law brought under Title VII of the Civil
Rights Act of 1964 has moved very slowly in defining these rights and
protections. Thus, while Title VII case law may be instructive in terms
of its trends and directions, the Court has progressed very slowly in
defining its standards for deciding sex discrimination.

Among the illustrative cases is *Griggs v. Duke Power Co.*,[37] also discussed in Chapter 4, which served to define "permissible types of employment criteria in terms of their effects on protected classes"[38] under
Title VII. The Court held that job "requirements which are facially neutral but operate in a discriminatory fashion are barred unless justified
by business necessity."[39] A central point in *Griggs* was the rejection of
"discriminatory intent" as a basis on which to seek relief under Title
VII in favor of a theory of discrimination based on "adverse effects."[40]
However, if the courts find a *prima facie* case, the employer can argue
that the challenged policy is a "business necessity," and the burden of
persuasion shifts to the victim of the discrimination.[41] Other decisions[42]
subsequently reiterated the emerging distinction between proving discrimination through constitutional (equal protection) and statutory
(Title VII) discrimination claims. However, in a 1989 case the U.S. Supreme Court issued a decision that significantly changed this distinction. In *Wards Cove Packing Co., Inc. v. Atonio*[43] the Court apparently
merged the "disparate treatment" standard, which requires claimants
to show discriminatory intent under Title VII, with the "disparate impact" or "adverse effects" theory, not previously believed to require this
burden of proof. Consequently, after *Wards Cove* it became as difficult
to prove discrimination under Title VII as it was to prove it under the
equal protection clause of the Fourteenth Amendment of the Constitution. The *Wards Cove* decision is important because it redefined the
"business necessity" doctrine of *Griggs*, which provided an affirmative
defense, putting the initial burden of proving an adverse (or disproportionate) impact of a company policy or practice on employees within a
protected class. *Wards Cove* established a new "business justification"
standard, subject only to "reasoned review." The result is that the "ultimate burden" now remains at all times with the plaintiff employee.[44]

In sum, the Court has largely clarified standards in sex discrimination
cases in the twenty-five years since the *Reed* decision. Equal protection
standards now appear to be more consistent, and while sex has not been

determined to be a "suspect classification," it has emerged as subject to an intermediate level of scrutiny. Similarly, Title VII decisions—including issues of equal pay, pensions, and pregnancy—evolved into interpretations of sex discrimination that have established solid legal precedent for women seeking redress for their employers' discriminatory practices. However, there remain numerous unresolved issues that require further Court review.

Subsequent litigation will face a more difficult challenge as a result of the current shift away from protecting the rights of victims of sex discrimination to protecting the rights of the employer. Furthermore, current congressional debate on setting limits in punitive damages awards in civil suits and the trend toward abolition of affirmative action programs are indicative that the growing conservative influence in the political arena will affect workplace equality.

SEXUAL HARASSMENT POLICY

Sexual harassment inflicts substantial social, economic, and psychological harm on working women and poses a serious threat to women's livelihood. It not only impedes job performance but also hinders employees' reasonable chances of advancement in the organization or workplace. While sexual harassment emerged as a major area of policy change in the 1980s, resistance to the standards set forth in various laws and policies, culminating in the Civil Rights Act of 1991,[45] remains throughout many sectors of the labor market—and there are a number of indications that it is increasing. In addition, the widespread media attention to Professor Anita Hill's testimony at the Clarence Thomas confirmation hearings and the publicity surrounding the navy's Tailhook incident have fueled a continuation of the debate over the legal protection against sexual harassment accorded to women. Clearly, the issue of sexual harassment in the workplace has emerged as one of the major women's issues of the 1990s.

The creation of the EEOC as a part of the Civil Rights Act of 1964 provided a foundation for the development of sexual harassment policy and guidelines. However, the EEOC has not always been effective in addressing sexual harassment complaints. Surveys reveal that approximately 90 percent of all women in the labor force have been victims of some form of sexual harassment.[46] A Congressional Caucus for Women's Issues report in 1993 found that 42 percent of women employed in the federal government experienced unwanted and uninvited sexual attention, deliberate touching, pressure for dates, and assault.[47] Private sector surveys report that between fifteen and twenty-one million women experience sexual harassment in their respective workplaces.[48] Consequently, sexual harassment affects the lives and livelihoods of millions of American women each year. Many women lose their jobs as a result of rebuffing sexual advances by supervisors or coworkers, and others are forced to quit after sexual harassment renders the workplace intolerable for them.

Sexual harassment clearly takes its toll in diminished worker productivity, increased employee turnover, and lost earnings and profits. According to a report on sexual harassment in the federal government, the government lost approximately $267 million as a direct result of sexual harassment.[49] Losses in private industry as a result of employee turnover, sick leave, and lost productivity are similar.[50] Sarah Burns, assistant director of the Georgetown University Law Center Sex Discrimination Clinic, testified before the House Subcommittee on Employment Opportunities that 90 percent of sexually harassed women suffer from chronic nervousness, fear, or anger and that another 60 percent experience physical symptoms such as headaches and nausea.[51]

Sexual harassment in the workplace appears to be not only pervasive but also increasing at an alarming rate. While they may not be the most accurate indicator, EEOC complaints are the best available baseline for reported incidents. The number of sexual harassment complaints filed with the EEOC has increased steadily since 1981. For example, 3,661 sexual harassment complaints were filed with the EEOC in 1981, 4,953 in 1985, 5,557 in 1990,[52] and 6,675 in 1991.[53] The EEOC reported that sexual harassment complaints filed in the first half of 1992 (4,754) had increased by over 50 percent compared with the same period in 1991. These increases reflect both a growing awareness of sexual harassment and a greater willingness of victims to report their experiences. However, while the number of formal complaints may be increasing, most women still do not report their sexual harassment or file formal complaints. For example, the EEOC reports that fewer than 1 percent of the estimated victims of sexual harassment filed charges under Title VII during 1989.[54] Similarly, a 1988 federal government study found that only 5 percent of women who had been sexually harassed took formal action.[55]

In 1980 the EEOC issued what has become the most widely cited definition of sexual harassment. According to the EEOC unwanted sexual advances, requests for sexual favors, and other verbal or physical conduct of a sexual nature constitute sexual harassment when (1) submission to such conduct is made either explicitly or implicitly a term or condition of an individual's employment, (2) submission to or rejection of such conduct by an individual is used as the basis for employment decisions affecting such individual, or (3) such conduct has the purpose or effect of unreasonably interfering with an individual's work performance or creating an intimidating, hostile, or offensive work environment.[56]

The U.S. Supreme Court issued its first sexual harassment decision in *Meritor Savings Bank v. Vinson*[57] in 1986, holding that sexual harassment in the workplace constitutes sex discrimination as prohibited under Title VII of the 1964 Civil Rights Act. In formulating its decision, the Court used the EEOC's definition to rule that sexual harassment may take the form of either "quid pro quo" (where an employee is promised a promotion, pay increase, continued employment, or some other work-related benefit in return for sexual favors) or a "hostile work environment," in which unwelcome sexual advances interfere with the employee's work performance.

The legal history of sexual harassment covers over two decades of litigation. However, nearly all of the early cases filed in federal district courts, which centered on quid pro quo harassment claims, were unsuccessful. Many of these courts viewed Title VII narrowly, as being limited to "discriminatory conduct arising out of company 'policy' rather than the 'personal proclivity, peculiarity, or mannerism' of a supervisor."[58] These courts reasoned that since the supervisor's conduct was not "company-directed policy" depriving women of federally protected employment opportunities, it was not actionable under Title VII.[59] Nearly all of the federal district courts during the early to mid-1970s failed to find sufficient grounds for Title VII violations.[60] A significant departure began with *Williams v. Saxbe*, in which a federal district court for the first time ruled that sexual harassment in the workplace constituted sex discrimination according to the meaning of Title VII.[61] Within a short time several federal appellate rulings affirmed that quid pro quo sexual harassment violates Title VII provisions "where gender is a substantial factor in the discrimination."[62]

In 1980 the EEOC issued guidelines that incorporated the *Williams* ruling into an interpretation of the Title VII prohibition against gender-based discrimination, of which one part addressed sexual harassment.[63]

The new EEOC guidelines were significant because they more clearly articulated the principle that rejection of unwelcome sexual conduct cannot be used as a basis for adverse employment decisions. Furthermore, the guidelines firmly reinforced the "hostile environment" case law by providing that unwelcome sexual advances, requests for sexual favors, or other verbal or physical behavior of a sexual nature violates Title VII whenever it "has the purpose or effect of unreasonably interfering with an individual's work performance or creating an intimidating, hostile, or offensive working environment."[64] Consequently, the volume of sexual harassment litigation alleging a "hostile work environment" began to increase.

Beginning with *Burdy v. Jackson*,[65] federal court decisions increasingly supported the 1980 EEOC guidelines by hearing cases against employers alleging that sexual harassment created an "intimidating, hostile, or offensive environment." With but a few exceptions, subsequent sexual harassment litigation prior to *Meritor* endorsed the EEOC principles of workplace privacy and protection.[66] Only a handful of federal cases expressed reluctance to adopt the hostile environment theory or failed to support emerging standards of liability.[67]

The 1986 *Meritor* decision by the U.S. Supreme Court was one of the most significant developments in the emerging legal protection against workplace sexual harassment. As stated earlier in this chapter, the Court in this case rejected the notion that only sexual harassment involving "a tangible loss" of "an economic character" could be used to support a Title VII claim and more clearly established the "hostile work environment" standard for all litigants.[68] *Meritor*, however, left several important legal questions unanswered, notably the "voluntariness" of sexual favors, the qualifications and conditions placed on workplace conduct, and the issue of employer liability. The Court stated that "not all workplace conduct that can be described as 'harassment' affects a term, condition, or privilege of employment within the meaning of Title VII."[69] At the suggestion that "mere utterance" of a sexually provocative nature that may promote "offensive feelings" in an employee would be sufficient for legal action, the Court asserted that sexual misconduct "must be sufficiently severe or pervasive to alter the conditions of employment and create an abusive working environment."[70] In regard to the issue of employer liability, the Court was divided as to what standard should be applied to sexual harassment. The majority indicated that in hostile environment cases, no employer, absent a formal policy against sexual harassment, should be made liable without actual knowledge of the conduct. Four justices concurring in the opinion argued that the "strict liability" rule of Title VII used in other forms of unlawful discrimination should be used to determine liability in sexual harassment cases.[71]

In an attempt to clarify remaining legal issues, the EEOC issued a new policy statement on sexual harassment on March 19, 1990.[72] This policy was intended to elaborate on legal principles set forth in *Meritor* and to update the commission's 1980 guidelines. These guidelines reasserted a distinction between "quid pro quo" and "hostile work environment" categories of sexual harassment and clarified the uncertain liability issue. The EEOC stated that an employer will "always be held responsible for acts of 'quid pro quo' sexual harassment of a supervisor," while the *Meritor* decision requires a "careful examination" of "hostile environment" cases to determine whether the harassing supervisor was acting in an "agency capacity."[73] Furthermore, the new EEOC policy stated that the commission would examine "objective evidence, rather than subjective, uncommunicated feelings" to "determine whether the victim's conduct is consistent, or inconsistent, with her assertion that the sexual conduct is unwelcome." Hence, the "unwelcomeness" issue was given greater clarity and the definition of what constituted a "hostile work environment" some degree of objectivity.[74]

As discussed earlier in this chapter, sexual harassment is both pervasive and destructive across virtually the entire spectrum of the labor force. Government policy may clearly determine the nature of sexual harassment, but that does little to stop the hostility, anger, resentment, and sense of male privilege expressed by a segment of the male work force. EEOC policy provides limited recourse for many victims of sexual harassment, who may choose to quit and look for another job rather than withstand the pressures and criticism resulting from filing a formal complaint with either state-level human rights agencies or the EEOC. This line of least resistance is especially likely to be taken by women working in minimum-wage or low-paying jobs, particularly within the service sector, or by those who are acutely dependent upon the income from their current employment. Just as some women do not readily leave hostile and abusive home environments, some women may endure sexual harassment for a wide range of psychological, social, and economic reasons. It is reasonable to assume that most of the cases that reach federal litigation represent only the most acute or chronic instances of sexual harassment and victimization.

In this regard, an examination of case law and remedies provides only

214   a partial glimpse into the experiences of sexually harassed women in the work force. However, these cases do offer a baseline from which to estimate the occurrence of less severe incidents. According to a private firm that tracks data on personal injury litigation, the amount of monetary awards for damages imposed on individual harassers can be substantial.[75] While many court awards are kept secret as a result of the agreement or settlement, the amounts of some awards remaining in the public domain appear to be substantial. According to the *Congressional Quarterly Researcher*, the sum of $3,100,000 was awarded to a woman who suffered emotional distress resulting from being forced to perform oral sex on a supervisor who threatened her with loss of her job.[76] In another case $2 million was awarded to a thirty-seven-year-old woman whose personnel manager position was eliminated (although she was transferred to a similar position at the same pay) after returning from workers' compensation leave for emotional distress caused by unwelcome sexual advances from her supervisor.[77] And $1,448,969 was awarded to a female executive who suffered emotional distress as a result of sexual discrimination in wages, sexual harassment from corporate managers, and subsequent termination.[78] It should be noted that these awards represent only the more recent top damage awards emerging from state courts. Furthermore, there is virtually no way to calculate the average award for sexual harassment or to determine what percentage of women who filed sexual harassment suits received an award or settlement.

In spite of more stringent government regulations and highly publicized court-ordered awards, American corporations appear to remain behind the trend of public awareness. While a growing number of companies have instituted sexual harassment training programs and seminars for employees, many have failed to establish clear standards of acceptable conduct in the workplace. Of course the economic costs of sexual harassment go well beyond those stemming from litigation and awards. As stated earlier in this chapter, losses due to absenteeism, reduced productivity, employee turnover, and poor morale can be staggering. *Working Woman* reported that the average company can lose up to $6.7 million a year due to sexual harassment.[79] In a survey conducted in 1992, more than 60 percent of the 9,680 readers responding stated that sexual harassment complaints are either ignored or result in merely token reprimands. Fifty-five percent of those who reported being sexually harassed in the workplace indicated that nothing happened to the harasser.[80] In contrast, 82 percent of the personnel executives surveyed at

106 *Fortune* 500 companies believed that most offenders in their companies are adequately punished.[81] Some management consultants view this disparity as being linked to employees' widespread distrust of internal grievance mechanisms and fear for possible effects on their careers.[82] Management analysts directed substantial criticism toward those corporate sexual harassment policies that fail to provide adequate protection for the complaining victim. Obviously, when victims of sexual harassment are required to confront their alleged harasser before the company will initiate a formal investigation, some women will be discouraged from pursuing internal remedies. Digital Equipment Corporation recently changed its sexual harassment policy to circumvent this dilemma. Consequently, a greater number of women were willing to report their sexual harassment experiences.

Facing severe criticism from consumers as well as from employees, a rapidly growing number of corporations are adopting tougher measures. For example, Honeywell and Corning have developed intensive seminars for their employees; DuPont has established a twenty-four-hour hotline and provides personal security for victims of sexual harassment; and AT&T has initiated a fast-track system for sexual harassment complaints.[83] The most effective corporate practice is to establish, publicize, and fully enforce a clear policy against sexual harassment. For example, once Honeywell removed the obscure and legalistic language from its policy in 1989 and began distributing handbooks and displaying posters in conspicuous locations in the workplace, the number of reported incidents increased substantially.[84] Similarly, corporate education and special training programs can be effective in sensitizing employees to the nature and effects of harassment, as well as informing them of the current legal ramifications. DuPont's program is a reasonably good example. In 1988 the company initiated a four-hour workshop led by teams of trained male and female workers representing all sectors of the corporation. The workshop, titled "A Matter of Respect," has been attended by well over 65,000 employees.[85] Furthermore, DuPont's hotline provides advice and personal security for victims fearful of retaliation. It also allows callers to remain unidentified, assures confidentiality, and does not automatically turn a call into a formal complaint. Prompt and responsive action is another key to successful intervention. The AT&T program attempts to complete the initial investigation within three to twenty days and provides security guards to protect against retaliation during the inquiry. The *Wall Street Journal* reported in 1991 that only 58 percent of *Fortune* 500 companies offered employees special training

216   for sexual harassment, but this number is expected to grow to over 90 percent during the 1990s.[86] A company that is responsive to complaints of sexual harassment, assumes responsibility for its employees' workplace conduct, and clearly articulates its guidelines and policies can provide a solid foundation for shaping employee conduct in the workplace. For example, Corning's guidelines, which date back to 1976, prohibit the display of nude pinups and calendars.[87] This policy establishes a standard of organizational intolerance, which in turn can alter the normative social climate surrounding symbolic and verbal communications, physical contact, and "game playing" of a sexual nature. As new adaptations and patterns of social interaction evolve from this social climate, employees should have more confidence that their work performance is the sole measure for personnel decisions, as well as having greater self-confidence and being more productive as a result of reduced sexual pressures.

The Civil Rights Act signed into law on November 22, 1991,[88] by President Bush included provisions for jury trials and damages for job discrimination. Its significance for victims of intentional sexual harassment was the provision for both compensatory damages (for example, reimbursement for medical bills and other costs directly associated with the harassment) and punitive damages.[89] However, damages for victims of sexual harassment, unlike those for other Title VII violations, were limited. The act "capped" the amount of damages that could be awarded according to the number of the company's employees: $50,000 for companies with fewer than 100 employees, $100,000 for 101 to 200 employees, $200,000 for 201 to 500 employees, and a maximum of $300,000 for companies with over 500 employees. In an effort to remedy the disparity between women and other minorities created by this legislation, Representative Barbara Kennelly introduced the Equal Remedies Bill in 1993[90] to end these limitations on compensatory and punitive damage awards. The bill proposed to compensate women fully for their losses and enable them to receive punitive damages based upon the nature and severity of the harassment rather than the size of the company. It was finally signed into law by President Clinton, making an important advance in the long and enduring struggle for sexual justice in the workplace.

The next important event in the evolution of law and policy governing sexual harassment was the 1993 U.S. Supreme Court case *Harris v. Forklift Systems, Inc.*[91] It was the first time since the 1986 *Meritor* decision that the Court had agreed to hear a sexual harassment case.

Teresa Harris was a manager at Forklift Systems, Inc., a construction equipment rental company, from April 1985 to October 1987. The U.S. Court of Appeals for the Sixth Circuit found that Charles Hardy, the company president, had made Harris the target of numerous unwanted sexual innuendos, demeaning remarks, and sexual gestures. Among the alleged acts were suggestions that they "go to the Holiday Inn to negotiate her raise," comments that she was a "dumb ass woman," and requests to her and other employees to remove the coins from his pants pockets. Hardy had allegedly committed these acts in front of other employees and had made repeated comments about her and other employees' clothing, intelligence, and sexual behavior. After Harris complained to Hardy, he expressed surprise that she was offended, apologized, and promised to stop. Believing that her complaint had ended the harassment, Harris decided to remain in her job, but in early September 1987, Hardy apparently renewed his sexually offensive conduct. Harris then quit and filed suit against her former employer, claiming that his conduct constituted "hostile work environment" harassment under Title VII of the 1964 Civil Rights Act.

In a unanimous decision written by Justice Sandra Day O'Connor, the Court held that employees do not have to show that they suffered severe or "serious" psychological injury to prove a "hostile work environment" case brought under Title VII of the Civil Rights Act of 1964. Justice O'Connor noted that "so long as the environment would reasonably be perceived, and is perceived, as hostile and abusive, there is no need for it also to be psychologically injurious."[92] The Court affirmed the "reasonable woman" standard and established a "middle path between making actionable any conduct that is merely offensive and requiring the conduct to cause a tangible psychological injury."[93]

While this decision is generally viewed as a major victory for women's rights in the workplace, as well as an asset for employers wishing to monitor and halt sexual harassment in their workplace, it has received some criticism from others who are concerned that it "ultimately may pit women against women when cases go before juries."[94] For example, Susan Deller Ross, director of the Georgetown University Law Center's Sex Discrimination Clinic, asserted that there will be "a lot of pressure from employers on other women employees to get up and testify that they weren't offended by what was happening."[95] The concern about "pitting women against women" emerges from the use of the "reasonable woman" standard, but it also concerns coercion by employers and coworkers.

218   While there may be instances in which some women may disagree with the allegations of women who have complained about sexual harassment, these differences would appear to be best resolved within the context of a clear and consistent legal standard and/or before a jury, rather than within the context of a workplace that has been deemed to be "hostile" and offensive by the victim. In such an instance, it is inevitable that some women would scrutinize other women, just as some men would scrutinize other men in any legal contest. The process merely places greater emphasis on the need to ensure that the investigation is not tainted by gender-based social and economic interests. It would appear that this task may be more readily accomplished with, rather than without, the *Harris* decision.

This is not to say that sexual harassment law, by itself, will alter normative workplace behavior reflecting popular (or dominant) attitudes and values governing appropriate gender roles, definitions of heterosexuality, use of power and control to resolve disputes, and gender-based conflict over shifting economic opportunities in the labor force. As stated earlier in this chapter, corporate victimization emerges from within a gender-based construction of harm. That is, the occurrence of sexual harassment in the workplace is fundamentally the manifestation of dominant cultural and social norms governing gender and sexuality. Whether or not legislation can change these attitudes and values remains unanswered. A number of scholars approach this issue with substantial skepticism, viewing the structural arrangements of gender, class, and power as forces stronger than the law.[96] However, greater awareness of the nature and consequences of sexual harassment and of the way in which the law is used to address victimization may help us formulate new interventions, remedies, and tools for monitoring the corporate workplace. Ultimately, it is the willingness of corporate decision makers, employees and their unions, and fellow workers to make the workplace reflect social and economic justice and, subsequently, eliminate normative support for sexually offensive conduct.

MATERNAL LEAVE AND WORKPLACE SAFETY POLICIES

Corporate victimization may also occur when women exercise their reproductive freedom.[97] Specifically, those women who become pregnant and give birth during full-time employment often face social and economic discrimination as a result of their decision to combine childbearing with employment. The Pregnancy Discrimination Act of 1978,[98] an amendment to Title VII prohibiting employment discrimination based on pregnancy, childbirth, and related medical conditions, was intended to expand women's protection from gender-based employment discrimination. Section 701(k) of the act provides that "women affected by pregnancy, childbirth, or related medical conditions be treated the same for all employment purposes, including receipt of benefits under the fringe benefit programs, as persons not so affected but similar in their ability or inability to work. . . ."[99] However, the act did not guarantee women a right to take family or maternal leave and did not protect those who lost their jobs after a leave of absence. Furthermore, Title VII prohibits employers from discriminating against women in hiring, firing, and other conditions of employment because they have chosen to have abortions. But because Title VII damage awards were designed to be "equitable" and limited to making the plaintiff "whole" for actual losses, Title VII is not seen as an effective remedy for women seeking damages for pain and suffering or punitive damages for intentional discrimination.

The first case on this issue to reach the U.S. Supreme Court is significant because it interpreted the Pregnancy Discrimination Act as applying to the dependents of both male and female employees. The Court, in *Newport News Shipbuilding and Dry Dock Co. v. EEOC*,[100] held that "male as well as female employees are protected against discrimination. Thus, if a private employer were to provide complete health insurance coverage for the dependents of its female employees, and no coverage at all for the dependents of its male employees, it would violate Title VII. . . ."[101] The Court noted that by "making clear that an employer could not discriminate (under the Pregnancy Discrimination Act) on the basis of an employee's pregnancy, Congress did not erase the original prohibition against discrimination on the basis of an employee's sex."[102] This decision left open the question of whether or not the "disproportionate impact" analysis is applicable to pregnancy discrimination with respect to women alone.[103] However, the Court clearly set forth the principle that company medical coverage must cover the pregnancy and related medical conditions of employees' wives to the same extent that it covered other dependents. Hence, failure to provide comparable coverage for dependents' pregnancies constituted illegal sex discrimination.

The next case in which the U.S. Supreme Court interpreted the Pregnancy Discrimination Act concerned a California statute that requires

220   employers to grant pregnant employees unpaid disability leave for up to four months and, specifically, its provisions for reinstatement to the same or similar job at the end of the leave period. In *California Federal Savings and Loan Ass'n v. Guerra*,[104] the Court upheld the California statute, asserting that the law was not invalid because it does "not compel California employers to treat pregnant workers better than other disabled employees"; it merely "establishes benefits that employers must, at a minimum, provide to pregnant workers."[105] Noting that employers were free to give comparable benefits to other disabled employees, the Court thereby sidestepped the difficult question of preferential treatment for pregnant workers.[106]

Generally, the Pregnancy Discrimination Act has given both women and men the ability to challenge discriminatory practices in employment. With the increase in the number of women in the work force, problems arising from gender differences have become more obvious, and the Court appears to have been largely effective in resolving these issues. However, the act protects pregnant workers from sex discrimination only if similar benefits are given to other workers. Hence, it left a significant gap in protection of pregnancy and maternity under the law.

This gap was addressed with the passage of the Family and Medical Leave Act of 1993.[107] However, this act applies only to businesses with fifty or more employees, requires thirty days' notice, and can be used only by employees who have worked at least 1,250 hours for the company over the previous year. Given the shifts in labor market participation and family structure described earlier, further study is needed to determine whether its provisions adequately protect the vast majority of women in the labor force. It is clear, however, that those women who depend upon the informal labor market to support their family will not enjoy the protection that is now accorded by larger employers in the formal labor market. Given changing economic conditions and the impact on household economies, maternal and family leave policies should be viewed as an essential part of women's employment rights.

Prior to legislation with provisions for maternal leave, many American women faced either voluntary or involuntary termination of employment for choosing motherhood. In spite of the passage of the Family and Medical Leave Act of 1993, eligible women still face the difficult choice of either taking twelve weeks of unpaid family leave (and possibly losing ground on opportunities for subsequent advancement) or returning to work even sooner after giving birth. The hardship associated with conflicts between employment opportunity and parental interests continues to have a negative effect on women, particularly those who depend on participation in the labor force for economic survival.

In contrast, all industrialized and many other nations long ago instituted maternal leave policies, many providing paid leave with full health care coverage, as part of their employment opportunity structure. The United States is clearly behind other industrialized nations in extending these rights to its workers. For example, the International Labor Office conducted a study in 1984 examining the parental and family leave policies of 121 countries.[108] The findings indicated that most countries prohibited termination during the leave period and guaranteed returning employees either their former position or a comparable assignment. While the length of leave varied, most nations provided between eleven and fifteen weeks of maternity leave.[109] The study, which also included an American cohort of women in the work force who gave birth between 1978 and 1986, found that approximately one-half of these mothers left the work force four weeks prior to delivery; almost one-third remained actively employed immediately before giving birth. Furthermore, it was reported that 74 percent of these women returned to the work force within one year after childbirth.[110]

Another form of corporate victimization affecting women is workplace safety, which historically has been given little attention by public officials and labor organizations but nevertheless represents a significant area of concern. With technological advancements in the workplace, many women are being exposed at work to environments that may have serious health consequences for a developing fetus. This form of victimization, discussed in detail in Chapter 5, may become more problematic as it extends across a wider segment of the labor market, particularly for hourly wage and production workers and those employed by multinational corporations operating in developing countries, which may have less stringent worker safety and environmental protection standards.

The Occupational Safety and Health Act of 1970 requires employers to guarantee workers safe and healthy working conditions and to maintain a workplace free from recognized dangers that would cause death or physical injury. The act also gives employees and unions the right to know about hazards in the workplace and allows workers, without penalty of loss of their jobs, to request an OSHA inspection. Since 1974, NIOSH has investigated reproductive hazards for women workers. As a result, some employers have adopted policies resulting in the exclusion of women from specific jobs, raising concern about a new generation of protective labor laws that effectively deny women access to employment opportunities more than they protect them from workplace hazards.

In 1980 the EEOC, the Department of Labor's Office of Federal Contract Compliance Programs, and OSHA attempted to establish a neutral policy to protect workers from reproductive hazards. After this joint effort received numerous critical comments during its review, the proposed guidelines were withdrawn. However, in 1988 the EEOC implemented new policy guidelines on reproductive and fetal hazards.[111] These guidelines provide for the use of the "business necessity" defense in cases where women employees are discriminated against to prevent their exposure to reproductive and fetal health hazards; but the employer must prove "whether there is a substantial risk of harm to offspring of employees through exposure to hazards in the workplace, whether the harm takes place through the exposure of one sex but not the other, and whether the employer's policy effectively eliminates the risk."[112]

Under the "general duty" clause of the Occupational Safety and Health Act,[113] intentional violations have been subject to a $70,000 penalty since 1991. This provision addresses employee injuries resulting from concealed dangers of which the company had previous knowledge. Thus, intentional concealment of workplace health hazards from workers has been given greater sanctions.

Long-term exposure to hazardous materials in many sectors of the workplace remains a serious concern. However, the effects on reproductive health may prove to be of equal concern for women and men.[114] Hence, the best remedy may be to establish an environmentally sound, safe, and nontoxic workplace for all employees, rather than to direct specific attention to possible fetal damage, which may further marginalize women's health issues.

DIRECTIONS FOR LAW AND SOCIAL POLICY CHANGE

The concerted and continuing efforts of women's organizations and the willingness of liberal political actors to move these issues and concerns into the legitimate governmental arenas of social policy development, legislative action, and case law decisions have brought about limited change favorable to women. However, there are many areas in which women's lives and experiences in American society remain at risk of corporate victimization. For example, unsafe consumer goods aimed at female consumers, continuation of sexual harassment in the workplace, hazardous working conditions in a number of industries that use piecework pay systems, exclusion of women from several areas of employment, and only scant attention to women's health needs and problems are but a few examples of corporate neglect and victimization. Within these forms of victimization, age, race, and class distinctions sometimes enhance the likelihood and/or impact of victimization. One clear example is the tobacco industry's advertisement campaigns targeting young female smokers. With available knowledge of the impact of smoking on fetal development, the corporate interest in competing for an expanded "market share," coupled with organized resistance to governmental attempts at further regulation of tobacco due to its health risks, illustrates the extent of corporate disregard for harm and reflects a business policy that does not include responsibility as a factor in the consumer-producer relationship.

In spite of several decades of policy change, the balance between women's and corporate interests remains tilted in favor of the latter. Women must therefore remain vigilant and maintain their scrutiny of government's role in ending all forms of gender inequality and discrimination. Within the context of changing political and ideological representation in both houses of Congress, a number of policies that have successfully promoted women's interests in the workplace are rapidly becoming the target of criticism by conservatives and others whose political ideologies place greater emphasis on cost-effectiveness and reduced governmental interference in private enterprise than on the quality of life of their female constituents. Among the many policies under attack are affirmative action programs, punitive damages awards in civil litigation, and some provisions of family and maternal leave policies and guidelines—cutbacks in which will have a significant impact on women as well as racial minorities.

New Republicans' emphasis on deficit reduction and eagerness to have a balanced budget by the year 2002, as stated in the "Contract with America," raise questions about the direction of social change for women in American society. Clearly, the political agenda of the late 1990s will be influenced by conservatives whose ideological views are opposed to abortion on demand, affirmative action, and a host of other social policies that they perceive as restricting corporate interests and

224 objectives, such as well-established environmental and consumer safety policies.

Before further changes favorable to women's interests can be pursued, there is an urgent need to develop new political alliances and strategies so that gains to date are not reversed in the swing toward the political right. Women's groups and organizations face renewed challenges, particularly given the growing conservative faction among some women and members of racial minorities who have realigned themselves with New Republicans' policy agendas. It is important to remember that social change favorable to women has historically been accompanied by substantial resistance and continuing challenges to the legitimacy of gender-based victimization. Further revisions of gender-based definitions of harm, along with efforts to limit regulatory powers and civil penalties, present a significant threat to the level of equality and freedom women have achieved since the early 1960s. Corporate victimization of women may continue unabated by law and policy as new proposals emphasize the removal of corporate regulations, restraints, and sanctions.

It is quite possible that we are entering a period in which law and government-sponsored policy will actually diminish rather than enhance the status of women in contemporary society. Given the already limited applications of the law, further efforts to control its ability to be an effective remedy for corporate harm may make sex discrimination and corporate victimization normative within the context of the law.

NOTES

1. G. Duerst-Lahti, "The Government's Role in Building the Women's Movement," *Political Science Quarterly* 104, no. 2 (1989): 249–68.

2. E. Paul, "The Women's Movement and the Movement of Women," *Social Policy* 23 (Summer 1993): 44–50. For sex discrimination see E. Traxler, "Sex Discrimination: Reasonable or Suspect," in *Historical U.S. Court Cases, 1960–1990: An Encyclopedia,* ed. J. Johnson (New York: Garland, 1992); T. Bach, "Gender Stereotyping in Employment Discrimination: Finding a Balance of Evidence and Causation Under Title VII," *Minnesota Law Review* 77 (May 1993): 1251–81; K. Duncan and M. Prus, "Starting Wages of Women and Men in Female and Male Occupations: A Test of the Human Capital Explanation of Occupational Sex Segregation," *Social Science Journal* 29, no. 4 (1992): 479–93; U.S. Department of Labor, *Pipelines*

of Progress: A Status Report on the Glass Ceiling (Washington, DC: Government Printing Office, 1992).

3. See B. Sinclair Decard, *The Women's Movement: Political, Socioeconomic, and Psychological Issues* (New York: Harper and Row, 1979); F. Davis, *The Women's Movement in America Since 1960* (New York: Simon and Schuster, 1991); R. Simon, *Women's Movements in America: Their Successes, Disappointments, and Aspirations* (New York: Praeger, 1991); R. Morgan, *The Word of a Woman: Feminist Dispatches, 1968–1992* (New York: Norton, 1992).

4. See S. Becker, *The Origins of the Equal Rights Amendment: American Feminism Between the Wars* (Westport, CT: Greenwood, 1981); M. Forster, *Significant Sisters: The Grassroots of Active Feminism, 1839–1939* (New York: Knopf, 1985).

5. B. Berg, *The Remembered Gate: Origins of American Feminism, Women and the City, 1800–1860* (New York: Oxford University Press, 1978); E. DuBois, *American Feminism and Suffrage: The Emergence of an Independent Women's Movement in America, 1848–1969* (Ithaca, NY: Cornell University Press, 1978); L. Gordon, *Woman's Body, Woman's Right: A Social History of Birth Control in America* (New York: Viking, 1977).

6. V. Sapiro, "The Gender Basis of American Social Policy," *Political Science Quarterly* 101, no. 2 (1986): 221–38; DuBois, *American Feminism and Suffrage*.

7. *Muller v. Oregon*, 208 U.S. 412 (1908).

8. N. Erickson, "Historical Background of 'Protective' Labor Legislation: *Muller v. Oregon*," in *Women and the Law*, vol. 2, ed. D. Weisberg (Cambridge: Schenkman, 1982), 158.

9. These developments within the early feminist movement are described in C. Harrison, "A 'New Frontier' for Women: The Public Policy of the Kennedy Administration," *Journal of American History* 67 (December 1980): 630–46; J. Sealander, *As Minority Becomes Majority* (Westport, CT: Greenwood, 1983); Duerst-Lahti, "The Government's Role in Building the Women's Movement," esp. 250–52.

10. Duerst-Lahti, "The Government's Role in Building the Women's Movement," 250–51.

11. D. Balser, *Feminism and Labor in Modern Times* (Boston: South End Press, 1987).

12. Harrison, "A 'New Frontier' for Women."

13. Ibid.; P. Zalman, *Women, Work, and National Policy: The Kennedy-Johnson Years* (Ann Arbor, MI: UMI Research Press, 1982).

14. Duerst-Lahti, "The Government's Role in Building the Women's Movement," 254–65.

15. Ibid., 255.

16. L. W. Gladstone, "Family and Medical Leave Legislation," *CRS Issue*

226   *Brief* (Washington, DC: Congressional Research Service, August 30, 1993), 1.

17. Ibid., 1.

18. Ibid.

19. For representative works on sexual harassment see A. Aggarwal, *Sexual Harassment in the Workplace* (Boston: Butterworth, 1987); E. Barnett, "Sexual Harassment: A Continuing Source of Litigation in the Workplace," *Trial* 25 (June 1989): 34–38; D. Bennett-Alexander, "Hostile Environment Sexual Harassment: A Clearer View," *Labor Law Journal* 42 (March 1991): 131–43; K. Neville, *Corporate Attractions: An Inside Account of Sexual Harassment with the New Sexual Rules for Men and Women on the Job* (Washington, DC: Acropolis Books, 1990); B. Ness, "The Road to Respect Which a Reasonable Woman Must Travel: Sexual Harassment in the American Workplace," *Federal Bar News and Journal* 40 (June 1993): 280–87. For women's health in the workplace see G. Kelly, "An Employer's Right to Health Protection or a Woman's Right to Equal Employment? A Critical Look at Fetal Protection Policies," *New England Law Review* 26 (Spring 1992): 1101–43; J. Morton, "Pregnancy in the Workplace—Sex-Specific Fetal Protection Policies: *UAW v. Johnson Controls, Inc.*—A Victory for Women?" *Tennessee Law Review* 59 (Spring 1992): 617–41; J. Kohl, "Small Business Compliance with the Pregnancy Discrimination Act," *Journal of Small Business Management* 21 (October 1983): 49–53; A. Duncan, "Fetal Protection and the Exclusion of Women from the Toxic Workplace," *North Carolina Central Law Journal* 18 (1989): 67–86.

20. The Wage and Hour Division of the U.S. Department of Labor is assigned enforcement responsibilities. Federal workers are regulated by the Office of Personnel Management.

21. Virtually all of the restrictive state laws have now been invalidated. Subsequent revisions of the Equal Pay Act extended its coverage to other workers. In 1974 the Fair Labor Standards Act extended protection to private household workers who are employed at least eight hours a week and whose earnings constitute wages for the purpose of social security. A provision enacted in 1980 allows employers to consider gratuities or tips as 40 percent of the minimum wage that must be paid. The following year the minimum wage was set at $3.35 per hour. Several exemptions were authorized, such as lower wages for apprentices, professionals, some salespersons, students, and those who work on a seasonal or casual basis.

22. The Equal Pay Act of 1963, 29 U.S.C. 206(d) is enforced by the EEOC, which was established in 1964 as part of Title VII of the Civil Rights Act of 1964.

23. C. Lefcourt, *Women and the Law* (New York: Clark Boardman, 1987), 2–33.

24. Ibid., 2–35.

25. *County of Washington v. Gunther,* 452 U.S. 161 (1981).

26. *AFSCME v. State of Washington,* 770 F.2d 1401 (9th Cir. 1985).

27. *Reed v. Reed,* 404 U.S. 71 (1971).

28. N. Erickson, "A Supreme Court First: Equal Protection Applied to Women," in *Historic U.S. Court Cases, 1960–1990: An Encyclopedia,* ed. J. Johnson (New York: Garland, 1992).

29. *Frontiero v. Richardson,* 411 U.S. 677 (1973).

30. See N. Morais, "Sex Discrimination and the Fourteenth Amendment: Lost History," *Yale Law Journal* 97 (1988): 1153–72; J. Dixon, "Constitutional Law—Due Process—United States Supreme Court in Plurality Opinion Names Sex a Suspect Classification Requiring Compelling Interest Test," *Creighton Law Review* 7 (Fall 1973): 69–91; L. D. Wiesenberger, "Constitutional Law—Equal Protection—Discrimination Based on Sex in the Provision of Armed Service Dependents' Benefits," *Case Western Law Review* 24 (Summer 1973): 824–45.

31. See for example *Kahn v. Shevin,* 416 U.S. 351 (1974); *Schlesinger v. Ballard,* 419 U.S. 498 (1974); and *Geduldig v. Aiello,* 417 U.S. 484 (1974).

32. *Craig v. Boren,* 429 U.S. 190 (1976).

33. K. Lewis, "Sex Discrimination and the United States Supreme Court Developments in the Law," *CRS Report for Congress* (Washington, DC: Congressional Research Service, August 22, 1989), 4.

34. See for example *Califano v. Goldfarb,* 430 U.S. 199 (1977); *Califano v. Sibowitz,* 430 U.S. 924 (1977); *Califano v. Webster,* 430 U.S. 313 (1977); *Orr v. Orr,* 440 U.S. 268 (1979); *Califano v. Wescott,* 443 U.S. 76 (1979); *Kirchberg v. Feenstra,* 450 U.S. 455 (1981); *Michael M. v. Superior Court,* 450 U.S. 464 (1981); *Rostker v. Goldberg,* 453 U.S. 57 (1981).

35. Lewis, "Sex Discrimination and the United States Supreme Court," 4–13.

36. K. DeCrow, *Sexist Justice* (New York: Random House, 1974), 91–92.

37. *Griggs v. Duke Power Co.,* 401 U.S. 424 (1971).

38. Lewis, "Sex Discrimination and the United States Supreme Court," 16.

39. Ibid., 16.

40. *Griggs v. Duke Power Co.* was the first case to articulate the "effects" test, which is also known as the "disproportionate impact" analysis.

41. See *Dothard v. Rawlinson,* 433 U.S. 321 (1977).

42. See for example *Washington v. Davis,* 426 U.S. 229 (1976); ibid.

43. *Wards Cove Packing Co., Inc. v. Atonio,* 109 S. Ct. 2115 (1989).

44. Lewis, "Sex Discrimination and the United States Supreme Court," 19.

45. Public Law 102-166 (1991).

46. See W. E. Terpstra and S. E. Cook, "Complaint Characteristics and

228   Reported Behaviors and Consequences Associated with Formal Sexual Harassment Charges," *Personnel Psychology* 38 (1985): 559–74.

47. Congressional Caucus for Women's Issues, *Sexual Harassment* (Washington, DC, October 1993).

48. E. Schmitt, "Two out of Three Women in Military Study Report Sexual Harassment Incidents," *New York Times* (September 12, 1990): A22.

49. U.S. Merit Systems Protection Board, *Sexual Harassment in the Federal Workplace: Is It a Problem?* (Washington, DC: Office of Merit Systems Review and Studies, March 1981); U.S. Merit Systems Protection Board, *Sexual Harassment in the Federal Government: An Update* (Washington, DC: Office of Merit Systems Review and Studies, 1988).

50. National Organization for Women, *Facts on Sexual Harassment* (New York: NOW Legal Defense and Education Fund, Inc., 1990).

51. Congressional Caucus for Women's Issues, "Sexual Harassment."

52. C. S. Clark, "Sexual Harassment: Men and Women in Workplace Struggles," *Congressional Quarterly Researcher* 1, no. 13 (August 9, 1991).

53. J. Gross, "Suffering in Silence No More: Fighting Sexual Harassment," *New York Times* (July 13, 1992): A1, D10.

54. Congressional Caucus for Women's Issues, "Sexual Harassment."

55. Ibid.

56. 29 C.F.R. 1604.11 (July 1990).

57. *Meritor Savings Bank v. Vinson*, 477 U.S. 57 (1986).

58. C. V. Dale, "Sexual Harassment: A History of Federal Law," *CRS Report for Congress* (Washington, DC: Congressional Research Service, May 7, 1993): 2–5.

59. Ibid., 2–3.

60. Ibid., 3.

61. *Williams v. Saxbe*, 413 F. Supp. 654 (D.D.C. 1976).

62. See for example *Barnes v. Costle*, 561 F.2d 983 (D.C. Cir. 1977); *Tomkins v. Public Service Electric & Gas Co.*, 422 F. Supp. 553 (Dist. NJ 1976); *Miller v. Bank of America*, 418 F. Supp. 233 (N.D. Cal. 1976).

63. 29 C.F.R. 1604.11(f) (1992).

64. Ibid.

65. *Burdy v. Jackson*, 641 F.2d. 934 (1981).

66. See for example *Henson v. Dundee*, 682 F.2d 897, 902 (11th Cir. 1982), which stated that

> sexual harassment which creates a hostile or offensive environment for members of one sex is every bit the arbitrary barrier to sexual equality at the workplace that racial harassment is to racial equality. Surely, a requirement that a man or woman run a gauntlet of sexual abuse in return for the privilege of being allowed to work and make a living can be as demeaning and disconcerting as the harshest of racial epithets.

67. See for example *Ross v. Communications Satellite Corp.*, 759 F.2d 355 (4th Cir. 1985); *Meyers v. I.T.T. Diversified Credit Corp.*, 527 F. Supp. 1064 (E.D. Mo. 1981); *Katz v. Dole*, 709 F.2d 251 (4th Cir. 1983).

68. In *Meritor* it was alleged that the complainant's supervisor fondled her in front of other employees, demanded sexual relations over the course of three years, exposed himself to her, and forcibly raped her on several occasions. The complainant argued that she submitted to protect her job. In this instance, there was no finding of quid pro quo sexual harassment, as the complainant had received several promotions that (disputedly) were based upon merit and not sexual favors.

69. Ibid., 62.

70. Ibid., 62.

71. Ibid., 72.

72. U.S. Equal Employment Opportunity Commission, "Policy Guidance on Sexual Harassment," *FEP Manual* 405 (1990).

73. Ibid., 6686–95.

74. Ibid., 6689. The commission emphasized the following factors: (1) whether the conduct was verbal or physical or both; (2) how frequently it was repeated; (3) whether the conduct was hostile and patently offensive; (4) whether the alleged harasser was a coworker or a supervisor; (5) whether others joined in perpetrating the harassment; and (6) whether the harassment was directed at more than one individual.

75. Court award data from Jury Verdict Research, Inc. were reported in Clark, "Sexual Harassment: Men and Women in Workplace Struggles," 542.

76. *Moore v. Cardinal Services, Inc.* (Richland, Ohio, settled December 1986).

77. *Bibun v. AT&T Information Systems* (Los Angeles, settled December 1986).

78. *Gaffke v. U-Haul of Oregon* (Multnomah, Oregon, settled February 1988).

79. R. Sandroff, "Sexual Harassment in the *Fortune* 500," *Working Woman* (December 1988): 74.

80. J. Lublin, "Corporate Efforts to Fight Harassment Face Credibility Gap, Survey Finds," *Wall Street Journal* (April 15, 1992): B4.

81. Ibid.

82. Ibid.

83. A. Deutchman, "Dealing with Sexual Harassment," *Fortune* (November 4, 1991): 145–48.

84. Ibid., 148.

85. Ibid., 148. Also see "Ending Sexual Harassment: Business Is Getting the Message," *Business Week* (March 18, 1991): 98–99.

86. J. Lublin, "Sexual Harassment Is Topping Agenda in Many Executive Education Programs," *Wall Street Journal* (December 9, 1991): B1, 6.

230

87. "Ending Sexual Harassment," *Business Week*, 98.

88. Public Law 102-166, 105 Stat. 1071. Title VII of the 1964 Civil Rights Act contained no specific provisions for damage awards. However, victims of discrimination could sue under the Civil Rights Act of 1866, 42 U.S.C., Section 1983.

89. Public Law 102-166, 105 Stat. 1071.

90. H.R. 224, 103rd Congress.

91. *Harris v. Forklift Systems, Inc.*, 126 L. Ed. 295, 114 S. Ct. 367 (1993).

92. Ibid.

93. Ibid., 302.

94. M. Coyle, "Workplace Policing to Be Easier?" *National Law Journal* (November 22, 1993): 3–4.

95. Ibid., 4.

96. G. Rosenberg, *The Hollow Hope: Can Courts Bring About Social Change?* (Chicago, IL: University of Chicago Press, 1991); also see C. MacKinnon, *The Sexual Harassment of Working Women* (New Haven, CT: Yale University Press, 1979); C. Smart, *Feminism and the Power of Law* (London: Routledge, 1990).

97. Women's reproductive freedoms, such as access to abortion and birth control, are relatively new rights that have been primarily defined by case law rather than by legislation. Since the *Roe v. Wade* (410 U.S. 113 [1973]) decision, the U.S. Supreme Court has been the major institution defining and limiting these freedoms. However, recent conservative political efforts—such as restrictions on the use of public funds for abortions, parental notification requirements for juvenile abortions, and other attempts to control and regulate women's reproductive freedom—have more squarely placed these issues in the political arena. The level of violence and terror directed at abortion clinics by antiabortionists and the religious right has not only endangered women's lives but has served to noticeably restrain individual choice and reproductive freedom.

98. Public Law 95-555, 92 Stat. 2076 (1978). This law was enacted to reverse the *General Electric Co. v. Gilbert* (425 U.S. 125 [1978]) Supreme Court decision, which held that discrimination based on pregnancy was not sex discrimination as defined by Title VII of the 1964 Civil Rights Act.

99. Section 701(k) of Title VII, 42 U.S.C. 2000e (k).

100. *Newport News Shipbuilding and Dry Dock Co. v. EEOC*, 462 U.S. 669 (1983).

101. Ibid., 682–83.

102. Ibid.

103. Lewis, "Sex Discrimination and the United States Supreme Court," 29.

104. *California Federal Savings and Loan Ass'n v. Guerra*, 479 U.S. 272 (1987).

105. Ibid.

106. Similarly, the Court in *Wimberly v. Labor and Industrial Relations Commission* (479 U.S. 511 [1987]), was unwilling to read a preferential treatment mandate into the 1975 amendment to the Federal Unemployment Tax Act (26 U.S.C. 3304 [a] [12]), which prohibits discrimination "solely on the basis of pregnancy or termination of pregnancy."

107. Public Law 103-3.

108. P. Garrett et al., "Working Around Childbirth: Comparative and Empirical Perspectives on Parental Leave Policy," *Child Welfare* 69, no. 5 (1990): 401–13.

109. Ibid.

110. Ibid.

111. U.S. EEOC, "Reproductive and Fetal Hazards," *Compliance Manual*, vol. 2, section 624 (Washington, DC: EEOC, October 7, 1988).

112. Ibid., 4–5.

113. Section 5(a)(1) requires employers to provide a workplace "free from recognized hazards that are causing or are likely to cause death or serious physical harm to employees."

114. See S. Sexton, "The Reproductive Hazards of Industrial Chemicals: Politics of Protection," *Ecologist* 23 (1993): 212–18.

REFERENCES

Aggarwal, A. 1987. *Sexual Harassment in the Workplace.* Boston: Butterworth.

Bach, T. 1993. Gender stereotyping in employment discrimination: Finding a balance of evidence and causation under Title VII. *Minnesota Law Review* 77(May): 1251–81.

Balser, D. 1987. *Feminism and Labor in Modern Times.* Boston: South End Press.

Barnett, E. 1989. Sexual harassment: A continuing source of litigation in the workplace. *Trial* 25(June): 34–38.

Becker, S. 1981. *The Origins of the Equal Rights Amendment: American Feminism Between the Wars.* Westport: Greenwood.

Bennett-Alexander, D. 1991. Hostile environment sexual harassment: A clearer view. *Labor Law Journal* 42(March): 131–43.

Berg, B. 1978. *The Remembered Gate: Origins of American Feminism, Women and the City, 1800–1860.* New York: Oxford University Press.

Clark, C. S. 1991. Sexual harassment: Men and women in workplace struggles. *Congressional Quarterly Researcher* 1(13, August 9): 538–59.

Congressional Caucus for Women's Issues. 1993. *Sexual Harassment,* October. Washington, DC.

232   Coyle, M. 1993. Workplace policing to be easier? *National Law Journal,*
       November 22: 3–4.

Dale, C. V. 1993. Sexual harassment: A history of federal law. *CRS Report
       for Congress,* 1–17, May 7. Washington, DC: Congressional Research
       Service.

Davis, F. 1991. *The Women's Movement in America Since 1960.* New York:
       Simon and Schuster.

DeCrow, K. 1974. *Sexist Justice.* New York: Random House.

Deutchman, A. 1991. Dealing with sexual harassment. *Fortune,* November
       4: 145–48.

Dixon, J. 1973. Constitutional law—due process—United States Supreme
       Court in plurality opinion names sex a suspect classification requiring
       compelling interest test. *Creighton Law Review* 7(Fall): 69–91.

DuBois, E. 1978. *American Feminism and Suffrage: The Emergence of an
       Independent Women's Movement in America, 1848–1969.* Ithaca, NY:
       Cornell University Press.

Duerst-Lahti, G. 1989. The government's role in building the women's
       movement. *Political Science Quarterly* 104(2): 249–68.

Duncan, A. 1989. Fetal protection and the exclusion of women from the
       toxic workplace. *North Carolina Central Law Journal* 18: 67–86.

Duncan, K. and M. Prus. 1992. Starting wages of women and men in female
       and male occupations: A test of the human capital explanation of occu-
       pational sex segregation. *Social Science Journal* 29(4): 479–93.

Ending sexual harassment: Business is getting the message. 1991. *Business
       Week,* March 18: 98–99.

Erickson, N. 1982. Historical background of 'protective' labor legislation:
       Muller v. Oregon. In *Women and the Law,* vol. 2, ed. D. Weisberg. Cam-
       bridge: Schenkman.

———. 1992. A Supreme Court first: Equal protection applied to women. In
       Historic U.S. Court Cases, 1960–1990: An Encyclopedia, ed. J. Johnson.
       New York: Garland.

Forster, M. 1985. *Significant Sisters: The Grassroots of Active Feminism,
       1839–1939.* New York: Knopf.

Garrett, P., D. Wenk and S. Lubeck. 1990. Working around childbirth: Com-
       parative and empirical perspectives on parental leave policy. *Child Wel-
       fare* 69(5): 401–13.

Gladstone, L. 1993. Family and medical leave legislation. *CRS Issue Brief,*
       1–12. Washington, DC: Congressional Research Service.

Gordon, L. 1977. *Woman's Body, Woman's Right: A Social History of Birth
       Control in America.* New York: Viking.

Gross, J. 1992. Suffering in silence no more: Fighting sexual harassment.
       New York Times, July 13: A1, D10.

Harrison, C. 1980. A 'new frontier' for women: The public policy of the

Kennedy administration. *Journal of American History* 67(December): 630–46.

Kelly, G. 1992. An employer's right to health protection or a woman's right to equal employment? A critical look at fetal protection policies. *New England Law Review* 26(Spring): 1101–43.

Kohl, J. 1983. Small business compliance with the Pregnancy Discrimination Act. *Journal of Small Business Management* 21(October): 49–53.

Lefcourt, C. 1987. *Women and the Law.* New York: Clark Boardman.

Lewis, K. 1989. Sex discrimination and the United States Supreme Court: Developments in the law. *CRS Report for Congress,* 1–51, August 22. Washington, DC: Congressional Research Service.

Lublin, J. 1991. Sexual harassment is topping agenda in many executive education programs. *Wall Street Journal,* December 9: B1, 6.

———. 1992. Corporate efforts to fight harassment face credibility gap, survey finds. *Wall Street Journal,* April 15: B4, 8.

MacKinnon, C. 1979. *The Sexual Harassment of Working Women.* New Haven, CT: Yale University Press.

Morais, N. 1988. Sex discrimination and the Fourteenth Amendment: Lost history. *Yale Law Journal* 97: 1153–72.

Morgan, R. 1992. *The Word of a Woman: Feminist Dispatches, 1968–1992.* New York: Norton.

Morton, J. 1992. Pregnancy in the workplace—Sex-specific fetal protection policies: *UAW v. Johnson Controls, Inc.*—A victory for women? *Tennessee Law Review* 59(Spring): 617–41.

National Organization for Women. 1990. *Facts on Sexual Harassment.* New York: NOW Legal Defense and Education Fund, Inc.

Ness, B. 1993. The road to respect which a reasonable woman must travel: Sexual harassment in the American workplace. *Federal Bar News and Journal* 40(June): 280–87.

Neville, K. 1990. *Corporate Attractions: An Inside Account of Sexual Harassment with the New Sexual Rules for Men and Women on the Job.* Washington, DC: Acropolis Books.

Paul, E. 1993. The women's movement and the movement of women. *Social Policy* 23(Summer): 44–50.

Rosenberg, G. 1991. *The Hollow Hope: Can Courts Bring About Social Change?* Chicago, IL: University of Chicago Press.

Sandroff, R. 1988. Sexual harassment in the *Fortune* 500. *Working Woman,* December: 74.

Sapiro, V. 1986. The gender basis of American social policy. *Political Science Quarterly* 101(2): 221–38.

Schmitt, E. 1990. Two out of three women in military study report sexual harassment incidents. *New York Times,* September 12: A22.

234   Sealander, J. 1983. *As Minority Becomes Majority*. Westport, CT: Greenwood.

Sexton, S. 1993. The reproductive hazards of industrial chemicals: Politics of protection. *Ecologist* 23(November–December): 212–18.

Simon, R. 1991. *Women's Movements in America: Their Successes, Disappointments, and Aspirations*. New York: Praeger.

Sinclair Decard, B. 1979. *The Women's Movement: Political, Socioeconomic, and Psychological Issues*. New York: Harper and Row.

Smart, C. 1990. *Feminism and the Power of Law*. London: Routledge.

Terpstra, W. and S. E. Cook. 1985. Complaint characteristics and reported behaviors and consequences associated with formal sexual harassment charges. *Personnel Psychology* 38: 559–74.

Traxler, E. 1992. Sex discrimination: Reasonable or suspect. In *Historical U.S. Court Cases, 1960–1990: An Encyclopedia*, ed. J. Johnson. New York: Garland.

U.S. Department of Labor. 1992. *Pipelines of Progress: A Status Report on the Glass Ceiling*. Washington, DC: Government Printing Office.

U.S. Equal Employment Opportunity Commission. 1988. Reproductive and fetal hazards. *Compliance Manual*, vol. 2, Section 624, October 7. Washington, DC.

———. 1990. Policy guidance on sexual harassment. *Fair Employment Practices*, vol. 8, February. Washington, DC.

U.S. Merit Systems Protection Board. 1981. *Sexual Harassment in the Federal Workplace: Is It a Problem?* Washington, DC: Office of Merit Systems Review and Studies.

———. 1988. *Sexual Harassment in the Federal Government: An Update*. Washington, DC: Office of Merit Systems Review and Studies.

Wiesenberger, L. D. 1973. Constitutional law—equal protection—discrimination based on sex in the provision of armed service dependents' benefits. *Case Western Law Review* 24(Summer): 824–45.

Zalman, P. 1982. *Women, Work and National Policy: The Kennedy-Johnson Years*. Ann Arbor, MI: UMI Research Press.

DIRECTIONS FOR SOCIAL CHANGE AND POLITICAL ACTION

Laureen Snider

 The purpose of this chapter is to address the question of social change and praxis. Can the situation described in the preceding chapters be changed and, if it can, how? This chapter will argue that lessening the corporate victimization of women is possible in certain circumstances. Creating the conditions that allow change to occur is a political process that involves changing the social and economic conditions, and the ideologies, that maintain the status quo. Dialogue, struggle, and resistance are the most effective tools that those outside dominant hegemonic orders can employ. Fortunately, as illustrated by the history of the women's movement itself, they can be very effective instruments for social change when employed in Western, capitalist democracies by dedicated, organized, and determined groups.

This chapter first analyzes how transformative change occurs and describes the process by which standards of corporate behavior can be raised over time. An understanding of the significance and role of patriarchy is an essential component of the analysis, because it examines operations that target women as consumers, employees, parents, and wives. Patriarchy, it will be argued, shapes the nature of corporate crime and the regulatory response to it. Finally, the chapter examines strategies for change with some potential for success at the macro, middle (organizational), and micro levels of social structures.

The types of corporate victimization discussed in this book are virtually all instances of corporate crime, that is, acts forbidden by law for which sanctions are prescribed. Since such acts all violate a law or set of laws, it should be straightforward to get the state and the regulatory agencies responsible for controlling corporate crime to take action against the offending corporations and executives. However, it is not

236   that simple. While the more conventional crimes of burglary and robbery are publicized extensively by the mass media, securing effective
enforcement of laws against corporate crime requires interested groups
to pursue strategies that both weaken the power of the corporate sector
economically and ideologically and simultaneously strengthen their
own oppositional forces. Given the continuing worldwide recession, the
prominence of free-market ideologies following the downfall of com-
munism, the antiregulatory climate dominating major Western democracies, and the ongoing backlash against feminism,[1] accomplishing this
is a major challenge.[2]

   We understand very little about the mechanisms necessary to change
deep-rooted and long-lasting values, norms, or practices on the individual, organizational, or societal levels. Why do well-adjusted, affluent
executives engage in antisocial behaviors guaranteed to hurt their fellow human beings? Why are corporate crimes so little understood and
ineffectively controlled? Why have sixty years of research on preventing
and controlling corporate crime—carried out by some of the best scholarly minds in Australia, the United Kingdom, the United States, and
Canada—been ignored or implemented in a manner guaranteed to render the laws ineffective? To answer this we must look at both the dy-
namics of the enforcement process (the political and economic factors
that shape regulatory patterns for corporate crime) and the roles of the
state, pressure groups, and academic research in shaping policy.

THE POLITICAL ECONOMY OF ENFORCEMENT

   The regulation of corporate crime by the state is an ever-changing
dialectical process, in other words, a struggle between opposing forces
at several different levels of analysis. The state,[3] government, or polity
is defined as encompassing the major institutions and top officials of
governing bodies at federal, provincial or state, and sometimes local or
county levels as well (depending on the degree of centralization of government power). At the micro level, the balance of power between a
particular offending firm and a relevant regulatory agency depends on
very specific mechanisms. A decision to ignore, advise, counsel, or prosecute will be influenced by a constellation of local factors. First, what
is the nature of the legislation governing agency behavior? The specifi-
cations of the actual legal text provide the bottom line for action, because both regulators and those regulated bargain within legislative pa-

rameters (or their concepts thereof), and neither side wishes its position to be weakened or overturned by a court challenge. Unless there is the potential of a precedent-setting legal decision, both parties usually prefer to avoid the time, expense, and publicity of litigation; a court case may force one side or the other to take positions it prefers not to take, or call attention to misdeeds each would prefer to conceal.

Second, when a regulatory agency suspects that an offense has been committed, its actions are conditioned by the power of the business or industry involved, its size, and the nature of its capital (is it local, national, or international?). The portability or mobility of the capital in question is crucial. Can the industry change location with impunity? Or is it, as is the case with resource-based industries, forced to remain in a particular place? If the latter, then the industry's ability to play one of its key cards, the implied or stated threat of pulling out its capital and removing the jobs and income it provides, is limited.

Third, the relationships that have developed between the regulated firm and the regulatory agency, and between both of these and broader political supervisory bodies, are important determinants of regulatory behavior. These relationships and the trust (or lack of it) established between regulators and executives can determine whether, for example, regulators will give a corporation the benefit of the doubt. How quickly does one side assume the other is operating in bad faith? Historically, regulators and regulated parties have been predominantly male and white; the ways in which gender, class, and ethnicity shape these relationships has never been examined in the literature. Lacking empirical evidence, then, we can only theorize about the influence of the increasing numbers of women or people of color in regulatory agencies and corporations on the regulatory equation.

The nature of the specific offense, particularly its visibility and the perceived harm it has caused or will cause, is a fourth factor affecting regulatory behavior. Pressure groups (both progressive and reactionary), politicians, and other observers are important in this context, insofar as they publicize the actions of the regulatory agency or the offending corporation and attract media attention to the consequences of corporate crime either on the public directly or on the environment. External groups do not necessarily support stricter regulation. They may be funded by business to represent business interests, and they may argue that "harsh" actions by regulatory bodies will have a deleterious impact on factors such as business climate and investor confidence. Finally, the local political environment plays a role in the regulatory equation.

238   Upcoming elections can prompt more or less enforcement action, depending on the visibility of a particular offense, the importance of the firm in question to the local employment picture, and the prosperity levels of the region or nation-state at that time.

As the above summary demonstrates, it is impossible to understand the enforcement and sanctioning process without looking at the regulatory agency, that is, the body charged with policing corporate crime. Laws typically grant regulatory agencies a wide array of powers and a large number of alternative courses of action when faced with an individual or organization believed to have broken the law. They can advise or counsel the offender, seek control through civil and administrative penalties, or advocate the laying of criminal charges. If their actions are sustained, agencies and/or judges may fine offending individuals or corporations, award double or treble damages to victims, demand changes in the firms' operations or methods of production, imprison offenders, or (the corporate equivalent of capital punishment) remove the corporate charter or license to operate. Typically, regulators do none of these. The first characteristic of enforcement through a regulatory agency is nonenforcement;[4] the second is a tendency to concentrate the most intensive enforcement efforts on the smallest and weakest parties. This pattern occurs partly because the latter are the easiest targets; they have the simplest organizational structures, and they are less likely to complain to political representatives or hire expensive law firms to obstruct and delay legal action. But it also occurs because regulators themselves believe that small "fly by night" operations are more likely to break the law than blue-ribbon corporations with their soft-spoken, well-groomed, upper-class executives. The fact that research evidence provides no support for this thesis—indeed, the reverse appears to be true[5]—has not altered these regulatory patterns. The third characteristic of regulatory agencies is that sanctions imposed on violators are typically the lightest allowed in that jurisdiction for that particular offense; it has been calculated that fines assessed for the typical corporate crime represent, for the average offending corporation, a tiny fraction of profits made in a single hour of operation.[6]

Switching from local factors to the macro level of analysis, the shape of regulation and control in Western industrial democracies is determined by a multitude of factors on this level as well. Overall, two basic factors shape regulation. The first is the level and nature of consent between the state (usually at the federal level) and business. Nation-states vary widely in this respect. For example, the state is allowed and expected to intervene in the affairs of business more in Canada than in the United States, and more in Australia, Germany, and Sweden than in the United Kingdom. Interventionist policies that would be anathema in some countries are therefore run-of-the-mill occurrences in others.

The second factor is the relationship between the state and the electorate, as represented by relevant pressure groups. Proregulatory pressure groups—whether environmental activists trying to curb toxic waste, "green" politicians trying to eliminate chemicals from farmers' fields, unionists working to secure stronger health and safety laws in the workplace, or feminists trying to control the pharmaceutical industry—are all central to achieving a successful regulatory process. The pressure that such groups can exert through a high level of activity, struggle, and publicity provides much of the leverage necessary to compel the state to maintain enforcement. Community groups can also delay, if not prevent, the phenomenon of "capture" (the name given to the process whereby regulatory agencies identify with the needs and interests of the industry they are regulating rather than the constituents whose interests they are supposed to be protecting).[7]

The significance of community pressure groups in curbing corporate crime is only now being recognized by the research community; and very few jurisdictions have thus far accepted them as full participants in the policy-making process.[8] One can expect industry actively to resist the inclusion of proregulatory groups, even to the point of funding captive "community groups" to lobby against regulation. Regulatory agencies and their political masters can also be expected to resist public "intrusion." Given the equivocal role played by the state and its regulatory agencies in capitalist societies (discussed below), and the tendency of bureaucratic structures to seek maximum control over information and operating procedures, such bodies may resent further surveillance from community groups, even—or perhaps especially—from those that support regulation. Nevertheless, Ayres and Braithwaite argue that the state ought to fund public interest groups and thereby empower them to become credible participants in tripartite regulation, on the grounds that their involvement will improve both the cost-effectiveness and the "decency" of regulation.[9]

Scholarly works that study regulation (such as Ayres and Braithwaite, cited above) themselves become part of the regulatory equation in that they are relevant to the political struggle between pro- and antiregulatory forces. The use of research is a complex and complicated business. At the risk of oversimplifying this process, however, research by "experts," be they social or natural scientists, plays an important role in the struggle for hearts, minds, and legitimacy. Such research can be sold to various publics as "objective knowledge." But of course it is not "objective"—if this means value-free, no knowledge is. All research is a reconstruction of reality from a particular point of view.[10] And because it has to be funded, publicized, and accepted as valid, forces with more money and power have a built-in advantage in securing public acceptance of their particular point of view. But research is not "merely" ideological, nor will it necessarily follow the agendas or support the positions of those who have sponsored or promoted it. The historical record reveals many instances in which a combination of physical evidence and social science documentation has produced changes in social policy and law against the interests of the strongest or richest. Struggles over banning asbestos, controlling ozone-depleting chemicals, limiting clear-cutting practices (only in the developed world thus far), and regulating the disposal of toxic wastes illustrate this process. Academic research, then, becomes part of the ammunition used by pro- and antiregulatory forces to buttress particular arguments and strengthen particular positions. Over several generations, this process of struggle and resistance has produced ideological change in regard to the accepted standards of "reasonable" working conditions and "acceptable" levels of risk. When such redefinitions favor increased safety levels for employees, as has been the case in the developed democratic states over the last century, they can result in considerable improvements in the lifestyle and life expectancy of less powerful groups.

The arguments above rest on a set of assumptions about modern states and about regulation itself. The first is that the typical state, left to its own devices, will not "automatically" enforce laws against corporate crime at the level required by legislation, even though this very body created, passed, and officially endorsed such laws in the first place. If permitted to do so, the state and its regulatory agencies will settle into an accommodation with the regulatory target, providing a level of enforcement that the target can live with. This level is unlikely to be high or rigorous, for reasons related to the political economy of the modern state, as discussed below.

Pressure groups have the potential to force the state's agenda, threaten legitimacy, and arouse and channel dissent, particularly in democratic societies with universal suffrage, authorized opposition parties, and active mass media. In such societies, pressure group politics works in the following way. Pressure is exerted through demonstrations, agitation, the dissemination of supportive information, and sometimes strikes. More is demanded at any particular time than the state, structurally and ideologically under the influence of strong anti-regulatory corporate forces, can allow. If the pressure is powerful enough, however, a mild form of regulation will be enacted. The new legislation may or may not be enforced; in fact mechanisms of enforcement are often absent at this early stage.[11] But with continuing public pressure and intermittent crises (such as Bhopal, Love Canal, Missouri Beach, and the Savings and Loan debacle in the United States, to name a few recent examples), stronger laws and enforcement can, and often have resulted.

This kind of overview once again oversimplifies a complex reality. Regulation does not always proceed in a linear fashion, nor does it necessarily develop from a weak initial position to a stronger one. As demonstrated in the 1980s in the United States under Ronald Reagan, in Canada under Brian Mulroney, and in the United Kingdom under Margaret Thatcher, regulatory reversals can occur. In these cases regulation became weaker, not stronger, and the backlash generated by the forces of capital undid generations of struggle, producing a less safe environment for employees and consumers and an income redistribution that took money from the poor and middle classes and gave it back to the rich.[12] Since a disproportionate percentage of the poor in North America and elsewhere are women and children, this effectively meant taking income from them and giving it to males and corporations. Hence we see the need for continuing struggle.

Nor can one assume that democratically elected governments will always be allies in this struggle. In many instances states have acted to promote rather than restrict corporate crime. They have drawn up ineffective laws and impeded regulatory agencies' attempts to enforce them.[13] And it would be similarly incorrect to assume that governments always have the resources to control corporate crime in those instances where the will *is* present—see, for example, the unsuccessful attempts by U.S. agencies to lay charges against multinational oil companies following the 1973 contrived oil "shortage."[14]

Indeed, it looks as though the development of larger and larger trading blocs, through arrangements such as the North American Free Trade Agreement and the European Union, may make states increasingly powerless to combat international capital. It has become fashionable to argue that regulation renders the nation (or area) that engages in it uncompetitive and, consequently, doomed to remain poor and unpro-

242   ductive.[15] The regulatory reverses of the 1980s, which set the clock back and redefined enforcement levels more leniently, look benign compared to the threat of unfettered global capitalism. Redefining the parameters within which enforcement levels are negotiated backwards in this way means that crimes that would previously have attracted the attention of regulatory forces may well be ignored.

"Better regulation" and "rigorous enforcement," therefore, are relative concepts whose meanings depend on the nature and level of consensus hammered out for that particular act at that particular time in that particular state; and events that change the content of these terms have significant effects. There are also large differences in regulatory policy and potential between different types of corporate crime, because some are much easier than others to discover and sanction. Similarly, differences are introduced by the nature of the capital involved—capital originating in one country may require a different control strategy than capital used for transnational corporations. And sometimes the corporate sector welcomes certain kinds of regulation. These factors also affect regulatory policy and the potential for reform.

The key elements in the regulatory process are the modern state and its role in the capitalist democratic system. Although initial formulations in the marxist literature conceptualized the state as the handmaiden of the bourgeoisie, these instrumentalist and deterministic modes of thought were justifiably criticized and have been extensively rethought. Nonetheless, it is clear to any observer that modern states take great interest in facilitating the development, growth, and accumulation of capital by the private sector and in providing optimum conditions for the extraction of surplus value. Socialist regimes justify this by pointing out that wealth must be produced before it can be redistributed. Whether this reality is dictated by the structural requirements of capitalism or created by the class origins of those who staff the machinery of the state is less obvious and, for the purpose of understanding regulatory ineffectiveness, less important. The empirical fact is that the survival of the nation-state; its revenues; and its social welfare, educational, and military programs (as well as the fate of the political party in power) are all dependent, directly and indirectly, on the profitability of the private sector.[16]

The attraction and retention of capital are therefore the central criteria by which policy initiatives are judged. These concerns may be articulated up front or remain unrecognized. Indeed, business power may play its most significant role here in the background, ensuring that policy options perceived as inimical to capital never make it onto state agendas where their exclusion would have to be defended in public debate. This initial "cut" shapes the kind of policy alternatives that are seen as possible well away from the arena of formal politics in which political actors in different parties compete openly for scarce resources. It underlies agenda setting, that crucial intermediary stage at which certain options get put on or taken off the table, by predetermining the shape and size of the table (to continue a rather mixed metaphor!). At this level, therefore, "radical" policy options—those that might cause capital to take flight—are weeded out. The real and perceived interests of capital, then, shape everyday government discourse at every policy level; they are an intrinsic part of government decision making, and they operate outside the public consultative process.[17]

The centrality of capital in the modern state means that those who own and control the means of production receive massive direct and indirect subsidies from government. States provide billions of dollars in grants, income tax loopholes, facilities for training, infrastructure, transportation, and "forgivable loans" to the corporate sector; they also engage with other states in fierce competition to lure and retain corporations.[18] After falling over each other to attract industries and bestow tax holidays and grants upon them, governments are reluctant to force industries to honor the few commitments they made—such as remaining in the area for a specified number of years (or even months!), or delivering a minimum number of jobs or level of investment. Forcing the corporate sector to keep its word might frighten off the new companies and result in the much-dreaded loss of business confidence.[19]

However, because the governing political party wants to be reelected, some leverage over its agendas is possible. Despite the extensive manipulation of public opinion that political and economic elites employ, democratic politics sometimes forces governments to pass (and occasionally even enforce) laws in the "public" interest to promote the "public" good, even though they contravene the wishes and interests of segments of the corporate elite. As delineated above, these policy alternatives are likely to be confined to those considered "feasible" and "realistic" at that time, and policies outside this conservative consensus will not be admitted to public forums. (The prevailing consensus does change over time, given high levels of ideological struggle, pressure, and open debate—a fact that makes dissent worthwhile.) However, policies opposed by capital (particularly when its various segments are united) are adopted with extreme reluctance, and only when action

244   is deemed necessary to protect the long-range stability of the state, its systemic hegemony, or the survival of existing means of production. Where states intervene against the expressed interests of capital, then, it is generally to save capital from its own excesses.

Most of the social policy reforms that have taken place in advanced capitalist democracies over the past century can be fitted into this explanatory frame. When powerful, organized working-class movements were in the ascendancy, as in the United States in the 1930s or in Canada and the United Kingdom immediately after World Wars I and II, governments passed laws providing unemployment insurance, workers' compensation, family allowances, and the like. The reforms were historically and culturally specific, sensitive to the interplay of local forces described earlier, but the mechanisms animating them were identical across different cultures and states.[20] Reforms raising the working standards of labor, for example, happened when organized workers' demands led certain countries to the edge of insurrection. Under such conditions, the interests of manufacturers as a class in minimizing production costs were compromised (betrayed, as the manufacturers saw it), and legislation forcing them to provide safer working conditions and setting maximum hours of work and minimum wages—thereby raising manufacturers' costs and arousing their ire—was passed.[21]

This thesis explains state timidity to pass, and reluctance to enforce, laws penalizing corporations, since both types of law potentially endanger profitability and accumulation.[22] Thus, laws banning false advertising or unfair labor practices do not operate under the same principles of political economy as standard criminal laws against bank robbery or assault. Their language, legal status, and history are markedly different. The state and its policing agencies maintain high levels of enforcement against traditional offenses because, structurally, such enforcement is in the interests of dominant forces. But to secure even minimal enforcement of laws against corporate crime, constant pressure on state bodies and continual vigilance over regulatory practices are required. Regulation must be minimized as much as possible, except in the rare cases where national or international capital needs it—to limit "excess" competition, for example, or eliminate "fly by night" companies from the marketplace.[23] This framework also explains the sizable differences in regulatory laws and enforcement that occur between and within apparently similar democratic countries. Real differences in levels of struggle and resistance and in the success or failure of battles for particular rights or concessions have produced substantial gains in the face of

heavy corporate and political resistance—and real losses where struggles have been unsuccessful.[24]

FEMINISM AND POLITICAL ECONOMY

States, then, do not have a direct and simple interest in controlling
corporate crime, whether it victimizes primarily female consumers of
pharmaceutical products or male factory workers. However, traditional
theories have been essentially gender-blind, written as though they
apply to men and women in the same way. As discussed in Chapter 1 of
the book, feminist theory argues that gender is a differentiation at least
as fundamental as class. All classes are gendered, and components of
the mode of production affect men and women of the same class in
different ways. Socialist-feminist theories try to reconcile gender and
class, arguing that gender systems are codetermined with economic systems.[25] Patriarchy—a system of institutionalized male dominance—has
historically been achieved through male control over sexuality, reproduction, the socialization of children, and production.[26] For many centuries ideology and religion, transmitted via the patriarchal family and
backed by the threat of male violence, were the key mechanisms for
achieving these ends. Women's major life activities were limited to the
private sphere, where their pivotal contributions were unpaid, unrecognized, and under male control. With the growth of the modern state and
the unleashing of productive forces under capitalism, women's labor
was increasingly needed outside the family to serve as cheap labor and
to supplement the inadequate wages of their husbands. Control over
women by family-based patriarchal systems, then, came to be supple-
mented by control through state forces and legal systems. Though these
latter forms of social control are also "male" in both composition and
structure, they are more public, more formal, and more explicitly gov-
erned by universalistic norms than family-based control. Law has become an increasingly significant component of patriarchal control in
Anglo-American capitalist democracies, moving in as the power of organized religion and individual male patriarchal power declined.[27]

Law and legality cannot be "read off" from an a priori analysis of the
"needs" of capital. Nor are laws necessarily repressive, although this is
a topic of much debate in feminist literature. Law is a site of struggle,
fought largely on the terrain of the state. Because law has historically
reinforced the dominant relations underlying capitalism and patriarchy

in both form and substance, some argue that it is an instrument of male control that cannot be modified to serve the needs of women.[28] For example, law posits "the reasonable man" as the basis of legislation and decision making, implying that male and female viewpoints and interests are the same, or that women's interests, should they be different, are inferior and therefore not worth discussing. Others have argued that law oppresses women because its content reflects male priorities and interests; such scholars seek therefore to rewrite existing laws in ways that affirm women's needs. These two theoretical positions lead to different policy positions: law reform in the latter case, and a total revision and rethinking of legal systems in ways that eschew hierarchy, confrontation, and competition in the former.[29] Feminists interested in social policy must come to terms with these debates to assess whether and how law can be used in delineating effective policies to combat the corporate victimization of women.

Attempts to apply feminist perspectives to the corporate victimization of women, however, are at a very early stage. In the nineteenth century, with women and children working eighteen-hour days in sweat shops and factories for minuscule wages, early feminists achieved considerable success by arguing that women needed legal protection because of their "special" roles in reproduction and the socialization of children. Skocpol, tracing the origins of social welfare in the United States, documents federally funded entitlements for only two groups in nineteenth-century America: women and veterans.[30] Veterans received full benefits and generous pensions (by nineteenth-century standards) because they had made an implicit contract with the state when they served in its wars. Such payments represented no more than "obtaining their due." And until women got the vote and the legal right to enter professional occupations and have careers, they also "deserved" special health programs and a mandated minimum wage because of their unique roles. This need to protect women as future mothers was used to advantage in struggles to secure protective legislation throughout North America and western Europe.[31]

Since the rise of modern feminism, women's groups have sometimes adopted a "differences" approach, analogous to that employed to such good effect in the nineteenth century, to argue that "true" differences between the sexes justify treating women differently in law—by providing them with extra protection in the labor force, for example, or allowing them to employ special defenses such as premenstrual stress or "battered women's syndrome" to justify homicides. At other times feminists have stressed legal equality, opposing special legislation for women and seeking an equalization of male and female power in every sphere as the preferred solution to discrimination and oppression.[32] The approach of emphasizing differences can backfire and produce lower standards of occupational health and safety in the workplace, particularly for men, and/or restrictive rules that discriminate against women. As discussed in Chapter 5, employers can, and have, used this approach to argue that women of reproductive age should be removed from high-risk workplaces unless they are willing to provide proof of sterilization. Women can then be transferred to jobs that carry lower health risks but often also entail lower wages and less responsibility. Meanwhile, the law expects male workers to risk *their* health and reproductive futures by exposure to dangerously high levels of radiation or lead. This situation polarizes workers and pits men against women to the advantage of neither. The most sensible approach is probably the more pragmatic and less doctrinaire one proposed by Kenney, who said: "I reject the view that feminists should always seek formal legal equality. Instead we should operate from the equality approach, that is, only advocate one standard for both sexes as a matter of strategy when it can be shown that the consequences promote a substantial equality for women and neither reduce their employment opportunities nor force them to choose between a job and healthy offspring."[33]

That women have frequently been victimized by corporate crime is beyond dispute. Women are the heaviest users of prescription drugs, and many drugs have been developed and marketed for women alone. Faced with two patients of different sexes with identical symptoms, medical doctors will typically seek psychological causes for the woman's disorder and organic causes for the man's. They prescribe more mood-altering drugs for women patients than for men,[34] and women are the prime recipients of birth control devices. Elderly people are the other group known to consume a disproportionate share of pharmaceutical products, and since women on average live longer than men, they make up the bulk of the elderly as well. With the pharmaceutical industry ranked as one of the most criminally disposed industries in existence (the others in the "top three" are the automobile and oil industries[35]), this fact also exposes women to a disproportionately high risk of victimization. Thus, it is not surprising, as discussed elsewhere in this book, that women have suffered more than men from defective pharmaceutical products and from products that were inadequately tested or fraudulently marketed.[36]

248   To make matters worse, women have traditionally been excluded as subjects from medical research projects on major killers such as heart disease and various kinds of cancer, usually because their reproductive cycles were seen as complicating the research design and raising costs. This exclusion made sense while it was widely believed that women's bodies—their circulatory systems, hearts, organs, and responses to stress—worked the same as men's for all but reproductive functions. Unfortunately, we now know that this assumption is incorrect in several important respects. It appears that the warning signals and presenting symptoms for women's heart attacks, for example, are quite different from those of men. Such factors further complicate the task of formulating policies to address women's health needs.

Finally, in countries without universal health care, poor people, especially the working poor, are denied adequate medical care. While the United States is virtually the only developed country that does not provide some sort of universal coverage, its vast population, topping 250 million, means that this failure affects the lives and life chances of millions of people. Since more women than men live below the poverty line, women in the United States are disproportionately victimized once again. Where women suffer because they are members of a group (such as the poor, the old, or the prime consumers of drugs), macro-level social change and policies that seek to empower the group as a whole, not just the women within it, will be the fairest and most effective stratagems.

Women are also victimized as employees. Since the majority of women still work in low-level jobs with lower wages and less power than male employees, they have less flexibility and fewer options when employers fail to pay minimum wages or provide benefits to which they are legally entitled. If they are sexually harassed in the workplace, they will probably have fewer financial resources to tide them over if they are fired or compelled to quit. Sexual harassment legislation works less well for the poor and vulnerable (like most legal remedies), because of the delays, costs, and uncertainties of compensation that even plaintiffs with ironclad cases face. And it is still perfectly legal in many jurisdictions, even in the developed world, to pay women less than men, a factor that remains a primary inducement for employers to hire women. Should equal compensation laws be passed and enforced, one result could well be higher female unemployment rates.[37] Race intersects with gender and class to produce even greater vulnerability for women of color. Race, gender, and class combine, then, to make women particularly vulnerable to corporate victimization.

Female corporate criminals have been virtually absent from academic literature. Looking at male versus female propensities to offend, Daly suggested that apprehended female white-collar criminals are more likely to cite family reasons and family-related motives for stealing from employers, while males are more likely to give individualistic reasons such as job advancement.[38] However, her research looked only at women charged with certain federal offenses in the United States, employed for the most part in low-level "pink collar" jobs such as bank tellers and clerks. These were not powerful female executives at the top of corporate hierarchies. Lacking empirically based knowledge of the role gender plays in corporate crime, then, we have had to fall back on speculation. It has been suggested that corporate crime is a typically male offense because men, particularly upwardly mobile male executives, are rewarded for espousing flexible ethical systems that encourage them to use others as tools, as means to particular ends. This Machiavellian value system, which calls for willingness to sacrifice individuals in the pursuit of long-term corporate goals, is effective in the corporate world and, therefore, strongly reinforced and rewarded. Motivationally, it is only a short step from taking ethical shortcuts and disregarding the resulting inconvenience and pain to taking legal shortcuts to enhance profitability.[39] Once the self-concept and self-esteem of males in the corporation become dependent on success as defined by the corporation, such men are psychologically vulnerable to corporate criminality should the right facilitating conditions arise.

The male corporate executive's masculinity is centered on the struggle for success, reward, and recognition in the corporation and community. This image of work, rooted materially in the corporate executive's gender and class status, helps to create the conditions for corporate crime. Devotion to achievement and success brings about the "need" to engage in such crime.[40]

To link ideas of masculinity and structures of patriarchy to corporate crime does not mean that a managerial class composed of women would behave any differently, particularly if the structures, ideologies, and competitive pressures that propel business under capitalism remain unchanged. There is no evidence that substituting executives with vaginas for those with penises would transform the organizational world. Indeed, the increasing presence of women (albeit mainly white and middle class) in the higher echelons of corporate America over the last dec-

250 ade has produced no noticeable decline in the competitiveness, rapacity, or criminal propensities of these firms. Nor have companies been transformed into law-abiding, socially responsible, user-friendly workplaces by the addition of female executives.

DEAD ENDS AND PROMISING BEGINNINGS

Drawing on the knowledge gained from feminism and political economy, and taking into account the dialectical nature of the regulatory process, how then can we challenge and reduce corporate victimization of women? Many suggestions have been made, some contradictory, some complementary. One group of scholars believes that the reluctance of the state and its regulatory agencies to assess realistic sanctions is the core of the problem. They advocate more criminalization, greater use of imprisonment, and higher, more punitive fines. As they see it, if criminal sanctions were to be deployed regularly, if corporations knew their chances of escaping criminal conviction were slight, if fines were based on the size of the firm and the profits yielded by the crime, if jail sentences were imposed, and if all these steps were backed up by enlarged enforcement staffs and realistic resource allocations, corporate crime against women *and* men could be effectively controlled.[41]

Unfortunately, such proposals are unrealistic.[42] Since the main obstacle to efficient enforcement is and always has been the power of the corporate sector over the state, those advocating criminalization must specify how corporate power can first be neutralized or overcome and incorporate these proposed mechanisms into their models. This is particularly important in light of the fact that Anglo-American democracies already have laws that direct or allow judges to impose much heavier sanctions than they actually mete out. Struggling to force legislators to pass even more laws, which experience suggests will be just as studiously ignored, is a waste of precious energy and time.

Scholars arguing for deregulation, the removal of criminal sanctions against corporations and corporate criminality, base their arguments on the aforementioned failure of the state to impose punishment or implement sanction-based policies. Advocates of deregulation maintain that the dependence of modern states on criminal law and the adversarial relationship this creates is a major cause of regulatory ineffectiveness.[43] But this belief that corporations would happily cooperate with regulators if only they weren't put off by nasty threats of incarceration is as misguided as the criminalization model discussed above. Deregulation models overlook the fact that corporate criminality is the most rational of acts: corporations commit offenses in the hope and expectation of greater profits. And they are seldom disappointed, as the average corporate crime nets millions of dollars for its perpetrators.[44] Most of the time, due to the nature of the offenses and the paucity of state efforts and resources expended in their detection, their crimes escape all official notice. And even when they are sanctioned, the penalties imposed seldom make a dent in profit margins.

Unfortunately, deregulation models are dangerous in another way. They appeal to dominant forces of capital and are taken up in ways their instigators never intended. The renaissance of the New Right in the 1980s and 1990s attracted enough supporters to launch a major attack on feminism, government regulation, antiracist policies (affirmative action in the United States, multiculturalism and immigration in Canada), gays, lesbians, unions, collective rights, and the like. Under the guise of promoting self-reliance and "family values," they advocated a stark reversal of the advances made since World War II. Adopting the position that postwar governments scapegoated business, these radical conservatives now argue that regulation is a socialist idea promoted by antibusiness forces and weak-willed, probably corrupt politicians. They further claim that governments caved in to the demands of such leftist groups, passing hundreds of unnecessary regulations and adding millions of dollars to the cost of running a corporation. According to this view, greedy unions and uppity women and minorities have compounded the evils of regulation and made American business, once the envy of the world, uncompetitive, allowing upstart countries such as Japan, Germany, and Saudi Arabia to overtake the United States. This combination of racist and nationalist views has had undeniable appeal, and academic critiques of regulation have made them appear respectable and mainstream, resulting in major behavioral and philosophical shifts. Thus, it is no longer fashionable in government or academic circles to argue that corporate crime is best controlled through tough regulatory action. The goal now is abolition, decriminalization, and downsizing. Economic incentives are the way to get compliance from industry; and the new buzzword is not *control* but *cooperation*. Given the high costs of regulation, the difficulties of documenting its benefits, and the deficits governments have decided they must eliminate, deregulatory policies have been pursued by political parties of every ideological stripe.

252   This trend is unfortunate. For despite the fact that many academic critiques of criminalization raise legitimate questions about the philosophy and effectiveness of traditional regulatory agencies, decriminalization would remove an important weapon from the puny arsenal regulators can deploy, further weaken the forces supporting regulation, and sabotage future efforts to force regulators to act against offenders. As discussed earlier, the delicate dialectical relationship between capital and the state within capitalist economies means that governments have to be persuaded, usually by external pressure, to enforce existing laws against corporations. Social movements and bad publicity are key mechanisms for making pressure effective. The fact that various forms of corporate victimization have officially been labeled criminal acts has crucial symbolic importance because criminal law, in Western societies, is universalistic and absolute. Those who offend against it are criminals, a term that connotes evil and villainy. This discourse carries no shades of gray, no sense that there might be a debate about the morality of the behavior signified. Because it is "criminal," its moral status is obvious, and attempts to justify it are labeled mere rationalizations.[45] The language of criminality, then, obscures the political process that originally transformed the act in question from a disputed behavior to an illegal one. This sleight of hand is highly significant, because "interests can be both constrained and enabled by the discourses through which they operate."[46] Social movements opposing corporate crime need this symbolic stigma. And they need the public attention criminality connotes. Criminal offenses are newsworthy; they are linguistically and socially defined as serious. Eliminating criminality would turn corporate criminals into "regulatory evaders"; their crimes would become value-free acts whose meaning is under negotiation, up for grabs. The implications this would have on coverage in the mass media, and the dampening effect on public education and consciousness raising, is obvious. Pressing a case against an "uncooperative executive" is a nonevent, whereas ignoring blatant examples of criminal acts by the corporate sector might well become a clear and outrageous example of government inefficiency or political bias in the eyes of an oppositional press.

The stronger and more universalistic the agency mandate, then, the greater the potential bargaining strength of proregulatory forces. The "capacity to escalate social intervention enables social control to work better at less coercive levels."[47] The potential to embarrass the regulatory agency and shame the offending corporation increases when there is a threat of criminalization, whether the state is in a position to carry it out or not. Winter put it this way:

> Without the clear power and duties to interfere with private interests, the administrative agency would not have a position from which to barter effectively. If legal doctrine allowed clear cut rules to be discarded whenever an agency preferred non-enforcement . . . the value of the legal rule as a bargaining chip would be diminished, for the regulatory process would begin with the assumption that full enforcement was not even a benchmark.[48]

Pressure groups also need the public access to information that has historically been attached to proceedings under criminal law. Laying or dropping charges is a public process in most developed democratic systems, as are hearings and trials. No comparable public right to know accompanies civil or administrative procedures. They are often swathed in secrecy from start to finish, a privilege corporations always seek to maximize and preserve.[49] Any official shift toward policies of cooperation with industry also affects the expectations of corporations themselves, providing them with additional excuses for continuing to offend. Because corporate crime is very profitable, the motivations for postponement and delay are strong.

One avenue we have not yet explored is the potential for crime-fighting change at the organizational level, within either the corporation or the regulatory agency. Once again, many ideas have been put forth. Cranston, focusing on regulation, suggests the following changes: states should introduce more controls to prevent the "revolving door" syndrome whereby executives move from jobs in a regulated industry into the agency responsible for it and vice versa; the number of public representatives on regulatory and industry boards should be increased; and regulators and corporations should hold bargaining sessions in public and publish the results. These are all good suggestions, but once again they do not address the root cause of regulatory inadequacy—the crucial power of the corporate sector to abrogate policies that challenge its profitability or dominance.[50]

Turning to corporate structure, because organizations perpetrate and benefit from corporate crime in a way that is not true of traditional offenses (usually committed by individuals to benefit individuals), researchers have looked at the degree to which different structural arrangements induce criminality. Specifically, they have asked whether

254   corporate goals such as profit maximization or the need to eliminate uncertainty from the business environment by controlling costs, suppliers, legislators, and the like lead executives to commit corporate crime.[51] The burgeoning field of corporate ethics, which approaches the problem from the individual or micro level, looks at the potential to reshape executives' values and norms to make law-abiding behavior more socially acceptable in corporate subcultures.[52] Different structural models have been examined to see whether variables such as the degree of centralization, the shape of corporate hierarchy, chains of command, or the distribution of responsibilities for compliance within corporations can be linked to corporate lawbreaking.[53] And the organizational environment—taxes, the competitive situation, the risks and benefits of lawbreaking in a particular industry and locale—has been scrutinized to determine its relationship to corporate criminality. However, given that profits are identified by everyone as a key corporate goal, potential remedies must either discuss ways to make this goal less central (a highly unlikely outcome, since this is the pivotal value of capitalist economies) or suggest ways of making corporate crime less profitable. Since corporations themselves can hardly be expected to embrace structural changes that render them less profitable, models of corporate reorganization must perforce deal with the role of the state. In particular, they must address state reluctance to challenge the corporate sector. And thus we come full circle because, as we have seen, traditional academic researchers have been slow either to incorporate this factor into their models or to consider its likely effect on the chances of getting ideas passed into law and then enforced.

What avenues do have potential, then? Several of the key ingredients in securing meaningful policy change have already been discussed, particularly the role of research and "scientific" knowledge, and the crucial importance of pressure groups. Ideological change and social restructuring, and eventually meaningful legal change, can be secured by changing minds and hearts through consciousness raising and social struggle. As one of the most thoughtful observers of corporate crime has stated, "crime rates are more responsive to patterns of community disapproval . . . than to state enforcement patterns."[54] And instituting procedures that shame corporate executives, hold them responsible for their acts, and force them to confront the human consequences of what they do is far more effective than passing laws to punish offenders. Braithwaite describes a process whereby top executives of insurance companies in Australia, involved in a death benefits scheme that defrauded thousands

of aboriginal people, were forced to travel to remote villages in the out-
back and work out solutions with their victims. Hearing the aboriginals
recount their distress apparently touched the perpetrators in a way no
punishment could have done—it reached them emotionally and allowed them to understand and respond to the consequences of their
actions. To quote Braithwaite once again: "Processes of dialogue with
those who suffer from acts of irresponsibility are among the most effective ways of bringing home to us as human beings our obligation to take
responsibility for our deeds."[55] But perpetrators will have to be compelled to expose themselves to restitution processes in the first place,
and this is where the real struggles will occur. Securing laws that require corporations to become part of the solution to corporate victimization, and then having such laws enforced, will require an extensive
campaign by social movements, populist and left-wing political parties,
and other progressive groups. Resistance will be massive. The fact that
laws are national (creatures of the now-embattled nation-state) while
capital is international will also complicate efforts of this sort.

Keeping criminal law in the regulatory process is not important because it will lessen rates of corporate victimization of women; it is important because of the role it can play in ideological change and because
of its potential to empower progressive social movements. This does
not mean that criminalization plays no role in the shaming process, but
its role is often a negative one because it is employed to stigmatize
and exclude rather than to shame and reintegrate. Because punishment
through criminal justice has typically pushed people out of their families and communities, it has been counterproductive, and certainly has
not fulfilled the "official" functions criminologists cite in its justification.[56] "Just desserts," the policy developed to eliminate judicial bias
and control discrimination by prescribing identical punishments for offenders charged with (apparently) identical offenses, could serve as a
textbook study on the dangers of advocating social reform without addressing its social context. Because the political economy of criminal
law was not considered, a "just desserts" approach has led to massive
increases in imprisonment for many innocuous—but poor and powerless—offenders.[57] Since the ability to respond to the different conditions
and circumstances that lead to criminal behavior has been destroyed,
judges have essentially been prevented from acting in merciful ways
and have willynilly reinforced the politics of vengeance.[58] Attempts to
apply "just desserts" policies to corporate victimization of women are
likely to founder on somewhat different structural realities—those

256 which shield the rich and powerful from punishment for their acts while ensuring that the poor are doubly punished.[59]

Overall, the most promising avenue of reform is empowerment, a concept that encompasses ideological, social, political, and economic change. One reason women suffer at the hands of corporate criminals is their relative inability to resist, to complain in ways that count, or to strike back effectively. Only social struggle, and probably decades of it, can bring about this kind of basic social change. The most effective techniques will vary widely, because each battle, each issue, each locale, is unique. But each battle has far-reaching, universal components as well, and one of these is the goal of empowerment, which should serve as an overarching criterion to guide decision making on the appropriateness of specific strategies. The history of feminism itself can guide future struggles, because it has been extraordinarily successful thus far in challenging centuries of patriarchy and righting a fair number of abuses in a very short time.

CONCLUSION

This chapter has examined reasons for the victimization of women by corporate crime, and strategies that might be employed to change this reality. We have argued that real progress can be made only through altering dominant ideologies and structures and through the empowerment of women. To understand why this is so, we looked at the political economy of law enforcement in democratic capitalist states and examined the role of women through feminist theory. It is clear that lessening corporate victimization will not be an easy process; however, it is equally clear that achieving this goal is an essential one.

NOTES

1. S. Faludi, *Backlash: The Undeclared War Against American Women* (New York: Doubleday, 1991).

2. Figuring out how to change hearts and minds, and knowing whether changing social structures and laws can ever accomplish this (A. Giddens, *The Class Structure of Advanced Societies*, 2nd ed. [London: Hutchinson, 1981]), is one of the great unresolved questions of social science. The disintegration of state structures was essential to the recent transformations of Communist states in eastern Europe, but the withdrawal of the consent of

those lacking power, those at or near the bottom of the social structure, was also a key component in achieving macro-level change. Feminists have always stressed the importance of reaching individuals, of seeking change from the bottom up rather than the top down, partly because they seldom wielded sufficient power to secure structural or legal changes.

3. Not to be confused with the geographic territory in a federally organized system, as in the fifty states that make up the United States of America.

4. R. Cranston, "Regulation and Deregulation: General Issues," *University of New South Wales Law Journal* 5 (1982): 1–29; B. M. Mitnick, *The Political Economy of Regulation* (New York: Columbia University Press, 1980); L. Snider, *Bad Business: Corporate Crime in Canada* (Toronto: Nelson, 1993).

5 I. Ayres and J. Braithwaite, *Responsive Regulation: Transcending the Deregulation Debate* (New York: Oxford University Press, 1992); M. Clinard and P. Yeager, *Corporate Crime* (New York: Free Press, 1980); J. Coleman, *The Criminal Elite: The Sociology of White Collar Crime*, 2nd ed. (New York: St. Martin's Press, 1989); P. Yeager, *The Limits of Law: The Public Regulation of Private Pollution* (Cambridge, U.K.: Cambridge University Press, 1991).

6. D. M. Ermann and R. J. Lundman, "Deviant Acts by Complex Organizations: Deviance and Social Control at the Organizational Level of Analysis," *Sociological Quarterly* 19, no. 1 (1978): 55–67.

7. J. Anderson, *Public Policy-Making* (New York: Praeger, 1975); P. Sabatier, "Social Movements and Regulatory Agencies: Toward a More Adequate—and Less Pessimistic—Theory of 'Clientele Capture,'" *Policy Sciences* 6 (1975): 301–41; P. Sabatier, "Regulatory Policy-Making: Toward a Framework of Analysis," *Natural Resources Journal* 17 (1977): 415–60.

8. See, however, J. Braithwaite and T. Makkai, "In and out of the Revolving Door: Making Sense of Regulatory Capture" (Research School of the Social Sciences, Australia National University, December 1991), and J. Braithwaite, "Corporate Crime and Republican Criminological Praxis," in *Corporate Crime: Contemporary Debates*, ed. F. Pearce and L. Snider (Toronto: University of Toronto Press, 1995) for accounts of attempts to empower nursing home residents to make them active participants in the regulation of their residences.

9. Ayres and Braithwaite, *Responsive Regulation*.

10. A. R. Edwards, *Regulation and Repression: The Study of Social Control* (London: Allen and Unwin, 1988), 51–2; D. E. Smith, "Women's Perspective as a Radical Critique of Sociology," *Sociological Inquiry* 44, no. 1 (1974): 7–13.

11. See examples in Snider, *Bad Business*, and E. Tucker, *Administering Danger in the Workplace: The Law and Politics of Occupational Health*

258   *and Safety Regulation in Ontario, 1850–1914* (Toronto: University of Toronto Press, 1990).

12. K. Calavita, "The Demise of the Occupational Safety and Health Administration: A Case Study in Symbolic Action," *Social Problems* 30, no. 4 (1983): 437–48; G. Kolko, *Restructuring the World Economy* (New York: Pantheon Books, 1988); D. Simon and D. S. Eitzen, eds. *Elite Deviance*, 3rd ed. (Boston: Allyn and Bacon, 1990).

13. K. Calavita, "Worker Safety, Law and Social Change: The Italian Case," *Law and Society* 20, no. 20 (1986): 189–229; W. G. Carson, "The Institutionalization of Ambiguity: Early British Factory Acts," in *White Collar Theory and Research*, ed. G. Geis and E. Stotland (Beverly Hills, CA: Sage, 1980); W. G. Carson, "The Other Price of Britain's Oil: Regulating Safety on Off-Shore Oil Installations in the British Sector of the North Sea," *Contemporary Crises* 4 (1980): 239–66; N. Gunningham, *Pollution: Social Interest and the Law* (Oxford Centre for Socio-Legal Studies, 1974); N. Gunningham, *Safeguarding the Workers* (Sydney: Law Book Co., 1984); N. Gunningham, "Negotiated Non-Compliance: A Case Study of Regulatory Failure," *Law and Policy* 9, no. 1 (1987): 69–97; M. Levi, "Giving Creditors the Business: The Criminal Law in Inaction," *International Journal of the Sociology of Law* 12 (1984): 321–33; M. Levi, "Crisis, What Crisis? Reactions to Commercial Fraud in the United Kingdom," *Contemporary Crises* 11, no. 3 (1987): 207–21.

14. A. Sampson, *The Seven Sisters: The Great Oil Companies and the World They Shaped* (New York: Viking, 1975).

15. F. Pearce and L. Snider, "Regulating Capitalism," in *Corporate Crime: Contemporary Debates*, ed. F. Pearce and L. Snider (Toronto: University of Toronto Press, 1995).

16. I. Gough, *The Political Economy of the Welfare State* (London: Macmillan, 1979); C. Offe, "Some Contradictions of the Modern Welfare State," *Social Policy* 2, no. 2 (1982): 7–16.

17. Offe, "Some Contradictions of the Modern Welfare State," 7–16; T. Schrecker, "The Political Context and Content of Environmental Law," in *Law and Society: A Critical Perspective*, ed. T. Caputo et al. (Toronto: Harcourt Brace Jovanovich, 1989), 182–83.

18. M. Hurtig, *The Betrayal of Canada* (Toronto: McClelland and Stewart, 1991); Simon and Eitzen, eds. *Elite Deviance*.

19. Gough, *The Political Economy*.

20. L. Panitch, ed. *The Canadian State: Political Economy and Political Power* (Toronto: University of Toronto Press, 1977).

21. M. Bliss, *A Living Profit: Studies in the Social History of Canadian Business* (Toronto: McClelland and Stewart, 1974); W. G. Carson, "White Collar Crime and the Enforcement of Factory Legislation," *British Journal of Criminology* 10 (1970): 383–98; T. Skocpol, *Protecting Soldiers and*

Mothers: The Political Origins of Social Policy in the United States (Cambridge, MA: Harvard University Press, 1992); Tucker, *Administering Danger.*   259

22. R. Miliband, *The State in Capitalist Society* (London: Quartet Books, 1969); J. O'Connor, *The Fiscal Crisis of the State* (New York: St. Martin's Press, 1973).

23. Kolko, *Restructuring the World Economy.*

24. The absence of organized pressure groups and resistance movements has been responsible, in part, for the generally abysmal record of passing and enforcing laws to protect workers, consumers, or the environment in many socialist countries.

25. H. J. Maroney and M. Luxton, eds. *Feminism and Political Economy: Women's Work, Women's Struggle* (Toronto: Methuen, 1987).

26. J. Mitchell, *Women's Estate* (Harmondsworth, U.K.: Penguin, 1971); see also Z. Eisenstein, "Developing a Theory of Capitalist Patriarchy and Socialist Feminism," in *Capitalist Patriarchy and the Case for Socialist Feminism,* ed. Z. Eisenstein (New York: Monthly Review Press, 1979), 5–40, who adds consumption to this list.

27. C. Smart, *Feminism and the Power of Law* (London: Routledge, 1989).

28. A. Howe, "The Problem of Privatized Injuries: Feminist Strategies for Litigation," *Studies in Law, Politics and Society* 10 (1990): 119–42; C. MacKinnon, "Feminism, Marxism, Method and the State: An Agenda for Theory," *Signs* 7, no. 3 (1982): 515–44; C. MacKinnon, *Feminism Unmodified: Discourses on Life and Law* (Cambridge, MA: Harvard University Press, 1987).

29. F. Olsen, "The Sex of Law," in *The Politics of Law,* ed. D. Kairys (New York: Pantheon Books, 1990), 453–68.

30. Skocpol, *Protecting Soldiers.*

31. S. Kenney, "Reproductive Hazards in the Workplace: The Law and Sexual Difference," *International Journal of Sociology of Law* 14 (1986): 393–414; L. Snider, "Criminalization: Panacea for Men Who Batter but Anathema for Corporate Criminals," in *Social Inequality, Social Justice,* ed. D. Currie and B. Maclean (Vancouver: Collective Press, 1994), 101–24; Tucker, *Administering Danger.*

32. Kenney, "Reproductive Hazards in the Workplace."

33. Ibid., 413.

34. P. Peppin, "Feminism, Law and the Pharmaceutical Industry," in *Corporate Crime: Ethics, Law and the State,* ed. F. Pearce and L. Snider (Toronto: University of Toronto, 1995).

35. Clinard and Yeager, *Corporate Crime.*

36. N. M. Chenier, *Reproductive Hazards at Work: Men, Women and the Fertility Gamble* (Ottawa: Canadian Advisory Council on the Status of

260   Women, 1982); W. DeKeseredy and R. Hinch, *Woman Abuse: Sociological Perspectives* (Toronto: Thompson Educational Publishing, 1991); M. Mintz, *At Any Cost: Corporate Greed, Women and the Dalkon Shield* (New York: Pantheon Books, 1985); S. Perry and J. Dawson, *Nightmare: Women and the Dalkon Shield* (New York: Macmillan, 1985).

37. J. Messerschmidt, *Capitalism, Patriarchy and Crime: Toward a Socialist-Feminist Criminology* (Totowa, NJ: Rowan and Littlefield, 1986).

38. K. Daly, "Gender and Varieties of White Collar Crime," *Criminology* 27 (1989): 769–94; see also L. Maher and E. J. Waring, "Beyond Simple Differences: White Collar Crime, Gender and Workforce Position," *Phoebe* 2 (Spring 1990): 44–54.

39. Messerschmidt, *Capitalism, Patriarchy and Crime.*

40. Ibid., 119.

41. J. C. Coffee, "Corporate Criminal Responsibility," in *Encyclopedia of Crime and Justice*, ed. S. Kadish (New York: Free Press, 1984), 1: 253–64; H. Glasbeek, "Why Corporate Deviance Is Not Treated as a Crime," in *Law and Society: A Critical Perspective*, ed. T. Caputo et al. (Toronto: Harcourt Brace Jovanovich, 1989); R. Nader and M. J. Green, eds. *Corporate Power in America* (New York: Viking, 1973); C. Reasons, W. Ross and L. Patterson, *Assault on the Worker: Occupational Health and Safety in Canada* (Toronto: Butterworth, 1981); J. C. Watkins, "White Collar Crimes: Legal Sanctions and Social Control," *Crime and Delinquency* 23 (1977): 290–303.

42. Reformers frequently have strategic reasons for advocating reforms they suspect are unattainable—public education and consciousness raising are two good ones. And, as Braithwaite ("Corporate Crime and Republican Criminological Praxis") has pointed out, "model mongering" can be an empowerment technique that helps the weak confront the strong. But many advocates of criminalization are employing it not as such a technique but in the naive expectation that governments will act as soon as the consequences of their inequitable behavior are pointed out.

43. B. Ackerman et al., *The Uncertain Search for Environmental Quality* (New York: Free Press, 1974); E. Bardach and R. A. Kagan, *Going by the Book: The Problem of Regulatory Unreasonableness* (Philadelphia: Temple University Press, 1982); R. Kagan and J. T. Scholz, "The Criminology of the Corporation and Regulatory Enforcement Strategies," in *Enforcing Regulation*, ed. K. Hawkins and J. Thomas (Boston: Kluwer-Nijhoff, 1984); A. V. Kneese and C. L. Schultze, *Pollution, Prices and Public Policy* (Washington, DC: Brookings Institution, 1975).

44. Clinard and Yeager, *Corporate Crime*; Coleman, *The Criminal Elite*; Glasbeek, "Why Corporate Deviance"; Levi, "Giving Creditors the Business"; Levi, "Crisis, What Crisis?"

45. Indeed, this symbolic power of criminal law has a dark side, for it makes mobilization against the excesses of criminal law and the criminal

justice system exceedingly hard. This is not a problem in the context of using criminalization to control corporate crime, because the groups one is seeking to control have political and ideological power equal to, and sometimes greater than, that of the state. But it is a major problem when addressing violence against women in other contexts (L. Snider, "Feminism, Punishment and the Potential of Empowerment," *Canadian Journal of Sociology of Law* 9, no. 1 [1994]: 75–104).

46. M. Condon, "Following Up on Interests: The Private Agreement Exemption in Ontario Securities Law," *Journal of Human Justice* 3, no. 2 (1992): 36–56, 36.

47. J. Braithwaite, "Inequality and Republican Criminology," paper presented at the annual meeting of the American Society of Criminology, San Francisco, November 1991, 33.

48. G. Winter, "Bartering Rationality in Regulation," *Law and Society Review* 19, no. 2 (1985): 219–250, 240–41.

49. This can be observed during public hearings to create new laws, and it can be more or less self-serving. Industry spokespeople typically plead that all information involving their business must be held in total secrecy, with no public access at all, to protect copyright information and keep trade secrets from their competitors. Their concern is justified in some circumstances; however, given the nature of the marketplace, with oligopolies the norm and monopolies not unusual, an observer can be forgiven for suspecting that this is a rationale to prevent the public from finding out the degree of industry pollution or predation. See, for example, the protestations of companies with the worst environmental records at parliamentary commissions responsible for coming up with the Canadian Environmental Protection Act in 1984–1985 (G. Chanteloup, "The Canadian Environmental Protection Act: A Critical Analysis of the Role of Industry in the Legislative Process" [M.A. thesis, Queen's University, Kingston, Ontario, 1992]).

50. Cranston, "Regulation and Deregulation."

51. S. Box, *Power, Crime and Mystification* (London: Tavistock Publications, 1983); F. Pearce, "Corporate Rationality as Crime," *Studies in Political Economy* 40 (Spring 1993): 135–62.

52. However, behavior modification that is not backed by deep structural and ideological change has been notoriously unsuccessful in venues ranging from weight loss clinics to prisoner rehabilitation centers.

53. B. Fisse and J. Braithwaite, *The Impact of Publicity on Corporate Offenders* (Albany, NY: State University of New York Press, 1983); M. L. Needleman and C. Needleman, "Organizational Crime: Two Models of Criminogenesis," *Sociological Quarterly* 20, no. 4 (1979): 517–28.

54. Braithwaite, "Inequality and Republican Criminology," 26.

55. Braithwaite, "Corporate Crime and Republican Criminological Praxis," 21.

262   56. S. Spitzer, "The Seductions of Punishment: Toward a Critical Criminology of Penality," paper presented at the annual meeting of the American Society of Criminology, Baltimore, November 1990.

57. R. Immarigeon and M. Chesney-Lind, *Women's Prisons: Overcrowded and Overused* (San Francisco: National Council on Crime and Delinquency, 1992); H. Pepinsky and R. Quinney, eds. *Criminology as Peacemaking* (Bloomington, IN: Indiana University Press, 1991).

58. N. Christie, *Crime Control as Industry* (London: Routledge, 1993).

59. D. Brants and E. Kok, "Penal Sanctions as a Feminist Strategy: A Contradiction in Terms?" *International Journal of Sociology of Law* 14 (1986): 269–86; J. Reiman, *The Rich Get Richer and the Poor Get Prison*, 3rd ed. (New York: Macmillan, 1990).

REFERENCES

Ackerman B., S. Rose, J. Sawyer Jr., and D. Henderson. 1974. *The Uncertain Search for Environmental Quality*. New York: Free Press.

Anderson, J. 1975. *Public Policy-Making*. New York: Praeger.

Ayres, I. and J. Braithwaite. 1992. *Responsive Regulation: Transcending the Deregulation Debate*. New York: Oxford University Press.

Bardach, E. and R. A. Kagan. 1982. *Going by the Book: The Problem of Regulatory Unreasonableness*. Philadelphia: Temple University Press.

Bliss, M. 1974. *A Living Profit: Studies in the Social History of Canadian Business*. Toronto: McClelland and Stewart.

Box, S. 1983. *Power, Crime and Mystification*. London: Tavistock Publications.

Braithwaite, J. 1991. Inequality and republican criminology. Paper presented at the Annual Meeting of the American Society of Criminology, San Francisco, November.

———. 1995. Corporate crime and republican criminological praxis. In *Corporate Crime: Contemporary Debates*, ed. F. Pearce and L. Snider. Toronto: University of Toronto Press, 1995.

Braithwaite, J. and T. Makkai. 1991. In and out of the revolving door: Making sense of regulatory capture. Unpublished paper, Research School of the Social Sciences, Australia National University, December.

Brants, D. and E. Kok. 1986. Penal sanctions as a feminist strategy: A contradiction in terms? *International Journal of Sociology of Law* 14: 269–86.

Calavita, K. 1983. The demise of the Occupational Safety and Health Administration: A case study in symbolic action. *Social Problems* 30(4): 437–48.

———. 1986. Worker safety, law and social change: The Italian case. *Law and Society* 20(20): 189–229.

Carson, W. G. 1970. White collar crime and the enforcement of factory leg-   263
islation. *British Journal of Criminology* 10: 383–98.

———. 1980. The institutionalization of ambiguity: Early British factory
acts. In *White Collar Theory and Research*, ed. G. Geis and E. Stotland.
Beverly Hills, CA: Sage.

———. 1980. The other price of Britain's oil: Regulating safety on off-shore
oil installations in the British sector of the North Sea. *Contemporary
Crises* 4: 239–66.

Chanteloup, G. 1992. *The Canadian Environmental Protection Act: A Critical Analysis of the Role of Industry in the Legislative Process*. M.A.
thesis, Queen's University, Kingston, Ontario.

Chenier, N. M. 1982. *Reproductive Hazards at Work: Men, Women and the
Fertility Gamble*. Ottawa: Canadian Advisory Council on the Status of
Women.

Christie, N. 1993. *Crime Control as Industry*. London: Routledge.

Clinard, M. and P. Yeager. 1980. *Corporate Crime*. New York: Free Press.

Coffee, J. C. 1984. Corporate criminal responsibility. In *Encyclopedia of
Crime and Justice*, vol. 1, ed. S. Kadish, 253–64. New York: Free Press.

Coleman, J. 1989. *The Criminal Elite: The Sociology of White Collar
Crime*. 2nd ed. New York: St. Martin's Press.

Condon, M. 1992. Following up on interests: The private agreement exemption in Ontario securities law. *Journal of Human Justice* 3(2): 36–56.

Cranston, R. 1982. Regulation and deregulation: General issues. *University
of New South Wales Law Journal* 5: 1–29.

Daly, K. 1989. Gender and varieties of white collar crime. *Criminology* 27:
769–94.

DeKeseredy, W. and R. Hinch. 1991. *Woman Abuse: Sociological Perspectives*. Toronto: Thompson Educational Publishing.

Edwards, A. R. 1988. *Regulation and Repression: The Study of Social Control*. London: Allen and Unwin.

Eisenstein, Z. 1979. Developing a theory of capitalist patriarchy and socialist feminism. In *Capitalist Patriarchy and the Case for Socialist Feminism*, ed. Z Eisenstein, 5–40. New York: Monthly Review Press.

Ermann, D. M. and R. J. Lundman. 1978. Deviant acts by complex organizations: Deviance and social control at the organizational level of analysis. *Sociological Quarterly* 19(1): 55–67.

Faludi, S. 1991. *Backlash: The Undeclared War Against American Women*.
New York: Doubleday.

Fisse, B. and J. Braithwaite. 1983. *The Impact of Publicity on Corporate
Offenders*. Albany, NY: State University of New York Press.

Giddens, A. 1981. *The Class Structure of Advanced Societies*. 2nd ed. London: Hutchinson.

Glasbeek, H. 1989. Why corporate deviance is not treated as a crime. In

264   *Law and Society: A Critical Perspective*, ed. T. Caputo et al., 126–145. Toronto: Harcourt Brace Jovanovich.

Gough, I. 1979. *The Political Economy of the Welfare State*. London: Macmillan.

Gunningham, N. 1974. *Pollution: Social Interest and the Law*. Oxford Centre for Socio-Legal Studies.

———. 1984. *Safeguarding the Workers*. Sydney: Law Book Co.

———. 1987. Negotiated non-compliance: A case study of regulatory failure. *Law and Policy* 9(1): 69–97.

Howe, A. 1990. The problem of privatized injuries: Feminist strategies for litigation. *Studies in Law, Politics and Society* 10: 119–42.

Hurtig, M. 1991. *The Betrayal of Canada*. Toronto: McClelland and Stewart.

Immarigeon, R. and M. Chesney-Lind. 1992. *Women's Prisons: Overcrowded and Overused*. San Francisco: National Council on Crime and Delinquency.

Kagan, R. and J. T. Scholz. 1984. The criminology of the corporation and regulatory enforcement strategies. In *Enforcing Regulation*, ed. K. Hawkins and J. Thomas. Boston: Kluwer-Nijhoff.

Kenney, S. 1986. Reproductive hazards in the workplace: The law and sexual difference. *International Journal of Sociology of Law* 14: 393–414.

Kneese, A. V. and C. L. Schultze. 1975. *Pollution, Prices and Public Policy*. Washington, DC: Brookings Institution.

Kolko, G. 1988. *Restructuring the World Economy*. New York: Pantheon Books.

Levi, M. 1984. Giving creditors the business: The criminal law in inaction. *International Journal of the Sociology of Law* 12: 321–33.

———. 1987. Crisis, what crisis? Reactions to commercial fraud in the United Kingdom. *Contemporary Crises* 11(3): 207–21.

MacKinnon, C. 1982. Feminism, marxism, method and the state: An agenda for theory. *Signs* 7(3): 515–44.

———. 1987. *Feminism Unmodified: Discourses on Life and Law*. Cambridge, MA: Harvard University Press.

Maher, L. and E. J. Waring. 1990. Beyond simple differences: White collar crime, gender and workforce position. *Phoebe* 2(Spring): 44–54.

Maroney, H. J. and M. Luxton, eds. 1987. *Feminism and Political Economy: Women's Work, Women's Struggle*. Toronto: Methuen.

Messerschmidt, J. 1986. *Capitalism, Patriarchy and Crime: Toward a Socialist-Feminist Criminology*. Totowa, NJ: Rowan and Littlefield.

Miliband, R. 1969. *The State in Capitalist Society*. London: Quartet Books.

Mintz, M. 1985. *At Any Cost: Corporate Greed, Women and the Dalkon Shield*. New York: Pantheon Books.

Mitchell, J. 1971. *Women's Estate*. Harmondsworth, U.K.: Penguin.

Mitnick, B. M. 1980. *The Political Economy of Regulation.* New York: Columbia University Press.

Nader R. and M. J. Green, eds. 1973. *Corporate Power in America.* New York: Viking.

Needleman, M. L. and C. Needleman. 1979. Organizational crime: Two models of criminogenesis. *Sociological Quarterly* 20(4): 517–28.

O'Connor, J. 1973. *The Fiscal Crisis of the State.* New York: St. Martin's Press.

Offe, C. 1982. Some contradictions of the modern welfare state. *Social Policy* 2(2): 7–16.

Olsen, F. 1990. The sex of law. In *The Politics of Law,* ed. D. Kairys, 453–68. New York: Pantheon Books.

Panitch, L., ed. 1977. *The Canadian State: Political Economy and Political Power.* Toronto: University of Toronto Press.

Pearce, F. 1993. Corporate rationality as crime. *Studies in Political Economy* 40(Spring): 135–62.

Pearce, F. and L. Snider. 1995. Regulating capitalism. In *Corporate Crime: Contemporary Debates,* ed. F. Pearce and L. Snider. Toronto: University of Toronto Press.

Pepinsky H. and R. Quinney, eds. 1991. *Criminology as Peacemaking.* Bloomington, IN: Indiana University Press.

Peppin P. 1995. Feminism, law and the pharmaceutical industry. In *Corporate Crime: Ethics, Law and the State,* ed. F. Pearce and L. Snider. Toronto: University of Toronto Press.

Perry S. and J. Dawson. 1985. *Nightmare: Women and the Dalkon Shield.* New York: Macmillan.

Reasons, C., W. Ross and L. Patterson. 1981. *Assault on the Worker: Occupational Health and Safety in Canada.* Toronto: Butterworth.

Reiman, J. 1990. *The Rich Get Richer and the Poor Get Prison.* 3rd ed. New York: Macmillan.

Sabatier, P. 1975. Social movements and regulatory agencies: Toward a more adequate—and less pessimistic—theory of 'clientele capture.' *Policy Sciences* 6: 301–41.

———. 1977. Regulatory policy-making: Toward a framework of analysis. *Natural Resources Journal* 17: 415–60.

Sampson, A. 1975. *The Seven Sisters: The Great Oil Companies and the World They Shaped.* New York: Viking.

Schrecker, T. 1989. The political context and content of environmental law. In *Law and Society: A Critical Perspective,* ed. T. Caputo et al., 173–204. Toronto: Harcourt Brace Jovanovich.

Simon, D. and D. S. Eitzen, eds. 1990. *Elite Deviance.* 3rd ed. Boston: Allyn and Bacon.

Skocpol, T. 1992. *Protecting Soldiers and Mothers: The Political Origins of*

266   *Social Policy in the United States*. Cambridge, MA: Harvard University Press.

Smart, C. 1989. *Feminism and the Power of Law.* London: Routledge.

Smith, D. E. 1974. Women's perspective as a radical critique of sociology. *Sociological Inquiry* 44(1): 7–13.

Snider, L. 1993. *Bad Business: Corporate Crime in Canada.* Toronto: Nelson.

———. 1994. Criminalization: Panacea for men who batter but anathema for corporate criminals. In *Social Inequality, Social Justice*, ed. D. Currie and B. Maclean, 101–24. Vancouver: Collective Press.

———. 1994. Feminism, punishment and the potential of empowerment. *Canadian Journal of Sociology of Law* 9(1): 75–104.

Spitzer, S. 1990. The seductions of punishment: Toward a critical criminology of penality. Paper presented at the Annual Meeting of the American Society of Criminology, Baltimore, November.

Tucker, E. 1990. *Administering Danger in the Workplace: The Law and Politics of Occupational Health and Safety Regulation in Ontario, 1850–1914.* Toronto: University of Toronto Press.

Watkins, J. C. 1977. White collar crimes: Legal sanctions and social control. *Crime and Delinquency* 23: 290–303.

Winter, G. 1985. Bartering rationality in regulation. *Law and Society Review* 19(2): 219–250.

Yeager, P. 1991. *The Limits of Law: The Public Regulation of Private Pollution.* Cambridge, U.K.: Cambridge University Press.

APPENDIX

Chronology of
Selected Law and Social Policy
Addressing Women's Rights and Concerns[1]

1963   *Policy Measures*
Report of the first Presidential Commission on the Status of Women.
Legislation
Vocational Education Act: A grant-in-aid program to help furnish assistance to state vocational agencies.
Equal Pay Act: Forbids unequal pay for individuals who work in the same establishment and whose jobs require equal skill, effort, and responsibility. Factors other than gender are allowed to differentiate wages.

1964   *Policy Measures*
Creation of the Equal Employment Opportunity Commission (EEOC) as part of Title VII (see below).
Legislation
Civil Rights Act: President Johnson signs the Civil Rights Act prohibiting employment discrimination and creating the EEOC to investigate complaints.
Title IV of the act prohibits discrimination on the basis of race or national origin in programs receiving federal financial assistance.
Title VII of the act prohibits discrimination based on sex, race, color, religion, or national origin with the exception of bona fide occupational qualifications (BFOQ) in hiring or firing; in wages or benefits; in classifying, referring, assigning, or promoting employees; in facilities; in training; or in any other terms, conditions, or privileges of employment. This section also includes protection from sexual harassment.

1965   *Policy Measures*
Executive Order 11246: Prohibits discrimination in employment based on race, religion, and alienage by federal contractors.

268   *Case Law*

Griswold v. Connecticut, 381 U.S. 479 (1965): Supreme Court holds that state statutes banning contraceptives violate the fundamental constitutional right to privacy of married individuals.

1966   *Policy Measures*

National Organization for Women (NOW) founded.

1967   *Policy Measures*

Executive Order 11375 Added "sex" to Executive Order 11246 of 1965: Prohibits racial, religious, and alienage employment discrimination by federal contractors.

Women's Equity Action League (WEAL): Founded to attack sexism in higher education.

Legislation

Age Discrimination in Employment Act: Prohibits discrimination in employment practices on the basis of age for individuals between forty and seventy. Only BFOQ exemptions (such as modeling "junior" fashions) are permitted. Affects only employment practices on the federal level.

Case Law

Loving v. Virginia, 388 U.S. 1 (1967): U.S. Supreme Court adopts the strict scrutiny standard of judicial review in situations where there is a suspect classification or a fundamental interest, requiring the government to demonstrate a compelling interest underlying the use of the suspect distinctions, classifications, or actions.

1969   *Policy Measures*

Executive Order 11478: Requires federal agencies to establish and maintain an affirmative action program of equal employment opportunity for all civilian employees.

The "Philadelphia Plan": Requires federal contractors to employ a targeted number of minority workers; Secretary of Labor George Shultz extends it to nine other cities.

Presidential Task Force on Women's Rights and Responsibilities established.

Presidential Committee on Population and Family Planning established.

Case Law

Weeks v. Southern Bell Tel. and Tel. Co., 408 F.2d 228 (5th Cir. 1969): The first Title VII sex discrimination case to reach an appellate court sets a precedent for using Title VII to supersede state protective legislation.

1970   *Legislation*
Occupational Safety and Health Act: Requires employers to ensure
safe and healthy working conditions and to maintain a workplace
free from recognized dangers that would cause death or physical
harm.

1971   *Policy Measures*
Congress considers amendments to Title VII and the addition of
Title IX to the 1964 Civil Rights Act.
Department of Labor issues guidelines requiring firms engaged in
government business to establish plans for hiring and promoting
women and authorizes the first compliance reviews of female hir-
ing practices and policies of educational institutions.
Executive Order 11478: Condemns sex discrimination within gov-
ernmental agencies.
Case Law
Sail'er Inn Inc. v. Kirby, 5 Cal.3d 1, 485 P.2d 529, 95 Cal.Rptr. 329
(1971).
Phillips v. Martin Marietta Corporation, 400 U.S. 542 (1971).
Sprogis v. United Airlines, 444 F.2d 1194 (7th Cir. 1971), cert. de-
nied, 404 U.S. 991, 92 S.Ct. 536, 30 L.Ed.2d 543 (1971).
Diaz v. Pan American World Airlines, 442 F.2d 385 (5th Cir. 1971),
346 F.Supp. 1301 (S.D. Fla. 1972).
Griggs v. Duke Power Company, 401 U.S. 424 (1971).
Reed v. Reed, 404 U.S. 71 (1971).
Rosenfeld v. Southern Pacific Co., 444 F.2d 1219 (9th Cir. 1971).

1972   *Legislation*
Equal Employment Opportunity Act: President Nixon signs the
act, giving the EEOC enforcement powers and expanding coverage
of Title VII.
Title IX of the Education Amendments of 1972: Prohibits sex discrimination in any educational program receiving federal financial
assistance. Discrimination because of pregnancy is deemed a violation of Title IX. The amendments cover sex discrimination in
grooming and appearance policies at schools, with some exemptions for private undergraduate institutions.
Title IV of the Civil Rights Act of 1964: Amended to establish regional sex desegregation offices to help schools conform to Title
IX.
Case Law
Eisenstadt v. Baird, 405 U.S. 438 (1972): Extends the *Griswold* decision to unmarried couples.

270 1973 *Legislation*

Rehabilitation Act of 1973 (amended in 1978): Provides employment protection for individuals with mental or physical handicaps.

Case Law

Roe v. Wade, 410 U.S. 113 (1973): Landmark Supreme Court ruling holds that the constitutional right to privacy can be extended far enough to grant a woman the decision to terminate her pregnancy. Does not allow women the unconditional right to terminate a pregnancy.

Frontiero v. Richardson, 411 U.S. 677 (1973): The Supreme Court overrules U.S. Air Force policy requiring servicewomen to prove their spouses' dependency in order for them to qualify for medical and dental benefits, but not requiring servicemen's spouses to show the same dependency. The Court stops short of declaring sex a "suspect classification." (Like the *Reed* case of 1971, the case focused on whether or not the Court would consider sex an immutable characteristic [suspect classification], which would put it in the same category as race, forcing the "strict scrutiny" standard to be used.)

1974 *Legislation*

Fair Labor Standards Act of 1938: Amended to extend to private household workers' social security benefits.

Age Discrimination in Employment Act of 1967: Amended to include age protection at the state and local level.

Comprehensive Employment and Training Act: Provides federal funding for employment and training programs for unemployed workers (expired in 1982).

Employee Retirement Income Security Act: Protects workers and their beneficiaries who depend on benefits from private pension plans.

Case Law

Cleveland Board of Education v. La Fleur, 414 U.S. 632 (1974): Supreme Court strikes down state legislation regarding forced leave and termination policies of pregnant teachers.

Geduldig v. Aiello, 417 U.S. 484 (1974): Supreme Court rules that the exclusion of pregnancy from an employee-supported insurance plan is not sex discrimination but a permissible means of achieving the "legitimate state purpose" of providing low-cost insurance coverage.

1975 *Policy Measures*

Regulations of Title IX take effect.

1976 *Legislation*

Title IX: Amended to allow more student and youth organizations to maintain their sex segregation status without penalty—

including the Boy Scouts, Girl Scouts, Boys State, Boys Nation,
Girls State, and Girls Nation.
Case Law
Planned Parenthood of Central Missouri v. Danforth, 428 U.S. 52
(1976): Supreme Court strikes down state laws requiring a spouse's
consent to terminate a pregnancy, effectively allowing a woman
the right to choose, even against the wishes of her spouse.

1977 *Case Law*
Barnes v. Costle, 561 F.2d 983 (D.C. Cir. 1977): The federal court
affirms that quid pro quo harassment violates Title VII, finding
that "gender is a factor contributing to the discrimination in a substantial way." The court holds that an employee's differential
treatment based on rejection of sexual advances violates the
statute.
Nashville Gas Co. v. Satty, 434 U.S. 136 (1977): The Supreme
Court rules that women's seniority and pension benefits cannot be
withdrawn because of maternity leave. The Court also holds that
employers may refuse sick pay to pregnant workers but may not
divest them of accumulated seniority.
Califano v. Goldfarb, 430 U.S. 199 (1977): Affirming a federal district court decision, the Supreme Court rules that a section of the
Social Security Act is unconstitutional because it constitutes "in-
vidious discrimination" against female workers by providing less
protection for their surviving spouses than for the spouses of male
wage earners.

1978 *Policy Measures*
Executive Order 12106: Consolidates federal fair employment enforcement under the EEOC.
Department of Health and Human Services issues regulations to
prevent the coerced sterilization of low-income, minority, and institutionalized women by social services and medical agencies.
Department of Health, Education, and Welfare establishes a policy
allowing students to be excused from coeducational courses if
there is a religious reason prohibiting them from doing so.
Legislation
Civil Service Reform Act of 1978: Prohibits discrimination on the
basis of race, color, religion, sex, or national origin in personnel
practices. The law creates the Merit Systems Protection Board.
Pregnancy Discrimination Act of 1978: An amendment to Title
VII, this act states that employment discrimination based on pregnancy, childbirth, and related medical conditions such as abortion
are illegal. This act does not guarantee the right of women to take

272   family or maternal leave and thus does not protect women who lose their job after a leave of absence. But Congress asserts that the "entire thrust . . . behind this legislation is to guarantee women the basic right to participate fully and equally in the workforce, without denying them the fundamental right to full participation in family life."

Rehabilitation Act of 1973: Amended in Sections 503 and 504 to cover discrimination by federal contractors (with contracts exceeding $2,500) and discrimination in programs or activities receiving federal funds, respectively.

1979   *Policy Measures*
Office of Personnel Management issues a policy defining sexual harassment.
Case Law
Bellotti v. Baird, 443 U.S. 622 (1979): The Court addresses the issue of parental consent and a minor's right to terminate pregnancy. The Court holds that state regulation of the right of a minor to seek an abortion must permit the minor to go directly to court without first consulting or notifying her parents. If a court decides that an abortion is in the minor's best interest, she is entitled to court authorization without parental involvement.

1980   *Policy Measures*
EEOC issues guidelines interpreting the Title VII prohibition against discrimination based on sex, one part of which addresses sexual harassment.
Legislation
Age Discrimination in Employment Act of 1967: Amended to prohibit the involuntary retirement of individuals under the age of seventy years.

1981   *Policy Measures*
U.S. Department of Education withdraws Title IX regulations regarding grooming and appearance, thus allowing local school districts to set their own standards.
Case Law
County of Washington, Oregon v. Gunther, 452 U.S. 161 (1981): The Court holds that women employees may claim gender-based wage discrimination under Title VII, even though jobs to be compared do not meet the equal work standard of the Equal Pay Act.

1982   *Policy Measures*
At the directive of federal initiatives, the Air Force Academy, the Naval Academy, the Coast Guard Academy, and the Merchant Marine Academy adopt a policy of voluntary inclusion of female students.
Legislation
Job Training Partnership Act: Replaces the Comprehensive Employment and Training Act of 1974; also provides job training for the unemployed.
Case Law
North Haven Board of Education v. Bell, Secretary of Education, 456 S.Ct. 512 (1982): The Court rules that Title IX provisions against sex discrimination in any educational program receiving federal financial assistance apply to employees as well as students.

1983   *Case Law*
City of Akron v. Akron Center for Reproductive Health, 462 U.S. 490 (1983): The Court reinforces the *Bellotti* decision striking down an Akron ordinance and thereby ensuring that all minors regardless of their age be allowed to circumvent parental notification regulations regarding abortions by receiving judicial consent, thus effectively proving their maturity.

1984   *Legislation*
Retirement Equity Act: Allows state courts to treat pensions as joint property in divorce proceedings. Also holds that women who take up to a five-year leave for childrearing will not be negatively affected by retirement benefits.
Women's Educational Equity Act: Revises and extends the Women's Educational Equity Act of 1974 by providing federal grants to enable educational institutions to meet the requirements of Title IX. It also funds educational projects for women who experience multiple discrimination.
Retirement Equity Act: Allows courts to consider pension plans as joint property in divorce cases, allows for the payment to an "alternate payee" through court order, protects women from breaks in pension benefits for maternity leave, and lowers the age at which pensions can start from twenty-five to twenty-one.
Case Law
Grove City College v. Bell, 465 U.S. 555 (1984): The Court rules that only the specific activity in which sex discrimination is determined is affected by Title IX, not the whole institution. This is considered a defeat by many women's rights groups.

274 1985 *Case Law*
AFSCME v. Washington State, 770 F.2d 1401 (9th Cir. 1985).

1986 *Case Law*
Meritor Savings Bank v. Vinson, 477 U.S. 57 (1986): The Supreme Court issues its first decision on sexual harassment. The Court holds that sexual harassment in the workplace is sex discrimination as prohibited under Title VII of the 1964 Civil Rights Act. In formulating its decision, the Court decides that sexual harassment may occur either as a quid pro quo, where an employee is promised a promotion, pay increase, continued employment, or some other work-related benefit; or as a hostile work environment, in which unwelcome sexual advances interfere with the employee's work performance. The Court further states that sexual harassment constitutes unlawful sex discrimination if it is unwelcome, based on gender, and sufficiently severe or pervasive to alter a term, condition, or privilege of employment. While *Meritor* was an important case, it left many questions unanswered regarding what types of sexual advances or behavior constitute a hostile work environment.

1987 *Case Law*
Guerra v. California Federal Savings and Loan Association, 479 U.S. 272 (1987): The Supreme Court holds that a California statute requiring an employer to reinstate an employee who takes a leave of absence to give birth is not in conflict with the Pregnancy Discrimination Act of 1978 or Title VII of the Civil Rights Act of 1964. The Court reasons that the Pregnancy Discrimination Act was intended to prohibit discrimination against pregnant women, but provided only a minimum standard. Thus, states may pass more stringent requirements and legislation without being in conflict with the act or Title VII. The claimant was reinstated to Cal-Fed after a lengthy delay and substantial losses.

1988 *Legislation*
Hyde Amendment: Modified to allow federal funds to be available for poor victims of incest and rape.

1990 *Policy Measures*
EEOC issues "Policy Guidance on Sexual Harassment," intended to elaborate on legal principles set forth in *Meritor* and its guidelines issued in 1980. These guidelines reassert a distinction between "quid pro quo" and "hostile work environment" forms of

harassment. The EEOC states that an employer will "always be held responsible for acts of 'quid pro quo' harassment" by a supervisor. The *Meritor* ruling requires "a careful examination in 'hostile environment' cases of whether the harassing supervisor was acting in an 'agency capacity.' "

The EEOC's criteria for determining whether a work environment is "hostile" are (1) whether the conduct was verbal or physical or both; (2) how frequently it was repeated; (3) whether the conduct was hostile and patently offensive; (4) whether the alleged harasser was a coworker or a supervisor; (5) whether others joined in perpetrating the harassment; and (6) whether the harassment was directed at more than one individual.

Legislation

Civil Rights Bill (vetoed): Proposed amendment to the Civil Rights Act of 1964 allows for the awarding of an unlimited amount of compensatory and punitive damages for those who prove willful bias. This bill was later vetoed by President Bush.

1991   *Legislation*

Civil Rights Act: One major provision of the new Civil Rights Act is its extension of jury trials and provision for compensatory and punitive damages as remedies for Title VII violations for sexual harassment claimants. Compensatory damages include "future pecuniary losses, emotional pain, suffering, inconvenience, mental anguish, loss of enjoyment of life, and other nonpecuniary losses." Punitive damages may be sought from private employers in cases where the employer acted "with malice and reckless indifference" to the claimant's federally protected rights.

The amount of recoverable damages is limited by the number of employees in the offending company during twenty or more calendar weeks in the current or preceding calendar year. Compensatory and punitive damages may not exceed $50,000 for 14 to 100 employees; $100,000 for 101 to 200 employees; $200,000 for 201 to 500 employees; and $300,000 for more than 500 employees.

Case Law

Robinson v. Jacksonville Shipyards, 760 F.Supp. 1486 (6th Dist. Fla 1991): The Sixth Circuit Court of Appeals in Florida holds that nude pinups in the workplace constitute illegal sexual harassment.

1993   *Policy Measures*

FDA lifts its 1977 ban on including fertile women in early clinical tests. Pharmaceutical manufacturers are now required in their

276   analyses of test data to identify gender differences that arise during drug development.

Legislation

Equal Remedies Act: Removes financial caps on compensatory and punitive damage awards for sexual harassment. This allows women to receive damage awards based upon the nature and severity of the harassment rather than on the size of the company.

Family and Medical Leave Act: Affects both public and private employers, allowing eligible employees to take up to twelve weeks of combined family and medical leave in any calendar year in the event of the birth, adoption, or serious illness of a child; illness of a parent; or medical disability. It also protects the employee's benefits and employment rights during and after leaves. It does not, however, mandate paid family leave, and it also includes fairly stringent eligibility requirements.

Case Law

Harris v. Forklift Systems, Inc., 126 L.Ed.2d 295, 114 S.Ct. 367 (1993): The Supreme Court, in a decision written by Justice Sandra Day O'Connor, holds that an employee does not have to show serious psychological injury in order to prove a "hostile work environment" case under Title VII of the 1964 Civil Rights Act.

NOTES

1. The material used for the development of this chronology of law and social policy changes has been adapted from a number of academic and government sources, including the following: J. Hoff, *Law, Gender and Injustice: A Legal History of U.S. Women* (New York: New York University Press, 1991), 236–43; V. Sapiro, "The Gender Basis of American Social Policy," *Political Science Quarterly* 101, no.2 (1986): 221–38; G. Duerst-Lahti, "The Government's Role in Building the Women's Movement," *Political Science Quarterly* 104, no.2 (1989): 249–68; C. Dale, "Sexual Harassment: A History of Federal Law," *CRS Report for Congress* (Washington, DC: Congressional Research Service, 1993); K. Lewis, "Sex Discrimination and the United States Supreme Court: Developments in the Law," *CRS Report for Congress* (Washington, DC: Congressional Research Service, 1989); R. Cherow-O'Leary and NOW Legal Defense and Education Fund, *The State by State Guide to Women's Legal Rights* (New York: McGraw-Hill, 1987).

CONTRIBUTORS

Joan Claybrook is the president of Public Citizen, a Washington, D.C., consumer advocacy group founded by Ralph Nader. Between 1977 and 1981 she was the administrator of the National Highway Traffic Safety Administration.

Susan M. Davis is an associate professor of economics and finance at State University College at Buffalo. Dr. Davis received her Ph.D. in economics from the New School for Social Research in 1987. As a labor economist, she has a special interest in women's economic status. She has published articles on labor relations systems in professional sports and labor-management cooperative systems and undertaken regional studies of women's changing role in developing and postindustrial economies. She is currently coauthoring a textbook on women in the global economy.

Lori Elis is a Ph.D. candidate in the Department of Criminology and Criminal Justice at the University of Maryland, College Park. Her research interests include the influence of informal sanction threats on intentions to engage in corporate crime, and gender and crime. Her coauthored publications on gender and crime have appeared in *Criminology* and the *Journal of Criminal Law and Criminology.*

Lucinda M. Finley is a professor of law at State University of New York at Buffalo Law School, where she teaches and researches in the areas of torts, products liability, reproductive rights, gender and the law, feminist legal theory, and labor law. She is working on a book project about the experiences of women injured by DES, in particular how the legal system has responded to their reproductive injuries. She has also been involved in the federal tort reform legislative arena, testifying on several occasions before committees of the U.S. Senate and House of Representatives to address how certain legislative proposals might adversely affect women. In addition, Pro-

278 fessor Finley has served as a lawyer on major reproductive rights cases, including efforts to protect women seeking reproductive health services from harassment and violence by antiabortion demonstrators.

James G. Fox is a professor of criminal justice at the State University College at Buffalo. Since receiving his Ph.D. in criminal justice from the State University of New York at Albany in 1976, he has held faculty and visiting faculty positions at Pennsylvania State University, the University of Oregon, and the University of Toronto. He has published several articles and has contributed to several books addressing the issues of women in confinement and public policy in criminal justice.

Nancy Frank is an associate professor of urban planning at the University of Wisconsin-Milwaukee. From 1981 through 1993 she taught criminal justice courses, including courses on female victimization and corporate crime. She received a Distinguished Dissertation Award in 1983 for her historical study of the use of criminal penalties in the areas of occupational safety, food safety, and water pollution legislation. She has written several books and articles on the subject of corporate crimes against health and safety. Recently, she has begun to focus her research efforts on risk assessment as it relates to environmental law and policy.

Donna M. Randall is dean of the Fogelman College of Business and Economics at the University of Memphis. Her research interests lie in the areas of organizational behavior, reproductive risk in the workplace, and the study of organizational commitment. Her publications have appeared in such journals as *Decision Sciences, Academy of Management Review, Journal of Business Ethics, Proceedings of the Academy of Management, Journal of Vocational Behavior,* and *Journal of Business Research.* She received both her Ph.D. (sociology) and MBA degrees from Washington State University.

Sally S. Simpson is an associate professor of criminology and criminal justice at the University of Maryland, College Park. She received her Ph.D. in sociology from the University of Massachusetts at Amherst in 1985. Her research interests include theoretical criminology, women and crime, corporate crime etiology, and crime control. Her recent publications have appeared in *Criminology, Journal of Criminal Law and Criminology,* and *Law and Society Review.*

Laureen Snider is a professor of sociology at Queen's University in Kingston, Ontario, Canada. She has written numerous articles on corporate crime, feminism, and criminal justice. Her most recent book is *Bad Business: Corporate Crime in Canada* (Scarborough, Ontario: Nelson, 1993).

Elizabeth Szockyj is an assistant professor at the Center for the Study of
Crime, Delinquency and Corrections at Southern Illinois University. In
1992 she received her Ph.D. from the University of California, Irvine, and
she continues to teach and publish in the area of white-collar crime.